BOREDOM AND THE ARCHITECTURAL IMAGINATION

BOREDOM AND THE ARCHITECTURAL IMAGINATION

Rudofsky, Venturi, Scott Brown, and Steinberg

Andreea Mihalache

University of Virginia Press
CHARLOTTESVILLE AND LONDON

The University of Virginia Press is situated on the traditional lands of the Monacan Nation, and the Commonwealth of Virginia was and is home to many other Indigenous people. We pay our respect to all of them, past and present. We also honor the enslaved African and African American people who built the University of Virginia, and we recognize their descendants. We commit to fostering voices from these communities through our publications and to deepening our collective understanding of their histories and contributions.

University of Virginia Press

Printed in the United States of America on acid-free paper

First published 2024

9 8 7 6 5 4 3 2 1

LIBRARY OF CONGRESS CATALOGING-IN-PUBLICATION DATA

Names: Mihalache, Andreea, author.
Title: Boredom and the architectural imagination : Rudofsky, Venturi, Scott Brown, and Steinberg / Andreea Mihalache.
Description: Charlottesville : University of Virginia Press, [2024] | Includes bibliographical references and index.
Identifiers: LCCN 2024000303 (print) | LCCN 2024000304 (ebook) | ISBN 9780813951560 (hardcover) | ISBN 9780813951577 (paperback) | ISBN 9780813951584 (ebook)
Subjects: LCSH: Architecture, Modern—20th century—Philosophy. | Boredom. | Rudofsky, Bernard, 1905–1988—Criticism and interpretation. | Venturi, Robert—Criticism and interpretation. | Scott Brown, Denise, 1931– —Criticism and interpretation. | Steinberg, Saul—Criticism and interpretation. | BISAC: ARCHITECTURE / History / General Classification: LCC NA680 .M445 2024 (print) | LCC NA680 (ebook) | DDC 724/.6—dc23/eng/20240126
LC record available at https://lccn.loc.gov/2024000303
LC ebook record available at https://lccn.loc.gov/2024000304

Cover art: Saul Steinberg, Untitled, ca. 1947–49. Ink on paper. Whereabouts unknown. Originally published in *The Art of Living* (1949), 6. Republished in *Journal of the American Institute of Planners*, August 1961. (© The Saul Steinberg Foundation / Artists Rights Society [ARS], New York)
Cover design: Adrianna Sutton

Lui Luca și părinților mei, pentru tot

CONTENTS

ACKNOWLEDGMENTS

Writing this book has been closer to a personal journey than I would have ever imagined, a journey that has been anything but boring. I turned in the final manuscript three days before the birth of our son, Filippo. Witty minds often ponder the similitudes between the birth of a book and that of a child—and while I used to find this metaphor clever, today it makes me smile. Writing is a craft you train for, practice, and refine over time; with patience and purpose, you learn how to build and defend arguments, how to stand your ground and show confidence. Nothing, however, prepares you for motherhood. It puts you in the humbling position of unknowing, of unlearning what you believed immutable. Your mind and body truly—finally—become one. You discover feelings you never knew you had, a power you always thought foreign. You open yourself to becoming vulnerable. And it is through this vulnerability that you begin a new journey.

The journey of this book started in the archives. I had access to invaluable primary sources through the Getty Research Institute, The Architectural Archives at the University of Pennsylvania, and The Saul Steinberg Foundation. This publication has been supported by a grant from the Clemson Architectural Foundation and by the Creativity Professorship awarded by the College of Architecture, Arts and Humanities at Clemson University. Years ago, the late Boyd Zenner from the University of Virginia Press approached me at a conference and asked whether I was working on a book manuscript on boredom and architecture. With gentle tenacity, she pushed me to turn in a book proposal. Her wit and imagination are the foundation stones of this work. Upon her retirement, Mark Mones took over with enthusiasm, rigor, and patience, and I thank him for seeing this project through.

I wish to extend my thanks to the anonymous reviewers of this manuscript for their feedback and to colleagues who helped me develop and refine my ideas. Parts of this book started in my dissertation, and Paul Emmons, Marcia Feuerstein, Amy Catania Kulper, and Jaan Holt have been invaluable in sharpening my mind and turning my curiosity into research. Paul Emmons continues to be a mentor and has become a friend. His *ingegno* operates at levels inaccessible to ordinary minds. With intuition and intelligence, he crafts not only future scholars but also, and perhaps more importantly, robust individuals. Maurizio Sabini (Drury University), the editor-in-chief of *The Plan Journal,* took the risk of publishing my writing on boredom and architecture ("Musings on Boredom, Midcentury Architecture, and Public Spaces," *The Plan Journal* 5, no. 1 [2020]: 119–38), which became an early version of chapter 5. Chapter 6 started as a paper ("On 'Deferred Judgment': Historical and Contemporary Perspectives") presented at the conference Architectural Theory Now?, which was organized by the Department of Architecture at the Stuart Weitzman School of Design at the University of Pennsylvania. Special thanks to the organizers: David Leatherbarrow, Peter Laurence, and Franca Trubiano. Chapter 9 is a revised and extended version of "Three Ghosts and a Baldachin: Boredom and (Day)dreaming in Two Drawings by Saul Steinberg," in *Ceilings and Dreams: The Architecture of Levity,* edited by Paul Emmons, Federica Goffi, and Jodi La Coe (London: Routledge, 2019), 197–211. Jaimie Johansson provided valuable feedback and sharp attention to detail. My thanks go to Kate Schwennsen, director emerita of the Clemson School of Architecture, a role model and inspiring leader, and to Jim Stevens, the current director of the school, who has fully supported me from the day he arrived at Clemson. All my colleagues make the school an incredible and inspiring place.

In my research (as in my life), I would have never accomplished anything without the support and patience of all the people who stood by me. This work was built on their friendship and unconditional trust. French artist Daniela Roman, Saul Steinberg's niece, shared with me her invaluable memories, and soon research turned into a friendship for which I am forever grateful. Sheila Schwartz, research and archives director at The Saul Steinberg Foundation, never ceases to amaze me with her encyclopedic knowledge of all things Steinberg and beyond. (I secretly believe she has superpowers.) Her intellectual generosity and personal warmth are like no other. I found in my friend Aga Skrodzka the ideal walking and thinking partner—everything looks sharper after our peripatetic chats. Anca and Virgil Nemoianu have become my family away from home, offering the support that one only finds in the closest kin. My warmest thoughts go to the Stavropoleos community in Bucharest for their joy and wit, along with their reassuring presence that makes the world a better place. My cousins Dana Bichianu, Camelia Petruc, and Marius Petruc are my safety net. Doina Cristina Ionescu has taught me more about life and what it means to be human than she will ever know—and not (only) because she has a beautiful mind but first and foremost because she is a wonderful person, living proof that miracles do exist. I am honored to be part of her world. My dear friend Muey Saeteurn remains my North Star. Her resilience, wisdom, and optimism make her one of the strongest people I know. I'm so glad you knocked on my door, Neighbor!

My parents are everything to me. Despite all the hardship they have seen in this tormented place called the Balkans, they move through the world with an elegance and dignity that I have never encountered elsewhere. Their vulnerability makes them invincible. They wrap me in a love so deep, forgiving, selfless, and infinite that it becomes the very fabric of my life. I owe them everything. Every day, my husband Luca shows me, quietly and unassumingly, the many forms of love. *Whereof one cannot speak, thereof one must be silent.*

Coming full circle, this manuscript will go to press a few days before our son's first birthday. His tiny world is bigger, fuller, and more exciting than anything I have ever experienced. Filippo, I don't remember life before you.

BOREDOM AND THE ARCHITECTURAL IMAGINATION

Prologue

INVITING TIME IN

Rather than pass the time, one must invite it in.
—WALTER BENJAMIN, *The Arcades Project*

Ennui. Langeweile. Acedia. Tedium. What do we mean when we talk about *boredom?* A pathological condition (Otto Fenichel), a mood conducive to philosophy (Martin Heidegger), "the dream bird that hatches the egg of experience" (Walter Benjamin), "a kind of bliss that is almost unearthly" (Siegfried Kracauer): the concept of boredom emerges in and is intertwined with modernity. Closely observed in philosophy, aesthetics, the social sciences, critical theory, literary studies, and the visual arts, boredom remains an ambiguous, vague, and barely examined concept in architectural scholarship.[1] Centering my inquiries on the middle decades of the twentieth century, I examine in this book the intersections of architecture with the study of boredom. Building bridges between architectural history, theory, and criticism and some major philosophical, social, and artistic explorations of boredom, I attempt to show how various concepts of ennui simultaneously undermine and reshape architectural Modernism at midcentury.

Psychologist Orrin Klapp has proposed that the increased use of the word *boredom* between 1931 and 1961 indicates a growing awareness of this particular mood in modern society. My thesis is that the underlying theme of the interest in boredom at midcentury, whether tacit or explicit, is a concern with time (the "long while" of the German *Langeweile*), threatened by the new pace of life after World War II. While an architecture qualified as "boring" typically conjures up banality, monotony, and repetition—in other words, spatial and aesthetic features that neither arrest our attention nor absorb us in any meaningful way—I propose that this sense of discontent emerges from a temporal disengagement. Simply put, we get bored in an environment that delivers itself immediately and instantaneously without building the anticipation and expectation of discovery.

Conceptually, my study draws on Heidegger's tiered structure of boredom.[2] Its first form (being bored *with* something) is exemplified by the tedium of waiting and is the most superficial form of boredom. The second form (being bored *by* something) leaves one in an inexplicable state of discomfort, like a merely pleasant, yet meaningless, social event. The third and most profound form of boredom is one of the "fundamental moods" of our age (along with anxiety and fright) that allow the human being to become attuned to the most genuine state of authenticity.[3] Boredom tests the ability of human nature to confront time and, ultimately, to find meaning and wonder. Wonder's fundamental trait, as Heidegger describes it, is that it lets the familiar, the habitual, the ordinary to appear unfamiliar.[4] In this awakening, wonder-struck, one rediscovers the world with fresh eyes.

Four main actors take the stage in this conversation about boredom, all trained as architects and practicing architecture in often unconventional ways: Bernard Rudofsky (1905–1988), Robert Venturi (1925–2018), Denise Scott Brown (b. 1931), and Saul Steinberg (1914–1999). Canonical historiography would place them under different labels and even in different disciplines: exhibition design, architecture, and graphic design. Examining them together, however, reveals the changes in architectural practice at midcentury, the role boredom plays in their work, and the evolution of the profession at large. Trained at the height of Modernism, they observe boredom as a condition of modern architecture and evolve into critics of its normative outcomes, repurposing the monotony and fatigue of modernist language as its critical tools. They all recognize this form of exhaustion and shallowness as a disease of the modern world, and their search is ultimately a search for meaning. Together they offer a comprehensive view of the alienated relationship of individuals with their world at three different, yet intertwined, scales: the body (Rudofsky), urban space (Venturi and Scott Brown), and the building (Steinberg).

The overarching ideas of this book emerge from a few lines that Walter Benjamin writes about boredom in the years leading up to World War II: "Rather than pass time, one must invite it in. To pass the time (to kill time, expel it): the gambler. Time spills from his every pore.—To store time as a battery stores energy: the flâneur. Finally, the third type: he who waits. He takes in the time and renders it up in altered form—that of expectation."[5] Taking apart and construing Benjamin's modes of understanding boredom through time, I offer three speculative readings of Rudofsky, Venturi and Scott Brown, and Steinberg, who all turn the displeasures of tedium into tools of creativity. A perpetual traveler, Rudofsky transforms the boredom of a commodified world into an act of physical and imaginary *wandering* that slows down time. Raised in the Quaker tradition of mindful expectation, Venturi introduces in his early projects moments of stillness and quiet *waiting* that seize the passing of time. Concurrently, Scott Brown develops her own theory of *deferred judgment,* a time-lengthening strategy of transforming the quick pace of decision making into a space for reflection. And Steinberg—a sharp and often ruthless critic of the built environment—folds the boredom of contemporary consumerism into acts of *wonder* that store and thicken time.

In one of the earliest references to boredom, a tongue-in-cheek first-century graffito in Latin found in Pompeii, tedium and architecture appear ontologically related: "Wall! I wonder that you haven't fallen down in ruin, when you have to support all the boredom of your inscribers."[6] While boredom, as the dissociation of person from place, has piqued architects' interest, especially during the middle decades of the twentieth century, most discussions on this topic have disregarded its ontological significance and, instead, have approached it mostly as a stylistic trope to draw attention to other, more pressing issues. A brief overview of the intersections of architecture with the discourse of boredom will show that, unlike most of their peers, Rudofsky, Venturi, Scott Brown, and Steinberg go beyond the provocative rhetoric of boredom and explore, instead, its potential as both a critical and a generative tool.

Some years after the first English use of the word *boredom* in Charles Dickens's *Bleak House* (1853), architecture professor Adolf Göller delivers a talk in 1887 at the Technische Hochschule in Stuttgart in which he offers a hypothesis for stylistic changes in architecture.[7] Mainly concerned with the formation of styles and the invention of architectural forms, Göller sees them as cyclical processes based on what he calls "the law of jading": as people become more familiar with certain forms, the style is exhausted and eventually becomes obsolete.[8] What he describes as the "law of jading" is the recognition of boredom as a link between architectural forms and human beings.

From the nineteenth century onward, boredom in architecture relates to either an excess or an insufficiency—of things, stimuli, sensations. Le Corbusier identifies the sources of contemporary boredom in the surplus of stuff amassed in people's dwellings and proposes new paradigms of inhabitation based on standards of minimal living. In *Toward an Architecture,* he describes how the unsuitable conditions of present-day homes spawn the tedium that drives people away from their houses.[9]

By midcentury, Modernism's motto of "less is more" is called into question. Disenchanted with the uniformity of modernist boxes, Austrian architect Josef Frank formulates his ideas about the role of happenstance in design in the article "Accidentism," published in the Swedish journal *Form* in 1958 and illustrated with three of his postwar projects.[10] Accidentism is a strategy to combat the dullness of mass-produced architecture and the monotony that ensues from modernist laws having become normative. After living in New York between 1941 and 1946, Frank and his wife move back to Sweden. There, in a letter to the Austrian painter Trude Waehner written in March 1946, he explicitly manifests his interest in the issue of boredom in art and architecture: "I am now preoccupied here with the problem of boredom in art and architecture." He asks himself, "Why are the streets and dwellings here so uninteresting?"[11] In two other letters to Waehner from the same year, Frank confesses that he prefers American "rawness" and inquires (rhetorically), "What good is the art here and carefulness in building if everything is so dull? I am now completely of the opinion that much that is good comes about merely through chance and not through careful planning."[12] His work continues to be a search for complexity as a form of resistance to the "boring, simplified mass production" of postwar architecture.[13] For Frank, people's everyday lives and habits offer the necessary resources to overcome both uniformity and ephemeral fashions. What he calls "accidents" are not exceptions to rules formalized as architectural objects but rather the coagulation of events, practices, people's individual choices, and preferences. Expressed through architecture, they constitute one's life: "A sitting room in which one can live and think freely is neither beautiful, nor harmonious, nor photogenic. It is the result of a series of random accidents; it is never really completed and it has sufficient scope to include whatever may be needed to satisfy its owner's shifting requirements."[14] Decrying modern uniformity, Frank envisions an "environment that appears to have arisen by accident."[15] For him, the answer to architectural boredom resides not in the search for the exceptional but in the careful examination of habits, daily routines, and commonplaces. (Formed at the Viennese school of architecture, Rudofsky will build upon the lessons learned from Frank and other prominent Viennese architects, such as Oskar Strnad and Oskar Wlach, who champion an architecture of the senses, informed by vernacular wisdom, as an antidote to the ennui felt by modern individuals.)

The postwar prospect of an excess of free time combined with a lack of engaging activities generates intense debates on the British architectural scene. Architect Cedric Price and Joan Littlewood, one of Britain's most radical theater directors, producers, and social activists, embark together on the challenging adventure of designing what they eventually call the "Fun Palace." In the postwar years, British society looks to capitalize on newfound free time and the economic opportunities this presents. In this context, Price and Littlewood attempt to erase the modernist distinction between education and leisure and make both accessible to the working class.[16] One of the underlying objectives of the project is to overcome the urban dweller's boredom. The Fun Palace challenges the conventional understanding of architecture as a fixed, immobile structure, proposing, instead, an "interactive machine" that the inhabitants themselves can change, modify, adapt, and reconfigure based on their own desires, needs, and actions. A publicity pamphlet that Price and Littlewood cowrite promotes the Fun Palace as a remedy to the problems of daily routines, urban boredom, and alienation. "Have you changed your job? / Did you want to? / Do you enjoy routine? / . . . / Do you suffer from boredom? / overwork? / loneliness? / overcrowding? / 12 or more yesses, read on."[17] An experiment in programmatically addressing large-scale boredom, the Fun Palace is built upon the indeterminacy of change and the idea of an open, never-completed work. The assumption is that people need variation and constant stimulation to overcome the dullness of their individual lives. Interpreted as one of the earliest examples of virtual reality, the Fun Palace prompts larger questions about the relationship of entertainment and boredom.[18]

The emerging field of environmental studies begins to look at the effects of monotonous environments on people's psyches. In 1963, Serge Chermayeff and Christopher Alexander publish *Community and Privacy: Toward a New Architecture of Humanism,* which describes the "fundamental monotony" and "anxiety-ridden existence" of the modern individual in terms of a lack of daily variety, contemplation, and introspection. As "more and more becomes less and less," overstimulation leads to boredom, a disease whose pathology they identify in the proliferation of artificial, machine-controlled environments. Approaching boredom from a scientific perspective, they find that mechanization and mass-produced commodities (along with electronic mass media, open-plan layouts, lack of properly defined enclosures, and transparent walls) are the most important causes of contemporary tedium.[19] "Mechanical extensions" lead to a double loss: on the one hand, confronted with the increasing automation of daily life (radios, air conditioning, mechanical devices, faster cars, and so on), people lose the immediate, sensuous experience of the world.[20] On the other hand, new forms of material transparencies (glass walls, picture windows, and the like) result in new forms of surveillance, and people lose the sense of privacy and intimacy at the core of human nature. The outcome is a debilitating boredom that not only erodes human life but also threatens to damage the environment.[21] The chapter "In Search of the Small" concludes with the section "Pathology of Boredom," a title borrowed from a study on boredom cited by the authors. Published in January 1957 in *Scientific American,* "The Pathology of Boredom" describes a study conducted at McGill University in 1951 to determine the results of prolonged exposures to a rigidly monotonous environment.[22] The experiment resembles a torture chamber: the subjects are kept in absolute physical and sensorial isolation, in a permanently lit room, lying on a bed for twenty-four hours a day, with time out only for meals and toilet use.[23] Not surprisingly, they begin to experience hallucinations and sensorial confusion. While these are without doubt extreme conditions, Chermayeff and Alexander use this study to support their thesis about the necessity of variety in the built environment.

Amos Rapoport and Robert E. Kantor's 1967 article "Complexity and Ambiguity in Environmental Design" identifies the problem of contemporary architecture in its lack of a whole range of meanings and possibilities: "It has been simplified and cleaned up to such an extent that all it has to say is revealed at a glance."[24] Boredom emerges as the underlying problem of the built environment. Making an argument for the right balance between simple and complex stimuli (called the "optimal perceptual rate"), the authors use scientific data to show that "stimuli which are too simple lead to boredom; those which are too complex lead to confusion and avoidance."[25]

The antidote to boredom is often sought in the change and novelty facilitated by rapid technological progress. While recognizing the problems of exhausted modernist language, Lewis Mumford and Sigfried Giedion express their concern about these responses to modern tedium. In "The Case against Modern Architecture" (1962), Mumford identifies and criticizes what he calls the "creativity of the kaleidoscope" as one of the design responses to the regimentation imposed by modern architecture.[26] Boredom is the specific disposition—or rather ailment—that engenders the fascination with this type of aesthetics: "When a child is bored or an adult is ill, the aesthetics of the kaleidoscope is enchanting."[27] Architecture is a discipline in crisis, and boredom is its disease. Like their fellow doctors, overwhelmed by the availability of an enormous quantity of drugs, architects feel compelled to prove their creativity by resorting uncritically to all the new and easily accessible materials and technologies. This approach results in shallow forms as the immediate response to tedium: "The desire for architectural originality through a succession of kaleidoscopic changes, made possible by modern technological agents, when the inner purpose and contents are ruled out of the equation, inevitably degrades the creative process."[28]

Giedion summarizes the state of affairs in midcentury architecture in his introduction to the 1967 edition of *Space, Time, and Architecture,* subtitled "Hopes and Fears." Giedion succinctly describes the situation as "Confusion and Boredom": "In the sixties a certain confusion exists in contemporary architecture, as in painting; a kind of pause, even a kind of exhaustion. Everyone is aware of it. Fatigue is normally accompanied by uncertainty, what to do and where to go. Fatigue is the mother of indecision, opening the door to escapism, to superficialities of all kinds. . . . A kind of playboy-architecture became *en vogue:* an architecture treated as playboys treat life, jumping from one sensation to another and quickly bored with everything."[29]

The basis of Giedion's position is a 1961 symposium at the Metropolitan Museum of Art in New York that discusses the future of modern architecture in terms of either death or metamorphosis. Criticizing the notion of fashion or style in modern architecture, Giedion foresees neither its death nor its metamorphosis; rather, he anticipates the development of a new tradition.[30] He recognizes that the answer to the exhaustion and boredom of contemporary architecture lies in paying close attention to people's habits, a position that the main figures in this book will themselves explore in different ways. Confidently, Giedion predicts that "the playboy attitude of the sixties will vanish too."[31] That his optimism is largely contradicted by history—and that architecture will continue to follow trends and fashions—is a topic for another book.

In this context, Rudofsky, Venturi, Scott Brown, and Steinberg discover an alternative to the usual way of reading boredom in architecture as the failure of an aesthetic language. By uncovering the temporal dimension of boredom, they shift the focus from form to habits, from space to the rituals of the everyday, which ultimately organize and give meaning to our practices of inhabitation. In the aftermath of World War II, when the discipline of architecture is redefining its goals and mission, they propose and exercise alternative modes of practice and criticism through exhibition design (Rudofsky), rhetorical building (Venturi and Scott Brown), and critical drawing (Steinberg). By expanding the boundaries of the field, they also challenge conventional notions about what constitutes architectural scholarship. The four of them, in different ways and in different contexts, specifically address the issue of boredom.

Although trained as architects, they are unlikely partners. Venturi and Scott Brown are the only ones who maintain an active architectural office. Rudofsky practices in the early stages of his career, when he works with Gio Ponti and Luigi Cosenza in Italy and then opens his own office in São Paulo, Brazil. Steinberg never works in practice, except for a very short time upon completing his architectural studies. From a traditional disciplinary perspective, he would hardly be considered an architect. Building his fame and reputation as a visual artist widely published in the *New Yorker* and numerous magazines and journals (including architectural ones), Steinberg produces a broad range of artifacts, from drawings, collages, and photomontages to murals, advertising art, fabric design, and stage sets. A visual storyteller, he describes himself as a writer and, despite the lack of a consistent body of written work, his interviews, personal notes, and journal entries reveal the same wit, imagination, and critical view as his drawings.

Venturi, on the other hand, who has always described himself as a practicing architect, first becomes known as an architectural writer. He has been working and teaching for several years when his 1966 treatise, *Complexity and Contradiction in Architecture,* truly puts his name at the forefront of the profession. The book most certainly plays a significant role in the public recognition of his practice when, the following year, the journal *Progressive Architecture* acknowledges the work coming from the firm of Venturi and Rauch. For the 1967 *P/A* Annual Awards, they receive one award for the Frug House and two citations for the Princeton Memorial Park and three buildings designed for downtown North Canton, Ohio—the Ohio project directly addressing the issue of boredom. Before her partnership with Venturi, Scott Brown publishes in professional journals, teaches at UCLA, and fights for recognition in a male-dominated field, activities that she continues to pursue throughout her career.

Rudofsky is interested in writing from the early stages of his career. Upon completing his doctoral dissertation in Vienna, he moves to Italy, where he works on the editorial staff of the prestigious journal *Domus* and, after settling in the United States, continues to write, publishing nine books and countless articles. Without explicitly mentioning Rudofsky's name, in *Learning from Las Vegas,* Venturi, Scott Brown, and Steven Izenour criticize his focus on the remote vernacular of traditional societies, advocating instead an appreciation of the American commercial vernacular (which Rudofsky dismisses).

Occasional collaborators, Rudofsky and Steinberg are friends, and their professional paths intersect often. As the curator of the American Pavilion at the 1958 Brussels World's Fair, Rudofsky commissions Steinberg to design the large-scale mural known as *The Americans.* In the 1940s and 1950s, he is also instrumental in introducing his friend to the New York architectural and artistic elite. Their shared interest in what constitutes the most intimate essence of the human being suggests an approach to architecture focused on embodied cultural practices and those habits and customs that define the nature of a place. While Venturi and Scott Brown glorify consumerism in its various forms, Rudofsky and Steinberg constantly challenge it.

Then why bring the four of them together?

In spite of their obvious and sometimes irreconcilable differences, Rudofsky, Venturi, Scott Brown, and Steinberg are nevertheless connected by multiple threads. Considering their work jointly sheds new light on the changing nature of the discipline at midcentury and on the role boredom plays in their work as well as in the evolution of the profession at large. What they have in common is also what shapes their shared interest in boredom.

Despite their unquestioned success, these architects deliberately position themselves at the periphery of the profession, a necessary move for gaining freedom from norms as well as the right distance to act critically. Capitalizing on their foreign origins (Rudofsky is born in Moravia, Venturi is of Italian descent, Scott Brown comes from South Africa, and Steinberg is from Romania), each of them creates a carefully crafted public persona in order to become relevant in the intellectual—not just architectural—world to which they aspire to belong.

They share a consistent attraction for the everyday and the ordinary in popular culture, most likely originating in their extensive travels around the world. From Greece to Japan and from Italy to Brazil, throughout his life Rudofsky spends time in various countries and on different continents, observing and engaging with local cultures and their environments. Venturi recognizes that his time in Italy and Europe as a fellow of the American Academy in Rome had a decisive influence on his views on architecture. Before coming to the United States, Scott Brown moves from

South Africa to England to study architecture at the Architectural Association in London. Steinberg leaves Romania to study architecture in Milan, and then, forced to flee fascist Italy, has to spend a year in the Dominican Republic waiting for his American immigration visa. An avid traveler, he equally enjoys visiting remote destinations and seeing America by Greyhound bus. Rudofsky, Venturi, and Steinberg have a common fascination with Italian architecture, culture, and lifestyle. Each of them spends time in Italy at a formative age, which leaves an indelible impact on their later work. Rudofsky lives and works in Italy, Venturi is at the American Academy in Rome, and Steinberg studies architecture at the Regio Politecnico in Milan.

Perhaps most importantly, all four of them, though working in different media and often communicating with different audiences, are simultaneously judicious architectural critics and ingenious designers.

Methodologically, I look at the work of these architects through the lens of microhistory, the research framework advanced by Carlo Ginzburg, which examines how small events contain and reveal larger truths.[32] Through microhistory, Ginzburg scrutinizes the overlooked, the disregarded, and the ephemeral on a small scale as a way to gain access to history on a large scale. Individual stories offer insight into wider collective histories. Within this framework, the relevance of a secondary character, of a minor incident or a missed detail, has the power to expose a broader network of significance. Not unlike the procedures routinely performed by doctors or detectives, this method requires a close reading of clues—piecing together speculative yet rigorous scenarios.[33] Similarly, by repositioning the work of these well-known designers, I unpack the overlooked notion of boredom as a mode to construct a "thick description" of midcentury architecture.[34]

Concurrently, I am making an argument for a positive valorization of boredom as a slow-paced mood of contemplation and introspection in a world that continues to move at a faster and faster pace. Why, one might ask, call this process "boredom" and not simply "contemplation"? The latter has an aura of inaccessibility and seems to require an uncommon disposition, but boredom begins in the everyday. Everyone experiences it; everyone connects to it. It is ubiquitous, pervasive, and unremarkable. Starting in the banality of the infra-ordinary, tedium relies precisely on the mundane to transcend its ordinary condition. Heidegger defines it as one of the fundamental moods of our age. Ennui has Janusian attributes: it begins either from a dearth or from an excess of experiences, actions, things, and stimuli. The more one tries to fight it through novelty or change, the deeper one falls back into its endless loop. Described as a malaise or a disease with enduring psychological consequences, ennui also conjures up Romantic visions of creativity. Both a collective and an individual condition, it is a measure of our discontent with and disengagement from the present moment. It is, at the same time, the present condition — available, accessible, and within reach — that might hold the key to resisting boredom not through the extraordinary, the uncommon, and the spectacular but through a stubborn persistence in discovering the immediate meaning of what surrounds us. A means rather than an end in itself, boredom opens up space for wonder, the "seesawing back and forth between the habitual and the inhabitual" that unexpectedly awakens us to and makes us present in the world.[35]

This study is organized into three parts and, perhaps unusually, is written in the present tense. Why this particular choice, one might wonder, in a work that looks at characters, events, and designs that belong to a time long gone? While the midcentury is a thing of the past, I argue that boredom and its relevance for architecture are more important today than ever. To talk about boredom in the past tense is to symbolically ignore its significance in today's world; I attempt, therefore, to situate it in the present. If the use of particular tenses is ultimately a convention, I would like to believe that the protagonists of my story continue to challenge, nudge, and engage with us today.

Part 1 looks at boredom's metamorphosis into acts of physical and imaginary wandering through Bernard Rudofsky's work. Starting with his 1955 book *Behind the Picture Window,* I examine his design projects, essays, and books from the 1940s through the late 1960s. Part 2 explores the transformation of boredom into mindful waiting through two distinct, yet intertwined, threads. Having its starting point in Robert Venturi's quip "Less is a bore," the first thread follows several projects designed in the early stages of his career: his thesis project for a chapel for the Episcopal Academy (1953), three buildings for the downtown of North Canton, Ohio (1965), the Guild House in Philadelphia (1963–66), and the Boston Copley Square Competition entry (1966). The second thread follows Denise Scott Brown and her career before her partnership with Venturi, when she develops the concept of *deferred judgment.* Finally, part 3 witnesses how boredom turns into wonder in Saul Steinberg's artwork. Specifically, I look at collections of drawings published between 1953 and 1968, including those in *The Labyrinth* and *The New World.* This period is bookended by two articles that engage with the theme of boredom and represent rare instances when Steinberg not only draws but also writes about architecture: "Built in U.S.A." (1953) and "Our False-Front Culture" (1968).

While each part has three chapters that can be read either sequentially or independently, there is a certain symmetry at work in this structure. The first chapter of each part examines genealogies of boredom in the work of the main protagonist(s). A systematic reader, Rudofsky's position on contemporary boredom as the malaise of modernity is informed by a series of early twentieth-century authors whose works he reads and meticulously annotates in his notebooks. Concurrently, in tune with contemporary Marxist critique, he sees mechanization and the commodification of leisure as major causes of modern boredom. Venturi, raised as a Quaker (a detail largely ignored in architectural scholarship), learns from an early age how stillness and waiting, attributes specific to the Quakers, shape human behavior. Steinberg brings into his art his personal experience of exile and refuge at a time when the visual arts turn toward boredom as an affectless state paradoxically eliciting interest. Unexpectedly, Steinberg finds in tedium his motivation to work.

The second chapter of each part unpacks each protagonist's critiques of contemporary tedium. Rudofsky finds evidence of boredom in the deterioration of domestic habits as well as in travel practices turned into consumerist tourism. The picture window, a feature common to midcentury residential architecture, stands for everything that is wrong with the modern home. Boredom and "disprivacy" sum up the condition of modern dwellings. One of the most cited yet largely overlooked references in *Complexity and Contradiction in Architecture* is August Heckscher, a liberal activist and writer, whose book *The Public Happiness* constitutes one of Venturi's main sources on boredom as an ethical concern in the public sphere. Informed by Heckscher, Venturi's unbuilt projects for three buildings in downtown North Canton, Ohio, and the proposal for Boston's Copley Square address the issue of collective tedium. Steinberg comments on the built environment through drawing. Repeatedly called a "critic without words," his drawings are modes of architectural criticism that, instead of separating and dividing matters, build bridges between the different forces at work in designing architecture and the city.

Each part concludes with a chapter on tactics of resisting ennui. Rudofsky offers an unexpected response to modern boredom. In his writings and design projects, floors are invested with the ontological function of building one's foundation in the world, horizons of inhabitation, and the mood of a place. In a more general sense, the ground is the unnoticed canvas onto which life unfolds, a place for physical and imaginative wanderings where, one step at a time, measured time becomes embodied time. Scott Brown's concept of deferred judgment restores a temporal dimension to our design actions. Active waiting and observing, as in Venturi's Quaker-inspired stillness, makes space for reflection. Finally, claiming the imprecise territory of visual riddles, Steinberg ponders the infra-ordinary of everyday life, those objects and practices that constitute the fabric of daily rituals and routines. Operating through inversions, he folds boredom into daydreaming, thus opening up a thick space of interpretations and wonders.

PART I

WANDERING

BERNARD RUDOFSKY

Only one thing is more boring than a showy display of vice: a continual search for novelty.

—BERNARD BERENSON, *CONVERSATIONS WITH BERENSON*

In 1955, Bernard Rudofsky publishes *Behind the Picture Window,* a collection of essays on the nature of the modern house that he unpacks through various domestic customs and activities, from cooking, eating, and sitting to sleeping, washing, and cleaning. Written as satires rather than academic papers, the book's chapters share the same goal: to expose the failure of the "American way of life" and to propose what Rudofsky has called elsewhere "a new way of living" based on lessons learned from past civilizations.[1] Replacing the conventional introduction and foreshadowing the critique of consumerism addressed later in the book, the "Advertisement" makes clear the author's intention to call into question the features of the modern, commodified house and to propose alternatives for healthier, more comfortable, and less mechanized living.[2]

Summarizing the main ideas of the book, the closing chapter has an intriguing title: "On Boredom and Disprivacy." On closer inspection, ideas about tedium are constantly present in Rudofsky's intellectual universe. Taking *Behind the Picture Window* as a starting point, I argue that the concept of boredom plays a central, yet overlooked, role in Rudofsky's critique of Modernism, a critique that demonstrates how architecture, specifically domestic architecture, offers the means to withstand ennui—the inevitable malaise of the modern world—through soft tactics that bypass the strategies of novelty or fashion usually associated with fighting boredom.

It is important to clarify a few facts. First, Rudofsky designs individual houses for a (real or imaginary) upper-middle-class clientele, people who can afford to occupy ample square footage, employ housekeepers, and maintain luscious gardens. Second, his books and articles, although well documented and well researched, maintain an ironic voice, ignoring the constraints of rigorous academic writing. As such, they belong to neither academic bookshelves nor bourgeois coffee tables. Third, despite his acclaimed interest in vernacular architecture and sustainable construction methods, Rudofsky's proposals do not withstand serious tests of sustainability and ecology. The value of his work for the twenty-first century resides elsewhere.

Although uninterested in the issue of midcentury affordable housing, Rudofsky's analysis of inhabitation articulates ideas about privacy and hospitality in residential architecture. Today, most contemporary studies on urban living disregard the need for domestic conviviality and social gathering, activities usually exported to venues outside the dwelling or found only in large, inefficient McMansions. Rudofsky, however, proposes that being social *at home* is a basic need for healthy living, part of what makes us human and maintains our ties with the community. Domesticity includes both privacy and conviviality, and only by acting *together* do they construct a happy mode of existing in the world.

The inaccessibility of scholarly writing to lay audiences continues to isolate academia. While Rudofsky's texts would hardly qualify as academic, they are also deceptively light. An avid and systematic reader (as his dozens of notebooks show), he conducts thorough research for his books, but his sarcastic style, not unlike Saul Steinberg's unconventional art, makes him an outlier in the academic world. And yet Rudofsky offers ways to bridge the gap between scientific texts and popular audiences through narrative and storytelling, a lesson that might be more useful today than it was in the twentieth century.

Despite his often biased and reductive readings of both traditional and modern societies, Rudofsky did not shy away from denouncing Modernism's failures. By looking at the *other,* he invites us to look critically at *ourselves.* The optimistic discourse of midcentury American architecture was neither ready nor willing to receive this criticism. While a non-pedigreed architecture might have been accepted in established circles for its exotic aura, Rudofsky's sharp critique of the state of affairs in architecture is uncomfortable. Therefore, while he enjoys consistent recognition, his career is anchored for decades in *Architecture without Architects* (1964), in many ways the most "mellow" of his works. Overshadowed by the 1964 exhibition, the merits of his other shows and writings remain largely unacknowledged.

Part 1 examines the presence of boredom in Rudofsky's work and comprises three chapters. Chapter 1 delves into the origins of Rudofsky's understanding of boredom as a modern malaise from two angles. First, it shows how his reading of late nineteenth- and early twentieth-century European authors informs a particular view of tedium as a clinical condition that eventually corrupts the human soul. Concurrently, midcentury studies on the relationship of boredom, mechanization, and the commodification of leisure reinforce his ideas about domestic architecture as a place to awaken the experience of the phenomenal world. Chapter 2 looks at Rudofsky's critique of the modern manifestations of boredom observed through a series of domestic and travel practices as well as through the subtle, yet significant, changes in domestic architecture, summarized under the overarching theme of the "picture window." Chapter 3 examines Rudofsky's design tactics to resist the pervasive tedium of the environment. Specifically, I argue that through indoor and outdoor floors and pavements he offers an architectural and existential way of anchoring us in the world. Floors have the potential to delay movement, slow down the pace, and, implicitly, expand time. Active agents of our engagement with a place, floors transform boredom (*Langeweile,* the "long while") into a form of physical and imaginary wandering.

1

GENEALOGIES OF BOREDOM

A Modern Malaise

A CLINICAL CONDITION

The final chapter of *Behind the Picture Window* reviews the two overarching and intertwined problems of the American house: boredom and "disprivacy," a term Rudofsky invents to describe the peculiar dialectic of voyeurism and surveillance present in suburban architecture at the time. Confronting the boredom of the built environment is not a casual concern but an urgent matter of life or death: "Defense against boredom ought to have the highest priority in our fight for survival. Boredom threatens to paralyze the heart beat of life."[1] Rudofsky approaches boredom from a medical perspective, both as a physiological condition and as a psychological state. Three authors (Jewish-German physician Martin Gumpert, who immigrates to the United States in 1936; French psychologist Émile Tardieu; and Belgian professor Marcel Kiven) inform his view of ennui as a modern disorder spreading throughout society.

Cited by Rudofsky and annotated in his notebooks, Martin Gumpert's book *The Anatomy of Happiness* (1951) is a collection of short essays that examine happiness and unhappiness from a biological and physiological perspective. The book offers practical advice and concrete methods to attain a state of well-being.[2] Along with physical conditions (such as being "sick") and psychological traits (like "secretive" or "timid"), one of the twelve aspects of unhappiness is boredom, "a crippling chronic disease," which, Gumpert maintains, is primarily a matter of individual agency.[3] Rudofsky's own fears echo Gumpert's conviction that a society suffering from boredom will soon go extinct.[4] According to Gumpert's pathology of unhappiness, the diseases and imbalances of the human body (constipation, ulcer, gout, allergies) are modern symptoms of emotional distress.[5] His musings on constipation as a sign of a larger societal malfunction resonate with Rudofsky's interest in bodily functions such as eating, sleeping, and bathing. In "On Boredom and Disprivacy," Rudofsky directly quotes Gumpert: "The time spent in the bathroom has become for many people in our civilization the only time which they spend in complete privacy and isolation."[6] This tongue-in-cheek remark draws attention to one of the main concerns shared by the two authors: the lack of privacy in contemporary houses. Neither a practicing architect nor an architectural theorist, Gumpert believes that houses indicate the state of individual and collective health. A *good* home reflects a *good* citizen who belongs to a *good* community; consequently, the absence of privacy in modern houses points to the deteriorating health of their residents and, on a larger scale, to society's declining health. Key to one's happiness, privacy has become, in modern times, an expensive and rare commodity.[7]

Tying together ideas about boredom, inhabitation, happiness, and health, Gumpert provides the framework for understanding the weakened well-being of the modern individual. Similarly, Émile Tardieu's 1903 study on ennui approaches boredom from a medical angle, this time as a psychological condition having six main causes: exhaustion, lack of variety, failure in life, monotony, excess, and a sense of nothingness or nonbeing.[8] Although Rudofsky never mentions this study explicitly in any of his published works, in a notebook from the early 1950s, he takes thorough notes on Tardieu's book.[9]

Tardieu's view of ennui builds upon Arthur Schopenhauer's philosophy and the nineteenth-century Romantic writers (Giacomo Leopardi, Charles Baudelaire, and Guy de Maupassant) who regard tedium as the privilege of highly creative, emotional, and sensitive individuals, the only ones who have access to the torments of the soul. Schopenhauer's position that life moves between pain and boredom surfaces in Tardieu's study, where life is described as a painful and vain endeavor, continuous suffering, and a ceaseless search for never-attainable happiness.[10] An extreme psycho-physiological condition, ennui holds a mysterious aura and, not unlike the aesthetic category of the sublime, generates intense feelings of fear and excitement, danger and appeal. While it provokes moral pain, it also affects the physical body, its symptoms ranging from visible and ephemeral manifestations, such as yawning, grimaces, and tics, to longer-lasting and more profound effects: sensitivity to cold, lack of appetite, weight loss, mental confusion, hallucinations, hypochondria, and loose muscles.[11]

Observing that the symptom of boredom in modern times is the decline of imagination, Tardieu's conclusion reverberates in Rudofsky's own work: the ally in the fight against boredom is a "modest and difficult art, the art of living well."[12] Informed by Tardieu and Gumpert, Rudofsky formulates a recurrent idea in his writings and design projects: as "we are all more or less missing our private lives," the lack of privacy becomes one of the main sources of modern tedium.[13] Expressed as "boredom and disprivacy," this notion is central to Rudofsky's critique of contemporary houses. While Gumpert focuses on the biological aspects of ennui and Tardieu delves into its psychology, the two of them share the same concern with the lack of privacy as a cause of contemporary boredom in modern life. At the same time, the art of living well constitutes for both writers a remedy to this malaise of modern times, and Rudofsky will translate it into his poetic residential architecture projects.

Along with Gumpert and Tardieu, another resource for Rudofsky's understanding of boredom is Marcel Kiven, a Belgian professor teaching at the American University in Cairo in the early decades of the twentieth century, whose article on the philosophy and history of ennui Rudofsky reads and annotates in his notebooks.[14] Kiven's approach resonates with Tardieu's: as a moral disorder, ennui is one of the most debilitating ailments of the soul, with devastating long-term consequences.[15] Caused by the malfunctioning of our intellectual faculties, boredom results either from a lack or from an excess of action.[16] In his own notebooks, Rudofsky engages in a conversation in the margins with Kiven, interspersing his own musings between notes from Kiven's article. To Kiven's observation that boredom, through excessive action, transforms habits into automatic gestures, and that fashion coerces individuals into constantly changing their clothes, residence, and location, Rudofsky replies: "A[merican] boredom is ten times more devastating than erosion, fire and floods. The [swinish?] blight of anti-intellectualism. . . . No conservation project in sight."[17]

Kiven adds a new dimension to the discussion of boredom. Addressing the tension between work and leisure that emerges at the beginning of the twentieth century from automation, mechanization, and mass production, he finds that the idea of vacation or holiday (*congé*) is a consequence of the ennui from excess of action manifested through the tedious activities undertaken during long periods of work. When spare time is conceptualized as quantifiable free hours, leisure becomes just another form of occupied time. While repetitive work requires programmed relaxation, another form of repetition has a different outcome: habits (*habitudes*) create comfort, safety, and well-being—an explanation for homesickness, an emotion that Kiven describes as "the ennui caused by the habit of one's distant country."[18] And yet, no matter how far away one travels, Rudofsky believes there is no way to avoid boredom: "But so ingrown is boredom in the industrial man that he cannot escape it anymore . . . pain killers and boredom killers," he scribbles in his notebook.[19]

As a Jewish-German immigrant to the United States, Gumpert writes in a midcentury America that has witnessed, though not on its own land, the horrors of World War II and is now experiencing both the angst of the Cold War and the exhilaration of a booming consumer culture. Gumpert's view is practical, if often cynical, and rarely lingers on speculative musings. Contrast this with Tardieu and Kiven, who, writing at the turn of the twentieth century, acknowledge the damaging outcome of ennui but romanticize it as a necessary part of artistic life and the creative process. Thus, Rudofsky is exposed to distinct yet intertwined traditions: a physiological examination of ennui, rooted in the biological processes of the human body, and a psychological and philosophical approach, based on the intricate functioning of the human soul and spirit. As a designer, he observes that under the increasing pressure of consumerism, nineteenth-century ennui becomes the empty boredom of midcentury American middle-class life (in commodified houses). While maintaining a view of boredom as the disease of modernity, Rudofsky gives both nuance and tangible form to a rather abstract notion through specific observations about the nature of domestic practices, human habits, and various forms of inhabitation. Since architecture, for him, gives shape to a worldview, its ultimate goal is to nurture one's body *and* soul. Tedium emerges at the junction of modern architecture (with its distinct transparency, achieved through the dissolution of the walls) and consumer culture (manifested through a wide range of labor-saving and leisure-producing devices, such as radios, television sets, and pocket recorders). Ironically called "containers for man" or "magnificently appointed pillories," modern houses are better suited for robots than for human beings.[20]

Rudofsky recognizes the inevitable ennui spawned from the constant exposure to an unchanging environment, but he opposes change as a conventional response to boredom (a position that both Gumpert and Tardieu seem to favor). He remains a consistent critic of the desire for continuous change, expressed in the modern world through tourism and fashion. Though Rudofsky is a passionate traveler and an observer of sartorial practices, his interest lies elsewhere. Through his travels, he searches for those immutable characteristics of individual cultures and places.[21] In clothing, he criticizes the ephemerality of trends and attempts to find the natural flow between clothes and the human body, a connection lost through centuries of constraints and conventions. Convinced that constant change only reinforces the circle of boredom, he notes that in nonindustrialized countries, people experience neither the malaise of boredom nor the superficiality of fashion.[22]

THE MECHANIZATION AND COMMODIFICATION OF LEISURE

Manifested through explicit and implicit pathologies, modern boredom also arises from the mechanization of the modern world. Once leisure deteriorates into "entertainment machines"[23] that offer meaningless distractions, its higher sense of the cultivation of the soul is obliterated, and it turns into quantitative free time spent outside working hours. Examining boredom and modernity, Elizabeth Goodstein explains the "democratization of leisure" and, subsequently, the "democratization of boredom" as an outcome of different forms of mass entertainment emerging toward the end of the nineteenth century, when boredom becomes "available" to the masses.[24]

In the first half of the twentieth century, the expansion of capitalist modes of production and the commodification of free time fuel a growing anxiety about the role of leisure in everyday life. If in industrialized societies work becomes linked with boredom through repetition, so does leisure. In response to the painful tedium of working hours, the recreation industry increases its presence in people's lives. Mechanized work finds its reward in mechanized leisure.[25] Writing a few decades apart, Siegfried Kracauer and August Heckscher share the same concern that contemporary leisure undermines human interaction. The former finds modern boredom disguised in the short-lived satisfactions of various forms of mass media (advertisements, movies, and radio) and argues that a cacophony of events claims simultaneous presence in the viewer's mind, thus eliminating interpersonal conversation and communication.[26] Heckscher (who has a critical influence on Robert Venturi) decries the abstract nature of leisure, which weakens the value of shared experiences.[27] The decline of meaningful human interaction lies at the core of Rudofsky's own discontent with modern forms of distraction that have colonized the domestic realm, substituting noise for music and listening for talking.[28]

The Frankfurt School's critique of capitalism exposes the techniques deployed in a consumer society to exercise soft forms of control. Herbert Marcuse sees technological progress and mass production as methods of social control, another form of totalitarianism that encourages "a comfortable, smooth, reasonable, democratic unfreedom," one in which people identify themselves with their commodities.[29] Theodor Adorno and Max Horkheimer argue that the mass culture industry, where business rules as the only ideology, operates as an instrument of social manipulation by reducing art to amusement. Because leisure comes to rely on the same processes of mechanization, standardization, and distribution, leisure becomes indistinguishable from work, losing the characteristics that once defined it—namely, its freedom and variety. As a result, the tedium of the workplace extends into the boredom of nonworking hours: "Pleasure hardens into boredom because, if it is to remain pleasure, it must not demand any effort and therefore moves rigorously in the worn grooves of association."[30]

Lewis Mumford diagnoses the paradox of modern life as a perpetual state of conflict between the technological props of one's outside world and the emptiness of the inner life.[31] Quoted by Rudofsky, he contends that the labor-saving devices invented in the modern world give rise to an abysmal boredom hardly imaginable in earlier civilizations.[32] Forced into forms of structured leisure, people lose the freedom of gratuitous play, the ability to make choices and celebrate differences. Examining boredom as a pathological condition, Mumford concludes that it looms large over modern civilization like a ticking bomb about to explode.[33]

A different meaning of leisure, lost in the modern world, offers an alternative to the mass tedium generated by the entertainment industry. In a book published only three years before Rudofsky's *Behind the Picture Window,* Josef Pieper reclaims leisure as meaningful time spent in contemplation and spiritual activities.[34] Retrieving the ancient Greek concept of leisure as the basis of civilization, he challenges the modern notion of leisure as amusement. His etymological observation that the English word *school* derives from the Greek word for leisure (*skole*) suggests a kinship between education and leisure. The latter is not, in other words, simply free time; rather, it possesses an intrinsic spiritual value and plays a decisive role in one's personal growth. The ancient world considered leisure (*otium* in Latin), rather than work (*neg-otium* in Latin), the main activity of a healthy society. Pieper contends that boredom is a direct consequence of losing the spiritual dimension of leisure: "One can only be bored if the spiritual power to be leisurely has been lost."[35] Similarly, advocating for more free time and fewer working hours in the 1930s, Bertrand Russell estimates that a four-hour workday for everyone would ensure enough jobs to eliminate unemployment and simultaneously free up enough time for everyone to enjoy leisure—whose wise use, he concedes, "is a product of civilization and education."[36]

The nature of leisure, and its relationship with work, constitutes a research topic of utmost interest at midcentury. The Twentieth Century Fund (today The Twentieth Century Foundation), a progressive think tank founded as a nonprofit public policy research institution, appoints a team of researchers to investigate the issue of leisure. Authored by Sebastian de Grazia, the study is published in 1962 as *Of Time, Work and Leisure,* a book that will become a classic reference in leisure studies—and with which Rudofsky himself is familiar. Starting from Aristotle's definition of leisure as wisdom, virtue, available time, and absence of necessity, de Grazia calls into question the assumption that time outside work qualifies as leisure.[37] Integrated within capitalist mechanisms of production, modern leisure is part of the work-time system that requires individuals to keep themselves occupied and constantly engaged in purposeful activities. Etymologically derived from the Latin *licere* (to be allowed), de Grazia observes, modern leisure has an underlying theme of permission and morality.[38] In other words, leisure is not a right but a favor granted outside work. Ever since the invention of the mechanical clock in medieval monasteries, time has been measured, controlled, and, more recently, industrialized.[39] De Grazia argues that true leisure—that is, freedom from time and freedom from goal-oriented activities—disappears in a world dominated by mechanization, production, and quantified time. Despite the progress it brings into the world, mechanization threatens individual freedom because it coerces people into regimented modes of existence. De Grazia concludes that contemporary life—ruled by mechanization and efficiency—lacks true leisure activities, which are the ones people engage in for their own sake.[40] If work can ennoble human beings, leisure perfects them. Understanding its nature is key to recalibrating the future and well-being of humanity.[41]

2

CRITIQUES OF CONTEMPORARY TEDIUM

Boredom and Disprivacy

Two conditions of the world underlie Rudofsky's architectural theory: a prelapsarian, premodern state and a current one, fallen, corrupt, and characterized by the gradual disintegration of a set of values deemed central to the human being. While deliberately emphasizing the rift between the two as a rhetorical strategy, he remains a modern architect, but his is a modernity with a twist. Educated in the Viennese school of architecture, which built upon rather than rejected premodern culture, he cultivates throughout his life a deep interest in and respect for history, traditions, customs, and the vernacular. At the same time, his own design projects—from architectural and exhibition design to footwear—employ an unmistakably modern language. Rudofsky does not reject the comforts of modern life but calls into question consumerism, whose most damaging effect is boredom.

Boredom threatens the fragile balance between the human body (with its sensuous experience of the world) and the human mind (with its rational understanding of the world). Rudofsky's implicit premise is that the Cartesian split between mind and body constitutes one of the causes of modern tedium. If many of his proposals (to eliminate chairs, to sit and eat on the floor, to eat with one's hands, to dress in flowing fabrics, to walk on uneven floors) appear impractical, sometimes naive, and often absurd, this is precisely Rudofsky's goal: to provoke, and thus elicit a reaction from, readers jaded by their own acceptance of tedium. Rudofsky takes note of the banal manifestations of boredom in various practices of everyday life, which occur at the same time as gradual but irreversible changes in the architecture of the home. Of particular interest to him are culinary habits and travel practices, each institutionalized and regulated through mechanisms of consumption.

Rudofsky is convinced that the built environment should reflect life itself and, therefore, that the architect needs to have a thorough understanding of people's customs, habits, and practices. The essays in *Behind the Picture Window* lay out some of the major themes that he will return to in future writings and projects: gastronomy and kitchens; bathing, washing, and bathrooms; and sleeping and bedrooms. Rudofsky ties together the different threads of his argument through the notion of "disprivacy." Neither a lack of privacy nor a condition of publicness, disprivacy indicates the separation of the self from the world and accounts for the modern collapse of different levels of intimacy into one flat layer. Boredom and disprivacy, Rudofsky concludes, find architectural expression in the midcentury picture window. "Disprivacy" indicates not a lack of privacy but rather a fabricated privacy, one designed to be showcased and put on display.

MODERN SHIFTS IN DOMESTIC AND TRAVEL PRACTICES

Rudofsky's attention to modern habits has a broader scope. By examining the bodily dimensions of our most mundane acts—postures, positions, movements—individuals can also redefine their relationship with time. Instead of fighting time, they might begin to reappropriate it through these embodied habits and thus resist the emptiness of boredom.

Rudofsky's criticism begins in the kitchen. "He [the architect] drew diagrams of imaginary traffic lines," he writes, "registering the navigable straits and channels of an apartment, of a house. On paper they looked as efficient as mariners' charts; put to the test, they turned out to be illusive."[1] The implementation of Taylorism and scientific management principles in the domestic sphere gain popularity at the turn of the twentieth century and lead to efficiency and time-and-motion studies, applied primarily to the space of the kitchen. The diagrams of Lillian Gilbreth and Christine Frederick, two of the pioneers in the field of home economics, directly influence the standardized layouts of early and mid-twentieth-century kitchens. (Paul Emmons describes these studies as "objective routing," privileging "spatial relations over individual actions.")[2] By midcentury, the American housewife is presented with a broad choice of appliances whose goal is to transform the erstwhile cozy kitchen into a scientific laboratory of efficient food production.

Rudofsky romanticizes the premodern kitchen (which he compares to a chapel where the hearth doubles as an altar and a sacrificial stone) and argues that the focus on scientific data related to food quality and production fails to address what constitutes the very core of a kitchen: the temporal act (and art) of preparing food.[3] The products of this workroom are bland, flavorless, and uninspiring. Although Rudofsky's observations are often generic and sometimes lack nuance, they gain new relevance decades later in the twenty-first century, when an increased concern with the ethics and quality of food emerges in new attention to locally grown food, food waste, food deserts, slow food, and overall accessibility to food. These contemporary conversations indicate that his writing might offer a framework for conceptualizing social and economic issues hitherto unforeseen in the mid-twentieth century.

Rudofsky's biases are explicit when he makes Eurocentric claims (e.g., that art has flourished in countries such as Italy and France, where good food is valued and appreciated) dismissing American cuisine, only acknowledging Southern food because of its French and Latin American influences (ignoring, however, its significant African and African American heritage).[4] As an alternative to warming up prepackaged food, he presents gastronomy as an art and a practice engaging not only all the senses but also the imagination and intellect.[5] By shortcutting the process of preparing and savoring food, the modern individual loses the immediate connection with the ingredients as well as the experience of enjoying the meal. No longer a pleasure, eating simply satisfies a basic need. While the mechanical props of the modern world might reduce the time one spends cooking, they also reduce the time for relishing the process itself. The decline of gastronomy is, for Rudofsky, immediate evidence of modern boredom.

The potential of culinary arts to engage both the sensual body and the rational mind contains the seeds of a modern resistance to tedium: "Work in the kitchen must go on, if only to banish that frightful spectre of modern life, boredom. The kitchen (restored to its old function) is the one place in the house where we still have a chance to use our brains and to test our senses."[6] It is the space that might offer "a last refuge from our aching boredom."[7]

Proper cooking, however, will not suffice. The ritual of sharing a meal, its lengthy enjoyment, and the company of others—in other words, the slow pace required to celebrate gastronomical delights—bring meaning and pleasure to everyday life. "Conviviality, rather than mere socializing, cultivates humaneness," Rudofsky writes.[8] He invites readers to challenge contemporary modes of eating while seated, often indecorously placing food on their laps, and to contemplate instead the possibility of adopting the reclining posture during eating, a well-documented ancient custom and an alternative that would impose a more leisurely pace on an otherwise hurried diner.[9] The lesson here extends beyond a debate about sitting up or lying down during a meal or about the pertinence of cultural transfers from the ancient to the modern world. Indeed, it brings forward the social and ritualistic dimension of eating and cooking, their temporal quality, and the potential of culinary arts to bring people together and create a community. In an unexpected historical twist more than half a century later, a global pandemic has forced people across the world to reconsider the very notion of community and has radically called into question our relationship with time and space, with each other, and with our own selves. Considering these drastic shifts, Rudofsky's midcentury rhetorical question appears uncannily premonitory: "Can you imagine that some day eating in company will be declared unlawful?"[10]

Modern boredom corrupts the relationship of the *self* to the *other* at the intimate level of the domestic sphere (expressed in culinary practices) as well as in the more public sphere of travel practices. A restless explorer, Rudofsky travels the world from a young age and remains throughout his life a perceptive observer of habits, customs, and traditions and their integration with the built environment. Several scholars have examined the role of travel in Rudofsky's professional work and personal life. Felicity Scott attributes his passion for discovering new places to an interest in nomadism.[11] Andrea Bocco Guarneri notices that, while following the routes of mass tourism, Rudofsky does it at a slower pace and with a deeper and more engaged eye.[12] Ugo Rossi explains Rudofsky's enthusiasm for travel as a desire to understand history and the works of the past.[13] Wim de Wit observes that although Rudofsky's passion for travel and his deep appreciation of customs might appear contradictory, it is precisely through his travels that he understands the continuity and flexibility of tradition.[14] Observing the similarities between Rudofsky's travel notebooks and his reading notebooks, de Wit proposes that traveling and reading are for him kindred processes, both nurturing his desire to understand the world.[15] This process of discovery simultaneously involves a close-up look and a bird's-eye view, and it is with this mindset that he approaches new places, unknown people, and unfamiliar habits.

I would argue that the themes of travel and boredom for Rudofsky are directly related (as Wim de Wit observes) and that modern changes in various domestic and travel customs have a common root: the disintegration of embodied habits in consumerist societies, where time matters only as a means of efficiency and productivity.[16] Rudofsky witnesses the transformation of travel into profitable mass tourism, which he attributes to the boredom of capitalist societies. Tedium plays a double role: on the one hand, feeling bored at home, people seek distraction elsewhere; their impulse to travel is not a genuine desire for discovery but simply another form of programmed entertainment. On the other hand, responding to the pressures of the industry, what were once places become tourist destinations. Gradually losing their character, they begin to look the same to offer the identical experiences set by travel guidebooks. The dullness of the modern tourist and the dullness of the destination constitute the tragedy of contemporary travel: "Travel, once the supreme tool for broadening one's horizons, has become a catalyst of boredom. Much that constituted travel's fascination—variety, strangeness, the direct access to a people's know-how and wisdom as exemplified in its folkways—is being obliterated by universal standardization."[17]

The recurrent themes of travel, boredom, and leisure are essential in Rudofsky's work. *Behind the Picture Window* is bookended by two chapters that discuss these themes at length. Consumerism makes people believe that their discontent with life can be cured by changing and upgrading their possessions, from the most banal objects of everyday use to their houses.[18] Invoked both at the beginning and at the end of Rudofsky's book, Arthur Townsend, a character in Henry James's novel *Washington Square* who constantly keeps up with new things and frequently changes his residence for a newer, improved one, is the epitome of the modern individual.[19] Townsend has the attitude and mentality of a perpetual tourist. Whether moving from one house to another or between different places, modern Townsends remain everlasting victims of boredom: "Many a man who seeks relief in travel cannot shake off boredom any more. At vacation time, when the empty hours stretch into days and weeks, he develops a most virulent form of it. The managers of resort hotels and cruise ships are familiar with the dangers of leisure and hire the services of so-called social directors."[20]

In his notebooks, Rudofsky muses about the emerging phenomenon of mass tourism (and of the American tourist in particular). Responding to Marcel Kiven's essay on the history and philosophy of boredom, he writes:

> Here is the whole tragedy of the A[merican] tourist. Neither curiosity nor eagerness drive him to travel abroad. Before he has even seen foreign ways, he will [regret them?]. With that good feeling to spread his wisdom, he is unable

> to communicate with the foreigner because he does not speak his language. Neither can he permit himself to learn languages because this would be the first step in an endless process of contamination not only with foreign words but foreign ideas. Sometimes his position will appear to him exasperated and hopeless. He will point out that he is eager to learn from others, even to assimilate his customs, to be willing to color his own ways with foreign [ways?], to like, nay, to adore, say, spaghetti and meat balls only to find out that Italians are totally ignorant of such a dish and, worse, unwilling to produce or eat it.[21]

The experience of food and that of travel share a temporal dimension. The inventions of modern life, from kitchen appliances to the mechanisms of mass tourism, offer the alluring promise of shortening both the time of culinary preparation and the time of travel. Fast gastronomy and fast travel are becoming a reality. Rudofsky's implicit question is, "To what end?" If efficiency becomes the norm at the expense of any other consideration, then what is life reduced to? In the early twentieth century, Lillian Gilbreth conceptualizes the home as a factory and the homemaker as a worker. Her efficiency studies claim to free "happiness minutes" for the homemakers—time spent outside domestic chores for leisurely pursuits. Just as with work, leisure is now quantified. However, by focusing exclusively on the outcome (the meal or the travel destination) and ignoring the process leading to it (food preparation or travel itself), one reduces the length of the experience to a fleeting moment whose enjoyment is brief and unsatisfying. Hence the desire to quickly gain another short-lived moment of pleasure. Unfulfilled, this desire leads to boredom. The paradox of modern life is that accomplishing tasks faster does not free up time but rather enslaves it to boredom. The "happiness moments" remain just that: inconsequential instances without depth.

THE TWO SIDES OF THE PICTURE WINDOW

The picture window—the popular midcentury architectural feature giving Rudofsky's collection of essays its title—becomes the overarching allegory of boredom. But what is a picture window, and more importantly, why is it associated with boredom?

While the *Oxford English Dictionary* traces the term's first use to an article published by Harriet Beecher Stowe in the *Atlantic Monthly* in 1864, it is originally applied in decorative arts rather than architecture. Although it generally indicates a framed view, in its original meaning this view is that of a stained-glass window or an artwork displayed in an interior space.[22]

By 1945, a "picture window" designates the framing of an outdoor view and is appropriated in the architectural vocabulary as a specific attribute of modern domesticity. However, by this time it already carries the tension between lowbrow and highbrow architecture. A 1942 issue of *Architectural Forum* dedicated to the house of the future recognizes its popularity, conceding that it is acceptable as long as it does not create problems with lighting, heating, and ventilation.[23] On the other hand, the curator of the 1945 architectural exhibition *Tomorrow's Small House,* organized by the Museum of Modern Art in New York in response to the post–World War II housing crisis, praises the virtues of the glass wall but mocks the "the silly artifice of the 'picture window.'"[24] By the early 1950s, to have a house with a picture window is to embrace a modern lifestyle, even when opening one into the wall of an old house is but an ironic pretense of modernization.[25]

The picture window acts as an interface between the indoors and outdoors, allowing these two worlds to coexist yet remain independent of each other—a position constantly reinforced in period advertising, where cheerful housewives, always portrayed indoors, look outside at an environment generally depicted as hostile, either too cold or too hot. Their clothes remain the same, regardless of seasonal changes outdoors. Thanks to the interface of the picture window and the convenience of HVAC systems, the homemaker can perform her household duties undisturbed by snow, rain, or excessive heat or cold, all while keeping a vigilant eye on the outdoors. As she carries on inside with her domestic chores, her children play outside in a beautiful garden.[26] Primarily targeting and featuring housewives, the advertisements for insulating glass (such as Twindow) promise a perpetual domestic heaven, undisturbed by the uncertainties of nature.

In advertising, the term "picture window" designates a particular type of page layout, the most popular one in the 1930s and 1940s (and represented in nearly half of all the ads of the 1960s).[27] It is worth pondering the implicit meaning of this term as it relates to advertising throughout this period. While the interchangeable use of "picture window" in advertising and architecture might simply appear to be a consequence of the visual similarities between the frame of an ad and that of an architectural element, it also indicates the commodification of the latter. Owing its pervasiveness to bold marketing campaigns, the picture window itself becomes an advertisement for prescribed lifestyles and cookie-cutter houses. The commercials promote the picture window, which in turn commercializes a particular standard of living.

In the most comprehensive history of the picture window to date, Sandy Isenstadt argues that its popularity emerges from the aggressive advertising campaigns conducted by glass manufacturers in the early and middle decades of the twentieth century in popular and professional magazines. By aligning the small-scale domesticity of the American house with the vastness of the American landscape, the picture window becomes the expression of larger democratic ideals.[28] Isenstadt shows that throughout the 1930s, the Libbey-Owens-Ford glass company implements "the picture window idea" as the articulation of access to nature (as a traditional American value) and technological progress (as a trademark of American "forward thinking"). In the post–World War II decades, the company continues to promote the picture window as a condition for modern happiness achieved through light and spaciousness.[29]

New technologies and construction materials enable the separation between the traditional functions of a window: visibility and ventilation. On the one hand, thanks to insulating glass such as Twindow or Thermopane, windows can expand to the size of an entire wall without the danger of thermal loss. On the other hand, HVAC systems create an artificially controlled environment where hot and cold air are mechanically activated, no longer requiring operable windows. A 1945 design manual specifically encourages homebuilders not to take for granted the traditional dual function of the window and instead to accept the new technological possibilities: while mechanical systems take care of ventilation, cooling, and heating without the need to open a window manually, large glass panes—reinforced, insulated, and energy efficient—bring in ample views and generous lighting.[30]

Large windows not only enable views of the outside but also create increased visibility for the activities taking place inside the house, an implicit form of double surveillance. The modern window fulfills the aspiration for perfect clarity; its lack of ambiguity carries the promise of moral and intellectual enlightenment. By midcentury, "picture window" designates "a large window in a house usually dominating the room or wall in which it is located, and often designed or decorated to present an attractive view as seen from inside or outside the house."[31]

While real estate developers and glass manufacturers promote the picture window as an elegant sign of a progressive lifestyle, for the critics of the American suburb, it stands for everything that is wrong with the society: consumerism, conformism, numbing repetition, and uniformity. Rudofsky uses this term as an allegory of specific social and cultural changes surfacing or already developing in post–World War II American society. Midcentury boredom emerges from the combined effects of the commodification of architecture and shifts in the notion of privacy.

COMMODIFICATION AND CONFORMITY

Under the pressure of increased production, consumerism becomes the norm for social integration. To buy, and to have, is to belong. Present at all levels of society, conformism and uniformization lead to the commodification of individual houses. House typologies, types of furniture, and appliances are concrete expressions of one's status. Lifestyles, customs, and habits exist within the parameters defined by the rules of consumption. Presented as a unique feature of the modern house, the picture window is the tangible expression of a new standard of living.

While in theory, post–World War II suburban developments attempt to respond to real demands emerging in the society (i.e., the need for affordable housing), the newly built houses (simplified versions of nineteenth-century homes) reduce inhabitation to a series of mere necessities, stripping off elements of play, conviviality, and pleasure.[32] These houses now provide the bare minimum needed for a modest life (living room, kitchen, two bedrooms, and a bathroom), while spaces deemed superfluous and unnecessary are eliminated.[33] Gone from the body of the house are those spaces where socializing at home used to take place, the rooms where the family would gather with friends: formal dining rooms, sun porches, or guest rooms. What is left is the living space dedicated to the nuclear family, where only the most basic needs are met: eating, sleeping, washing, and—a novelty—watching television. The family is thus forced into a lonesome existence by the very spaces it occupies and the configuration of its house.

As a surface, the (mostly suburban) picture window negotiates the connection between constructed forms of domesticity and a staged outdoors. The proliferation of picture windows coincides with the democratization of television sets, as both types of screens mediate the relationship between individual and reality. Daniel Boorstin remarks that the picture window has replaced "the friendly front porch" in domestic architecture.[34] A liminal place where the inside greets the outside and the familiar ponders the unfamiliar, the porch is the thick space where waiting is not boredom and where various social practices are enacted. (Steinberg will show this space as a place for daydreaming.) Keeping the domestic interior out of reach for the *other,* the porch creates the promise of unveiling it to those allowed to cross the threshold. The picture window, on the other hand, eliminates the tacit rituals taking place on the porch and offers, instead, a shortcut to the image of a staged interior, a condition of mutual surveillance.

Typically situated along the back wall of the living room, the picture window has standardized dimensions: eight feet high and sixteen feet wide.[35] As real estate interests dictate high densities of occupation in suburban developments, the picture window ends up looking not toward a view but toward another picture window.[36] "The picture in the picture window, for example, is what is going on *inside*—or, what is going on inside other people's picture windows," observes urbanist and journalist William H. Whyte.[37] Not unlike the newly acquired television sets, the picture widow is itself a screen that displays both the dramas and the sitcoms of everyday life.[38]

In the society of the picture window, conformity becomes a core value. Writing at midcentury, several scholars observe that the process of democratization, unfolding at multiple levels, is occurring simultaneously with a process of uniformization and leveling of taste. Whyte describes the era as the age of conformism, where any deviation from the norm, whether it is about having more or having less, is cause for notice and concern.[39] What he calls the "new packaged suburbs" are not simply assemblies of mass housing but structures that engender "a new social institution."[40] Sociologist David Riesman argues that what characterizes the new middle-class American society is conformity with the expectations and preferences of the social group to which one wishes to belong.[41] He proposes a three-tiered evolution of societies in time. Unlike the previous stage of society (inner-oriented and focused on production), the current phase is outer-oriented and focused on consumption. Individual goals no longer relate to ideals of self-fulfillment and personal growth but respond to the peer pressure exercised by the social group.[42] Theodor Adorno and Max Horkheimer see in advanced industrialized societies evidence of social control disguised as the promise of democratization. Conformity to the norm is key to achieving this new mode of compliance with the political and (more importantly) economic apparatus. While everyone is free, individuals are regimented from an early age in a system of various organizations (such as churches, clubs, or professional associations), which act as instruments of social control.[43]

To have a choice is also to exercise critical judgment and thus resist the facile path of conformism. Advocating this position, Rudofsky closes *Behind the Picture Window* with a quote by Judge Learned Hand, a significant figure in the American judicial landscape of the first half of the twentieth century: "Our dangers . . . are not from the outrageous but from the conforming; . . . from those, the mass of us, who take their virtues and their tastes, like their shirts and their furniture, from the limited patterns which the market offers."[44] Under the pressure of consumerism, the dwelling becomes one of the most visible and quantifiable expressions of compliance with norms. The proliferation of picture windows in environments where common sense would advise otherwise embodies the obedience to normative standards for the sake of conveying social status and a sense of belonging.

DISPRIVACY

Indicating a shift in the notion of privacy, the picture window is a concrete step toward the "society of the spectacle." In 1962, five years before Guy Debord coins this term, Daniel Boorstin decries the transformation of American society in a collection of "pseudo-events" where the only thing that has value is the image one creates of oneself and projects into the world.[45] In a world where mass media shape people's experiences and individuals turn from active agents of their own lives into passive observers, the thresholds between private and public spheres gradually disappear. The picture window eliminates the liminal spaces between interior and exterior, setting the stage for the spectacle, which "is . . . a social relation among people, mediated by images."[46] Rudofsky's notion of "disprivacy" illuminates this condition, characterized by an alteration of the relationship between the self and the world.

On either side of the picture window, the viewer remains in expectation, a mere observer of a possible event that never occurs. Framing a view, the picture window outlines the framework of expectation, of waiting for something to happen, and makes visible boredom and disprivacy as two concurrent conditions of the modern house and the modern individual: the ordinary boredom of the housewife waiting for her children to return from school and for her husband to come back from work; the apathy of children who have less and less direct interaction with the world; the tedium of husbands filling up nonworking hours with scripted leisure time.

No longer an architectural element, the picture window becomes an optical device that, quite literally, simply creates a picture. Art historian Julian Jason Haladyn observes that from Kepler's *Optics* onward there is a split between the *presence* of an object seen with the eye and the *image* produced in the eye by the same object.[47] Termed a "picture," the latter defines modern subjectivity as a process by which the world is known and represented through a constructed image.[48] The modern subject assumes this distance between the object and its representation, thus becoming an observer of the world rather than an agent of it. The picture in the picture window signals the passive role of the dweller in their own environment and the separation of the self from the world, which is no longer experienced directly but mediated through an image. By offering access to the most intimate moments of domesticity, the picture window contributes to the erosion of privacy in modern life.[49]

For Boorstin, the picture window is symptomatic of the current state of American society. Like a double-sided viewing device, it often opens toward another picture window, revealing "a large, ornate, tasteless electric lamp" on one side and "our neighbor himself" on the other.[50] Whether private (house) or public (store), the interior is staged for display thanks to the extensive use of glass, a modern material that acts as a democratizing agent.[51]

The new suburban house represents ideas about living, constructed and disseminated mainly through advertising as a means to create middle-class aspirations. The failure of "the image" comes from a profound disconnect between people's real needs and desires and what these dwellings actually have to offer, an underlying theme of a significant body of literature at midcentury. Published two years after Rudofsky's *Behind the Picture Window,* John Keats's book *The Crack in the Picture Window* (1957) is a fictional account of a generic middle-class family, the Drones (John, Mary, and their two children), who buy and move into the only house they can afford, only to be trapped in a frustrating existence of monotony and financial debt. Basing his book on newspaper and magazine articles and various studies published between 1944 and 1955, Keats, a journalist himself, identifies the main problems of suburban sprawl as financial and land speculation, manipulation through advertising, poor design, and lack of a true sense of community.

One of the central themes of the book is the deadening boredom of a uniform and repetitive environment that keeps the housewife, along with the rest of the family, in the infinite loop of ennui. All the families live in identical houses, with identical views, equipped with identical furniture and appliances. The symbol of this abysmal boredom is the picture window: "Through their picture window, a vast and empty eye . . . they could see their view—a house like theirs across a muddy street, its vacant picture eye staring into theirs."[52]

The house is inadequate for the life of the family: although brand new, it is poorly finished, undersized, and has an inefficient layout. It becomes Mary's archnemesis as she struggles and fails to make a comfortable environment for her family. She addresses her main problem—boredom—by watching television, which only pulls her deeper into the abyss of ennui. Along with visual monotony, tedium settles in surreptitiously as an overarching mood and state of mind: from houses, meals, television shows, and clothes that are all alike to identical Yummy Gummy mixes, available in "six distinctively similar flavors," diversity is only a controlled illusion.[53] Like Rudofsky, Keats observes that people's belief in change will cure their existential boredom. Predictably, however, Mary discovers the only significant difference between suburbs: the price of boredom is higher in another subdivision.[54]

The tedium of the suburban wife is a leitmotif in Betty Friedan's canonical *The Feminine Mystique,* in which she examines closely the sense of emptiness, incompletion, and profound boredom experienced by midcentury housewives.[55] Critical of an architecture designed primarily by men with no consideration for women's needs or desires, Friedan studies the psychological effects of architectural layouts and observes that the housewife is forced to spend most of her time in open-plan houses where the lack of doors and walls results in a lack of privacy and the impossibility of being alone.[56] Boredom and fatigue exacerbate the sense of profound loneliness.

Rudofsky's notion of disprivacy emerges, along with boredom, within the "society of the spectacle," wherein the self deliberately exposes itself to the world. Peeking at and spying on each other through picture windows, people construct and display fabricated scenes of domesticity as a way of showing their sense of belonging to a group and a social class. Along with the picture window, the front lawn completes the setting for this type of artificial social interaction. All the manicured front lawns look alike and perform the same decorative function, without inviting or allowing for spontaneous interactions. Just as picture windows are not designed to be opened or kept ajar, front lawns are not meant to be actively used. The picture window is not a window but a screen on which everyday life projects its boredom; the lawn is not a green space but a theatrical background that levels out the natural imperfections of topography or vegetation. Both features express what sociologist William M. Dobriner calls in his book *Class in Suburbia* (1963) the "visibility principle": they allow residents to observe and watch each other's behaviors and lifestyles. Barbara M. Kelly makes a distinction between the privacy of the Levittown house, centered on its own lot, and the lack of privacy within the house itself, where the nuclear family has no other choice than to be together all the time.[57] Rudofsky never explains the notion of disprivacy. However, it could be situated between Dobriner's "visibility principle" and Kelly's interpretation of domesticity, giving a more nuanced account of the complex social relationships unfolding in the suburban house between the front lawn and the picture window.

Rudofsky finds his allies not among architects but among writers from other disciplines. His interest in human behaviors, habits, and material culture direct him toward contemporary anthropologists such as Margaret Mead and her student Geoffrey Gorer, who offer valuable perspectives on both the strengths and the weaknesses of American society. Gorer argues that people's fear of being by themselves is manifested in specific architectural features, such as open plans and a lack of doors both in private houses and office spaces.[58] He notices the lack of boundaries or transition areas such as hedges, walls, or gates: "In the normal American house . . . nearly everything is open to the inspection of the world."[59] Houses become mechanisms of display and voyeurism. If privacy is intimacy, disprivacy is loneliness.

What are, then, possible tactics to resist environmental ennui? What is Rudofsky's response to the discomforts of modern boredom? How can individuals regain their sense of self deeply affected by ennui? The answer resides in the same place that generates the problem: the architecture of the house. *Behind the Picture Window* becomes a manifesto for retrieving the intimate connections between individuals and their homes through embodied habits and bodily rhythms as a means to address modern ennui. The last chapter of part I will examine Rudofsky's specific design strategies formulated around ideas about leisure as a state of being free of everyday necessity, a central aspect of the art of living well.

3

TACTICS OF RESISTING ENNUI

Floors and "Our Fingertip Feeling"

Ubiquitous in industrialized and modern societies, boredom emerges as a state of discomfort with and alienation from the environment. When they are not chasing fads or trying to keep up with the Joneses, people often find themselves unable to enjoy a life outside the consumer bubble. Bored, they lose contact with and interest in the world. Two divergent phenomena are unfolding simultaneously. On the one hand, projects such as John Entenza's Case Study Houses promote modern architecture through designers like Richard Neutra, Eero Saarinen, and Ray and Charles Eames, and advertising entices people to consume lifestyles constructed through impeccable images (such as Julius Shulman's artful photographs). On the other hand, architects begin to question Modernism's promised land of progress, comfort, and social equity that seems oblivious to the reality of segregation, suburbia, and lack of affordable housing.

ON FLOORS

Rudofsky responds to the conundrums of Modernism not by negating its principles but by redefining the primal elements of architecture. While scholars such as Andrea Bocco Guarneri and Ugo Rossi note his interest in an architecture of the senses, they overlook how modern boredom is integral to his approach. Rudofsky's implicit claim is that consumerism lies at the origins of modern tedium and that architecture—and more specifically, the dwelling—is its first victim. Resistance to boredom begins with a sensuous architecture that awakens the body, resituates it in the world, and restores the broken connection with the environment.

Like other midcentury architects, Rudofsky recognizes that modern architecture—in tandem with consumer culture—has become normative, alienating people from their places. He offers perhaps the most unexpected way for modern consumers to overcome their jaded existence. At a time when most architects look *up* above the ground to *see* as a prevailing mode of perceiving the environment, he looks *down* to *feel* the touch of the floor. As the only surfaces that constantly engage our sense of touch, floors are never merely functional nor merely aesthetic. We rarely see them, but we always feel them, and they carry an inherent contradiction: for them to function properly, they need to go unnoticed, but as they go unnoticed, they diminish our awareness of the ground.

I argue that Rudofsky's attention to floors and pavements, which scholarship has only marginally examined despite its consistent presence in his work, reflects an ethical concern with defining one's place in the world.[1] If to be bored is also to lose a sense of belonging, becoming aware of the surfaces we step on might reconnect us to a deeper sense of the self. Three implicit themes underlie his explorations of floors. First, they inform our grounding (in the most basic sense of growing roots), connecting the human body and the architectural body with the earth and making present the forces of gravity. Second, both interior and exterior horizontal surfaces define and frame the horizon as a cultural stance within a specific place. Last, as the canvas against which life itself unfolds, floors construct the mood of a place by being active agents of our various practices of inhabitation.

GROWING ROOTS. For Rudofsky, every building begins with floors and walls that give human beings the ontological status of their upright posture. "A wall is the bread of architecture," he argues. "Building his first wall, he [the man] became, mentally, a biped."[2] Elsewhere, he writes: "The floor is, literally and figuratively, the touchstone of a civilization. A good floor is much more than a delight to the eye; it appeals to that most sensuous of our senses, touch."[3] In the February 1938 issue of *Domus,* Rudofsky publishes what looks like an old illustration of an architectural foundational moment: builders have laid out the foundations of the outer walls of a house and are now setting the stones to stabilize the structure. Rudofsky's caption states the primordial role of floor, and floor plan, as the organizing force of the building: "Architecture begins with a pavement: the architect inscribes order in the freedom of nature."[4]

The drawing recalls ancient practices of inscribing the plan of a building at full scale onto the site itself.[5] While in premodern times the floor *was* the actual floor plan of a new construction, this intimate relationship has been gradually lost with the changing practices of architectural drawing, construction, and technology. As Paul Emmons observes, the construction of the plan on site anticipates the future building, establishing an intimate connection between drawing, site, and architecture.[6] No longer viewed as an embodied footprint but primarily as a horizontal section, today the floor plan bears little, if any, affinity with the architectural floor.[7]

Challenging these modern forms of representation, Rudofsky explores drawings and buildings as embodied phenomena. The surface of the page, the surface of the building floor, and the surface of the site itself become one, and thus the pavement is invested with an ontological role. In a disenchanted world increasingly perceived through new media, by rediscovering the primeval sense of touch, individuals experience the unmediated presence of the land while gaining a sense of belonging to a larger community. A floor grounds human beings in the earth and situates them within the horizon of a specific culture. Because "every culture has its perfect pavement," the floors—experienced by walking barefoot—teach more about a certain civilization than any writings or indirect accounts.[8]

Connected through the intimacy of the sole, feet and floors are inseparable in Rudofsky's work, a relationship celebrated in architectural as well as footwear designs. Bernardo Sandals, originating in 1946, make manifest the bodily awareness of the horizontal plane. Designed to accommodate rather than constrain the anatomy of the foot, the sandals aspire to remain timeless pieces, comfortable and wearable beyond fashions and fads. Building upon the multiple meanings of the Italian word *pianta,* Rudofsky notes the attraction between the sole of the foot (*la pianta del piede*) that caresses the sole of the house and also its plan (*la pianta della casa*).[9] Departing from modernist notions about functionality and efficiency, he establishes an affinity between the plan of the house and the materiality of its pavement: "The pavement will control the plan. Only on a good plan can one make a good pavement."[10] The floor thus becomes the articulation of the architectural body and the human body.

Floors establish connections among the personal scale of the body, the convivial scale of the community, and the larger one of the environment, as shown in the Neolithic houses in Lindenthal, Germany, discovered in the early decades of the twentieth century. Far from primitive, they reveal to Rudofsky a methodical architectural strategy that is neither accidental nor clumsy.[11] Central to their design is the sculpted floor that celebrates the intimate encounter of the body with the earth and, as the author infers, situates the individual in the world.[12] What Rudofsky calls our lost "fingertip feeling" (*Fingerspitzengefühl*) suggests not only the sensitivity of our limbs (now numbed) but also a certain intuition about place, space, and materiality that humans forgot as they became modern.

In 1938, Rudofsky publishes in *Domus* the drawings of a project for a (never-built) house on the island of Procida, off the coast of Naples.[13] Titled "What We Need Is Not New Technologies, but a New Way of Living," the article represents, as Rudofsky himself will later acknowledge, the kernel of "half a dozen books on architecture, apparel and related matters."[14] Designed for a piece of land that he and his wife, Berta, bought on the island in 1935, the project constitutes Rudofsky's manifesto on the ideal dwelling. A harmonious encounter between architecture and lifestyle, the ideal home eliminates the unnecessary prostheses of consumerism, seeking an intimate relationship between inhabitants, nature, and the man-made environment (fig. 1).

The article begins with a recurrent idea in Rudofsky's writings: people lost contact with the ground long ago.[15] More than a rhetorical trope, this statement indicates a deeper loss: the erosion of our grounding in the world and the dissolution of tectonics, understood as an intimate connection between body, building, and the earth. Lacking this foundation, the modern individual becomes bored. In

Figure 1. Bernard Rudofsky, project for a house on the island of Procida, Italy (unbuilt), axonometric view. Published in *Domus*, no. 123 (March 1938). (© 2023 Artists Rights Society [ARS], New York / Bildrecht, Vienna)

the nineteenth century, Søren Kierkegaard describes the concept of boredom as the result of constantly sliding over surfaces and never growing roots. Born from discontent with a current situation, this constant desire to move only feeds people's dissatisfaction with their lives, providing momentary—but never sufficient—relief from boredom.[16]

As Rudofsky writes elsewhere, modern houses, with their transparent walls, appear so light that they could fly away at any moment, like a magic carpet.[17] The gradual loss of tectonics translates into human uprootedness. This sense of displacement is present in the matching suburban houses that simultaneously respond to and create the need for identical environments, irrespective of location, living customs, or individual habits. As the characters in John Keats's *Crack in the Picture Window* come to realize, the urge to move to a different, supposedly better house is a pressure artificially created by consumer culture. Never living in the present and perpetually bored with it, the users of these houses have lost their grounding. Rudofsky's implicit claim is that to become aware of the floor is, in a larger sense, to become aware of and live in the present moment, resisting the boredom that society inflicts upon us.

Designed in a modern vocabulary, the Procida project nonetheless challenges modern assumptions about function and program. The rooms are designated with conventional nomenclature (living room, dining room, bedroom, bathroom, and so on), but they respond to the activities taking place rather than to the programming logic. Those activities are shown in various forms of architectural representation: model photographs and drawings ranging from hand-drawn sketches, perspectives, and axonometries to a more rigorous plan, all inhabited by real and imaginary characters (fig. 2).

The boundary between indoors and outdoors is blurred not through the modernist trope of glass walls but through practices of living in and occupying the space. People's movements between inside and outside are choreographed through the materials and textures of walls and floors. In a subtle play of scales and textures, furniture turns into architecture and architecture into furniture. Rudofsky eliminates the dining table, the desk, the night table, the kitchen table, and the bathtub, considering them superfluous.[18] Having the entire floor made of mattresses, the whole bedroom becomes an oversized bed (not unlike Japanese rooms covered in *tatami*), where one can only walk barefoot.[19] At the same time, the mosquito net hanging from the ceiling and hovering above the entire room evokes both a baldachin and an archetypal primitive hut (fig. 3).

Figure 2. Bernard Rudofsky, project for a house on the island of Procida, Italy (unbuilt), composite drawing. Published in *Domus*, no. 123 (March 1938). (© 2023 Artists Rights Society [ARS], New York / Bildrecht, Vienna)

In Rudofsky's theory of inhabitation, there is an essential distinction between washing (as the modern, utilitarian act of removing dirt and grime) and bathing (as an ancient form of ritual or cultivated leisure). The chapter "Our Indecorous Bathroom" from *Behind the Picture Window* explains this difference at length, describing it as an unintended outcome of the schism between mind and body. In the Procida house, the toilet and sink are in one space and the bathtub in another, and the bathroom itself becomes a bathtub: dipping into the ground, the floor carves out

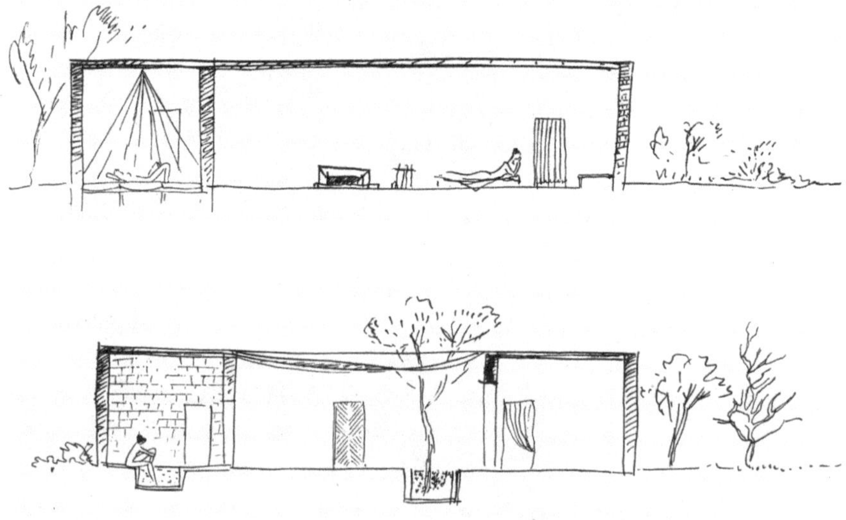

Figures 3–4. Bernard Rudofsky, project for a house on the island of Procida, Italy (unbuilt), section. Published in *Domus*, no. 123 (March 1938). (© 2023 Artists Rights Society [ARS], New York / Bildrecht, Vienna)

the bathtub from the ground plane, creating an intimate relationship between the body of the bather and the earth (fig. 4). One could trace the inspiration for this gesture back to the Lindenthal houses, whose living rooms had a sunken space in the middle, "a sort of square womb for faltering souls."[20] (A few years after the Procida project, Rudofsky will once again take cues from Neolithic architecture for the floor of his 1944 exhibition *Are Clothes Modern?* at New York's Museum of Modern Art, where the uneven floor, made of wood and plaster and meant to suggest an irregular, undulating stone pavement, did not have the impact he was anticipating: "An uneven floor was inimical to our footwear."[21])

People are represented lying down or sitting directly on the floor in a space similar to a Roman *triclinium,* where an assemblage of three stones with a marble slab in the middle replaces conventional chairs and tables (fig. 5). This furniture not only removes people from the comforting proximity of the ground, but, Rudofsky warns us, also causes poor digestion, stomachaches, and an unaesthetic belly![22]

With its natural pavement of grass, daisies, violets, and orchids, the patio is the true living room of the house, which itself "grows" from the floor plane. A tent in the summer and a fireplace (shared with the music room) in colder weather allow for year-round inhabitation. Rooted in the ground, the body of the house and the bodies of its inhabitants find their place on earth. Boredom, as the dissociation of

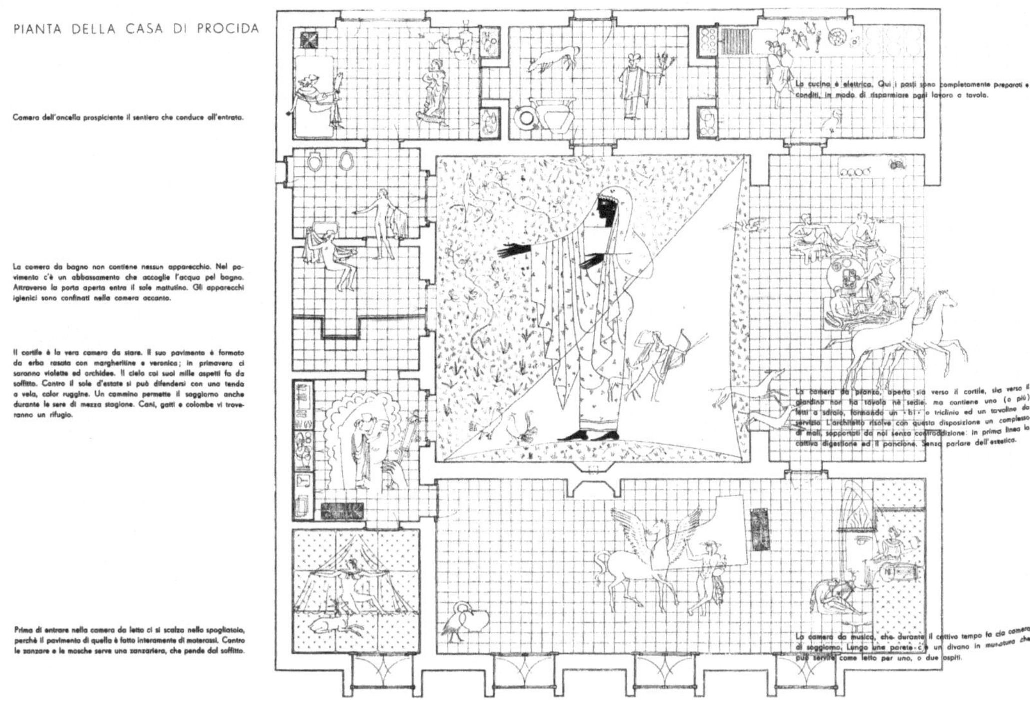

Figure 5. Bernard Rudofsky, project for a house on the island of Procida, Italy (unbuilt), plan. Published in *Domus*, no. 123 (March 1938). (© 2023 Artists Rights Society [ARS], New York / Bildrecht, Vienna)

people from places, is transformed through the everyday rituals of inhabitation, enacted on the horizontal planes of the house.

BUILDING HORIZONS. David Leatherbarrow observes that the fluid spaces of modern architecture need to be understood not as a function of walls, which begin to disappear, but, instead, in relation to floors, which he calls *levels* or *horizons:* "planes of reference or, more fundamentally, of existence."[23] Moreover, sections, rather than plans, reveal the "multiplication of levels" that did not exist in premodern buildings.[24] Rudolph Schindler's Kings Road House (1922), Frank Lloyd Wright's Fallingwater (1936), and Richard Neutra's Tremaine House (1948) create spatial differentiation through horizontal planes that float, meander, move, and undulate, thus offering what the modern dissolution of walls has eliminated: the complexity of spatial experiences.

Rudofsky's work tacitly makes present the horizons of inhabitation that Leatherbarrow uncovers. The ground and the sky, particularly the expansive skies of the

Mediterranean, are the two levels that position us as humans in the world and confront us with our finitude. While practicing in Italy, Rudofsky has several collaborations with the architects Luigi Cosenza and Gio Ponti. Designed with Cosenza, Casa Oro (Naples, 1934–37) remains one of the most notable examples of modern Mediterranean architecture (fig. 6).

Not only does it embrace the topography of the site but it also celebrates the

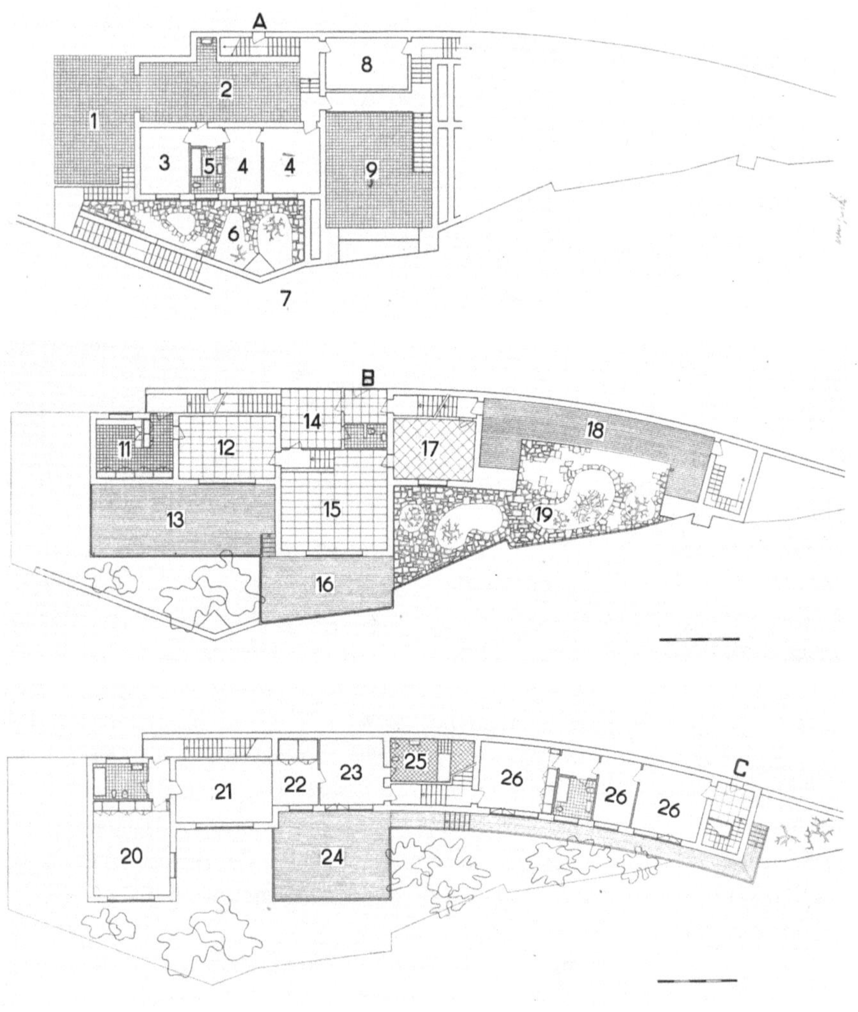

Figure 6. Bernard Rudofsky and Luigi Cosenza, Casa Oro, Naples, 1934–37, floor plans. (© 2023 Artists Rights Society [ARS], New York / Bildrecht, Vienna)

horizon of the Gulf of Naples, along with horizons of living in a particular time and place. Implicit in plans, section, and axonometric drawings, the dialogue with the topography is evident in the one-point interior perspectives, where the flat, strict surfaces of floors and ceilings frame the skyline that thus becomes the focus of the space. In sketches and photographs, carefully framed views insist upon the relationship with the distant horizon that is consistently brought inside the space. Particularly telling are floor and furniture details. Two photographs point the camera lens toward the "great majolica floor, representing the Gulf of Naples."[25]

In another sketch, a long horizontal bench makes full sense only next to the deep sunbreaker, both framing the window and the view of the horizon, suggesting a specific relationship with the landscape. Casa Oro exemplifies Leatherbarrow's thesis that "the building and its interior are co-determined by the wider landscape that envelops them," creating what he calls "the inner horizon."[26]

The unbuilt project for a house in Positano (Salerno, 1937, coauthored with Cosenza) reduces the architectural elements to a minimum and introduces a theme that Rudofsky will return to throughout his entire career: the patio, with colorful and fragrant vegetation, as an outdoor living room. The role of the patio is not only to create horizontal movements and connections between indoor and outdoor spaces but also to make the sky present inside the house. Imagined as an ideal dwelling for "a good oarsman, an expert fisherman and a diver," this simple structure brings in the infinity of the sky as an essential element of inhabitation.[27]

The sectional studies for Casa Guarujá (São Paulo, 1939–40) show a series of cascading platforms and tell micro-stories about how people inhabit the different levels. The plan recalls the configuration of Casa Oro. A man looks down into the main living room space from a mezzanine floor. Father and child are about to lie on a *chaise longue* on the open terrace. The space where two women sit at a table on a higher platform is defined as "here one has breakfast." Someone peeks through the door left ajar in the entrance façade. The same plane folds from the garage into the kitchen and higher up to the bedroom, where a man sits at a table in front of the window. A woman climbs up the stairs. A man leans against a column on the open terrace.[28] The sequence of indoor and outdoor platforms creates opportunities for the inhabitants to move, rest, hide, and peek through—in other words, to engage with the house and its surroundings, nestled into the hillside.

Casa João Arnstein (São Paulo, 1939–41) (fig. 7) unfolds between two planes that balance one another: the synesthetic garden floor and its counterpart, an implied ceiling suggested by "sun sails and pergolas, rustic and carpentered."[29] The

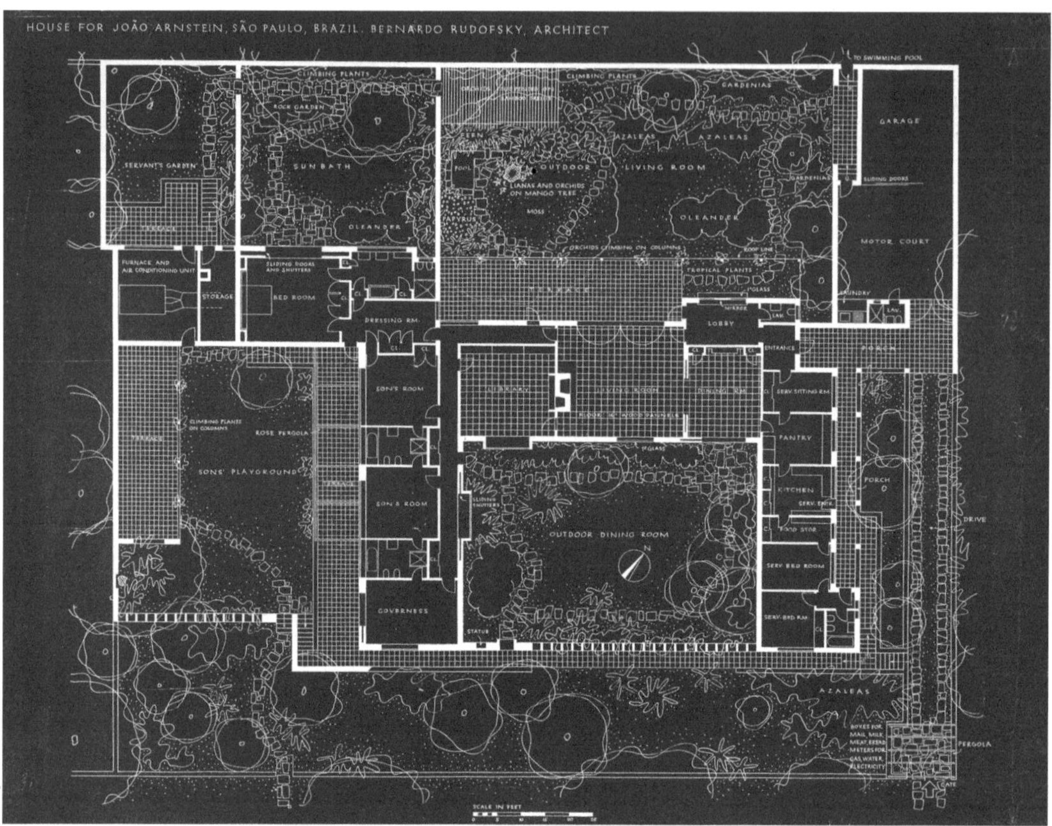

Figure 7. Bernard Rudofsky, Casa João Arnstein, São Paulo, 1939–41, blueprint. (© 2023 Artists Rights Society [ARS], New York / Bildrecht, Vienna)

house constructs environments adapted to the passage of time: "By varying light-, temperature- and humidity- controlling means, perfectly conditioned settings are achieved for the different hours of the day and the transitions of the seasons."[30] In the blueprints, pergolas and vegetation are drawn freehand, unlike the precise outline of the walls. Naturally, one wonders whether they are natural or man-made—indeed, some photographs indicate that the pergola is made of natural-looking logs, spaced at narrow intervals to create a textured ceiling. Other photographs show the play of horizontal planes—pavements, pergolas, low walls—as a deliberate design decision.[31]

In 1950, Rudofsky and his friend Constantino Nivola, an Italian-born sculptor, build a series of interventions in the spacious yard of Nivola's house in Amagansett,

New York. (Friends with both, Saul Steinberg will purchase a summer house across the street in 1959.) Published in the July–August 1952 issue of *Domus,* the project offers Rudofsky an opportunity to discuss one of his most cherished ideas about inhabitation: retrieving the ancient role of the garden as the center of gravity of the house, rather than the decorative feature it has become in modern houses.[32]

The project, modest in size, consists of outdoor walls, a solarium, a pergola, and a fireplace that organize the garden space, creating the fluid relationship between architecture and nature that Rudofsky praises in his writings. An aperture in a freestanding wall allows a tree branch to grow through, a playful condition captured in a photograph that Rudofsky will reproduce in several publications. (The tree has died in the meantime, but the opening still frames a specific view of the garden.) A sunroom accessible through a ladder only from above creates a room open to the sky, separated from the environment yet still part of it. Condensed to elemental pieces—vertical and horizontal plane, posts and beams—architecture is not an end but a means toward celebrating nature and timeless rituals of wholesome living.

Another key element is the presence of the sky. "The spectacle of the forever changing sky can be enjoyed only outdoors," Rudofsky remarks. "One has to contemplate the sky not in a shapeless garden, but rather from within four possibly white walls that form an edge as defined as a picture frame."[33] This gesture of delineating a slice of the sky to bring it closer (which James Turrell will later reinvent in his Skyspaces) is a way of defining and making sense of a horizon of inhabitation. Domesticity is neither routine nor fashion. Rather, it is a ritual that, once established, is performed over and over again without the constant need for change.

CREATING MOODS. The emergence and frequency of the terms and concepts we employ indicate tacit concerns underlying our everyday lives as well as broader societal and cultural anxieties. The increased frequency of the terms "atmosphere" and "mood" in contemporary architectural discourse indicates not that architecture has not been concerned with them in the past but that a certain discontent with our current experience of the environment is prompting us to seek answers outside the tangible and the measurable. A sign of our disenchantment with the quotidian, it speaks about the dissatisfaction with the banality of everyday experiences constantly mediated through screens and simulated realities. Like many of the terms we often employ casually, "atmospheres" and "moods" are less a matter of language and more one of culture, society, and history, because the language does not simply reflect the processes of society and history—instead, these processes take place *within* the language itself.[34]

Commenting on the walls and floors of Roman rooms, Rudofsky writes, "Stone mosaic, marble slabs, stucco reliefs, mural decorations from the simplest geometric ornamentation to elaborate paintings, were employed to establish a mood particularly conducive to spiritual composure."[35] Though architects rarely imagine the floor as instrumental in creating moods, Rudofsky assigns to pavements the role that walls play in defining the character and atmosphere of a room: "Do you know the Faun House in Pompeii? Here we understand why the Pompeiians who inherited the Greek culture could easily give up the frescoes: they had paintings of profound beauty on the floor." He suggests that the banal horizontal plane has the unexpected potential to generate spiritual dispositions and celebrates it as the "most noble part of the house."[36]

Moods, affects, atmospheres: appropriated in the architectural vocabulary from psychology and physics, they have become recurrent themes in the work of many contemporary architects and theorists. Among the most notable, Peter Zumthor and Juhani Pallasmaa have unpacked them in writing and practice as essential design elements. The former defines the atmosphere as an almost mystical quality of a space, intrinsic to those architectures that move you, and discovers it in "the magic of things, the magic of the real world."[37] The latter believes that it was only from the mid-1990s onward that an experiential view on architecture has begun to replace a long-established formal approach to design.[38]

Ideas about constructing the atmosphere of a place have always been present in architecture. Alberto Pérez-Gómez observes that in Vitruvius's *Ten Books on Architecture,* a tempered and balanced environment was at the core of a healthy life, and it was achievable through the right positioning in the world.[39] During the Middle Ages, the transfiguration of light through stained glass in Gothic cathedrals created an environment meant to elevate the spirit and redeem the soul. Intimately connected with existing natural caves, Renaissance villas in the Italian Veneto breathed the air that circulated through the caves through a sophisticated system of vents and ducts, thus being quite literally filled with a healthy atmosphere (from Greek *atmos* = vapor and *sphaira* = globe). Etymologically, the term "atmosphere" originally designated the ring of vapor supposedly "exhaled from the body of a planet."[40] From the eighteenth century onward, it has also conveyed a certain mood hanging in the air.[41] In early modern architecture, the materiality of Adolf Loos's designs embodies not only a concrete manifesto against ornament and decoration but also, and equally important, a carefully designed atmosphere. Eileen Gray's marvelous E.1027 house is centered on experiencing the space through sensuous materials and textures that define the atmosphere of each room. Le Corbusier's *espace indicible* suggests a phenomenal and subjective experience of the space, akin to the concept of atmosphere.

Theorizing these unquantifiable concepts has emerged as a relatively new phenomenon.[42] Adrian Forty's *Words and Buildings: A Vocabulary of Modern Architecture* (2000), a volume that eruditely traces the philosophical and intellectual history of architectural terminology, does not include an entry on architectural moods or atmospheres. This "atmospheric turn" has various explanations that range from deterministic views to social and political arguments, from subjectivity to scientific evidence. Whether a follow-up to current fads or fashions, a matter of "architectural quality," or a response to scientific evidence demonstrating the role of feelings, emotions, and moods that architecture engenders in our psychosomatic health, the interest in atmosphere is generating an important body of work.[43] While philosopher Gernot Böhme considers atmosphere the subject matter of architecture, David Leatherbarrow emphasizes, in response, that atmospheres emerge from concrete, material conditions and are intimately correlated with habits and practices of everyday life.[44]

Central to Rudofsky's ideas about domestic architecture, habits and embodied practices constitute the scaffolding from which the atmosphere of a place emerges. Moreover, the orchestration of different horizontal levels and their materiality and textures draws attention to the pace of a place, the way it is experienced and lived. Boredom as the malaise of modern individuals stifled under the excess of consumerism vanishes once people engage with their environment. Floors and pavements play an active role in this interaction. In Rudofsky's projects, the ground plane receives special attention through textures and specific indications of materials that themselves suggest specific modes of inhabitation and deliberate relationships between the interior of the house and the landscape. I will turn once again to the Procida project, where these intentions become manifest.

The project chronicles a way of living, and the plan view is where the practices of inhabitation are enacted, the floor plane revealing the "temperament" of each room. A rather unusual drawing, this view combines an architectural plan as horizontal section with depictions of people and mythical characters. Wrapped in loose fabrics, various figures engaged in domestic activities are projected against the surface of the floor, which itself becomes one of the main actors in the complex orchestra of the house (fig. 5).

Dominating the image, a dark-skinned female silhouette represented in an Egyptian profile pose—the lady of the house?—occupies the central patio. Spread

Figure 8. Bernard Rudofsky, project for a house on the island of Procida, Italy (unbuilt), plan and section. Published in *Domus*, no. 123 (March 1938). (© 2023 Artists Rights Society [ARS], New York / Bildrecht, Vienna)

throughout the spaces surrounding the courtyard, other characters narrate the living practices of the household. Situated at the top left corner, the entryway is the space of the *ancella,* an Italian word that designates an apprentice—who is shown lying on a low *cline* (deck chair), overlooking the pathway to the entrance and acting as the guardian of the house. From here, one has the choice of moving either toward the (fully electric and modernized!) kitchen or toward the bathing room, preceded by an ablution space. These acts are rituals that situate the individual in a horizon of existence bound to a particular place and a particular community (fig. 8).

In vividly depicted scenes, male and female characters interact among themselves as well as with real and mythical creatures and inanimate objects (fig. 5). A winged horse trots gracefully while deer glide from space to space and birds hover in the air. Some inhabitants are feasting in the dining room (a *triclinium* true to its name), while others play the piano or the harp in the music room, a space that transforms into a living room during inclement weather or a guest room when needed. A couple bathes leisurely in the bathroom. Profiles of mythical figures emerge as muses of different spaces. Holding a bow and arrows, a fearless Diana stands naked in the courtyard (fig. 5).

What are we to make of these domestic scenes? The story is not complete without the last pages of the article. A photograph of a model of the house is placed next to close-up photographs from the island of Procida.

In a cinematic twist, the drawings from the previous pages come to life: fish, boats on the shore, people, light filtered through tree leaves. We understand that the intentions suggested in the plan drawing reflect the reality of the island. The sailing curtain hovering in the courtyard has its counterpart in the floating fabrics of the fishermen. The architectural elements, textures, light, and air rendered in the project are part of the actual landscape. The lady of the house materializes as a mysterious woman whose right and left foot, respectively, traverse the left and right pages of the journal spread. Wearing open sandals, the woman's feet are photographed on a grass bed with flowers. All these fragments constitute the "tabella delle materie prime di Procida." A pun between "tabella di materie" (table of contents) and "materie prime" (resources), this collection is an inventory of resources, both physical (such as tuff, mosaic, wood) and experiential (a walk with a mule on the shore, going grocery shopping, the beach), that one encounters on the island.

The Procida house proposes a model of inhabitation that is both real and ideal. The visual field of the photographs from the island frames either floors of different kinds or views of the sky, implicitly building the horizon of the place. Looking down: grass and flowers, tiles in a courtyard, mosaics, a sandy beach, the shimmering sea, a rocky shore. Looking up: floating fabrics, a canopy of trees, a delicate wooden pergola. Naturally emerging from this symphony of materials, colors, smells, and tastes and intertwined with centuries-long customs, the atmosphere of the place—reflected in the house design—offers the most ordinary form of resistance to modern boredom. This mood accounts for everything that is human. At the same time practical and poetic, the house is firmly anchored in its place, yet it also inhabits another magical, mythical dimension. "The new way of living" urged in the article's title proposes to reposition modern individuals in close contact with the phenomenal world. As Rudofsky writes elsewhere, "Today, when some of our dearest beliefs are questioned, when well-established half-truths are being shaken, when we have second thoughts about attributing man's happiness to an unending supply of things he does not need, the time seems propitious to reassess those of our habits and usages that regulate daily life down to minute details. This is by no means the grim business it may look in cold print; on the contrary, it provides moments of hilarity, tempered by lulls of melancholy, which in turn put us into the proper mood for shedding the more indefensible of our prejudices."[45]

WANDERING: EMBODIED TIME

Consumerism engenders a tedium that devours time, and Rudofsky's nostalgia for a pre-industrialized society is more than anything a nostalgia for time as embodied duration rather than instantaneity. While he clearly idealizes a far-from-perfect world, he presents architectural ideas (especially for domestic spaces) whose ultimate goal is to slow time. The floor is the architectural element with the immediate potential to make people tarry and linger as they move through space. The most inconspicuous yet most direct in its engagement with the body, the floor constructs the physical measure of our pace. By slowing its pace down, the body readjusts to its environment. The floors Rudofsky imagines are often impractical, inaccessible to everyone, unsuited to comfortable walking, whimsical, and useless, but what is at stake in his emphasis on the horizontal plane is the awareness of time as embodied experience.

An outcome of an increasingly mechanized environment, boredom threatens to alter human beings' most intimate connections with their world. The architecture of the house, Rudofsky proposes, has the agency to reposition this relationship and resist everyday ennui. With the underlying motif of time as embodied experience, three themes emerge from Rudofsky's theory of dwelling. First, the function of the house is to foster privacy and conviviality, habits and customs slowly developed and appropriated in time. Second, a house, like clothing, is a series of veils or layers wrapped around the bodies of its inhabitants. And last, indoor and outdoor floors cultivate a sense of wandering as both a physical and imaginative act.

CONVIVIALITY. Although never addressed explicitly, Rudofsky's approach to domestic architecture departs from the strong (and often divergent) meanings of the modern concept of function. Ever since Louis Sullivan inadvertently created one of the mantras of modern architecture, the much-quoted and largely misinterpreted "form follows function," function—and its derivatives, such as functionalism or functionality—has remained among the most debated concepts of the discipline.

In his comprehensive study of architectural concepts and vocabulary, Adrian Forty argues that the polemics surrounding the notion of function emerge at the same time as the midcentury critique of Modernism.[46] The difficulty in tracing the word's meanings arises from its use as a metaphor that borrows from other fields (e.g., mathematics, biology, sociology) and from the word itself, which is a concept translated from German, French, and Italian.[47] In contrast, in Rudofsky's theory, function appears as a soft and fluid trace of inhabitation rather than a prescribed and predetermined purpose. His approach does not align with any of the various scientific paradigms of function that Forty identifies in the architectural discourse from the eighteenth century onward.[48] He often replaces the established nomenclatures that signify function and program (bedroom, living room, bathroom, and so on) with the practices that take place in those rooms (such as room for sleeping, room for bathing, room for music). In so doing, Rudofsky destabilizes the very notions of function and program, prompting us to imagine what a room can be beyond norms and expectations. In this realm of imagination, rooms are conceived as gratuitous and playful spaces. To be a good designer, an architect needs to possess the spirit of play.[49]

If, as Walter Benjamin writes, "to live is to leave traces," then the function of a house is to nest these ephemeral marks.[50] Among Rudofsky's most evocative examples is the stone-walled enclosure on the Italian island of Pantelleria whose sole purpose is to protect a lemon tree from the gusty winds.[51] For him, the function of the dwelling, like that of the enclosed garden, is to foster inhabitants' sense of *privacy* (which is distinct from being by oneself) and *conviviality* (which is distinct from socializing or, to use the preferred real estate term, entertaining). His implicit claim is that through these domestic practices the modern individual resists the boredom spawned through consumerism and scripted leisure, thus getting closer to a never-boring phenomenal world.

"Conviviality, rather than mere socializing, cultivates humaneness," Rudofsky writes.[52] The ideal house offers the resources to transform the tedium of meaningless leisure into conviviality as a practice of togetherness. In his study on leisure, de Grazia makes a clear distinction between modern leisure—anti-boredom time dedicated to entertainment—and leisure as purpose-free time spent for pure enjoyment. Similarly, Rudofsky aims to retrieve the gratuitous and playful character of architecture: "Clearly, architecture means more than a roof over one's head and the constraints of walls. There was a time when men got together for no other purpose than to put up mile-long processions of good-for-nothing but enchanting monoliths."[53]

In tune with Martin Gumpert (who aligns the health and happiness of individuals with those of the community), Rudofsky encourages us to ponder larger issues of houses and housing. Twenty-first-century debates about downsizing, living in small versus large houses, and urban versus suburban continue to examine what constitutes a "basic need" in a minimal dwelling. Rudofsky suggests that conviviality is, in fact, a fundamental necessity and a critical function of the dwelling. Being together with others at home cultivates civic practices that will later be exercised in the public sphere.

VEIL. Criticizing those tenets of Modernism that have eroded the intimate relationship between people, habits, and architecture, Rudofsky asserts that "we do not think of our houses in terms of a wrap but of a box."[54] Eventually conducive to banal architectures, the restraint implied in "less is more" has resulted, paradoxically, in an excess of useless gadgets. "The house ended up as a storeroom for household goods." To Modernism's enchantment with consumerism and to mechanization "as the answer to our prayers," he presents the alternative of the house as an embodiment of practices and habits.[55] Whether an *instrument* rather than a *machine,* or a *wrap* rather than a *box,* the dwelling should be in tune with its inhabitants' bodily experience of the world.

One's (ideal) house and one's (ideal) clothing are both homes to the human being and share proximity with the human body, its peculiarities, and its imperfections, which the rigid, modern box levels out and ignores. Failing to engage the body, contemporary houses are "hard-edged containers with perfectly level floors, and no deep-pile carpets, no water beds will confer sensuousness upon them."[56] The veils Rudofsky choreographs in his designs do not translate into a formal lexicon of fluid shapes, as one might infer, but rather in subtle tactics of articulating relationships: between spaces, between spaces and their inhabitants, between the inhabitants themselves, and between materials. These tactics often come to life, as we have seen already, in the way floors are deployed as horizontal layers that undulate, fold, bend, and move, connecting interior and exterior spaces and rooms for different activities.

Casa Arnstein shows how these veils create a sense of privacy, on the one hand, and a sensuous relationship between architecture and nature on the other. Rudofsky admits that the goal of the architecture was not to show off but to enhance the luscious vegetation. His description of the "garden floor" takes a synesthetic approach that engages sight, touch, and smell through "red tile, soft stone, and varieties of moss and blue grass."[57] Reading the blueprint, one experiences the fragrances of azaleas, oleanders, gardenias, orchids, tropical plants, and roses, while papyrus, lianas, moss, and bamboo complete the visual and olfactory landscape (fig. 7).

Challenging the conventions of how we define inhabitable spaces, Rudofsky explains Casa Arnstein as a "sequence of outdoor rooms."[58] The interior rooms become filters or veils through which one moves toward the main spaces of the house: the outdoor living room, the outdoor dining room, the sunbath, and the playground. The natural and the man-made converse and make each other present. A quick glance at the floor plan makes it difficult to distinguish the outdoors from the indoors—not because they blend into each other but because they are given equal weight. Similarly, the photographs intentionally amplify the ambiguity between inside and outside, closed ceiling and open sky. Defying the artificial need for a fully mechanized environment, the project uses passive strategies such as orientation, materials, light, vegetation, sun sails, and pergolas to create a comfortable ambience for every time of day and every season.[59]

The veil-like house ("that static outer garment for all seasons") indicates the state of the individual and, more generally, the state of the society. In a world forgetting that good living is built upon rituals rather than sets of prepackaged products, tedium threatens to corrupt the very nature of inhabitation: "Our tendency to confuse feeding with eating, washing with bathing, boredom with leisure, has debased the substance of domesticity."[60]

WANDERING. A lifelong *flâneur,* Rudofsky travels the world on journeys lasting anywhere from a few weeks to a few years, but he also embarks upon equally fascinating imaginary voyages. Critical of modern travel practices, he decries the tourism industry's dependence on fads and fashions that dictate what is or is not worth seeing. The obsession with quantifiable leisure time only reinforces the ennui of the modern individual, who continues to fall back into the loop of boredom: "Many a man who seeks relief in travel cannot shake off boredom any more. During vacation time, when the empty hours stretch into days and weeks, he develops a most virulent form of it. . . . Fashion, for instance, is engineered and controlled change; fashion and boredom are mutually dependent. Where boredom is not endemic—as in non-industrial countries—fashions do not thrive."[61]

Wandering indicates, perhaps more truthfully, the nature of Rudofsky's attitude toward travel. If the latter often entails a clear plan, a destination, and a set of pre-established expectations, the former is looser (more open to chance and random encounters), lacks a fixed course, and implies an unhurried pace. In the act of wandering one can cover vast territories, the expanse of a neighborhood, or simply the span of one's own house. Both a physical and an imaginative act, wandering can be performed anywhere and anytime, outside the constraints of fashion and advertising. A way of exercising internal freedom, this form of travel ensures the dignity of the human being and often finds its physical support, quite literally, on the ground. If by embracing an architecture of the senses one can resist the capitalist tedium of fashion and advertising, then the first step is to become aware of what unfolds under our feet.

Wonderful places for wandering, Rudofsky's floors awaken people's awareness of the world. Writing about architectural experiences, Henry Plummer draws attention to the dullness of the built environment resulting, in part, from the inability of buildings to support "the spontaneous powers of human beings to act in space." He asserts that these actions "originate in simple endeavors such as opening a door or closing a window, climbing a stair or crossing a bridge, changing level along a footpath or emerging in an urban square to find multiple routes and attractions ahead from which to choose. Regrettably, these countless undertakings have become so dull and uneventful that we barely notice them anymore."[62]

Acting upon rather than simply observing the environment constitutes one of the most vital modes of resisting boredom. Plummer argues that through ground planes (described as "floors of agility"), the body has the first opportunity to know and experience its world. Engaging with or ignoring the floors makes the difference between experiencing boredom or the "vital forces" of the world: "When omnipresent and despite its necessity, a predictably uniform ground of flat floors and repetitive steps subjects us to monotonous, mechanical movement, dissociating power from the body." Echoing Rudofsky, Plummer observes that the flat, leveled floor is only suited "to the routine behavior of mass culture."[63]

Whether in a private residence or a public exhibition, the floors in Rudofsky's projects invite people to act in space and wander in the realm of imagination. The uneven, wavy floor for the 1945 exhibition *Are Clothes Modern?* and the floors covered in tweed for the 1956 exhibition *Textiles, U.S.A.* aim to restore the lost sense of tactility of the feet.[64] "Nobody had ever walked on tweed before," writes Rudofsky in his notes for a lecture to be delivered in Japan.[65] Similarly, the private residences designed over the years, from the Procida house to the Long Island intervention, continue to engage the horizontal planes as places where our sense of grounding is born.

The last project to discuss here is Casa Frontini, designed in 1934–41 for Dr. Virgilio Frontini in São Paulo (fig. 9). An outer wall separates the domestic realm of the house, which includes both indoor and outdoor spaces, from the outside world. Although low, this wall is perforated by openings covered in wooden louvers situated at eye height to allow the inhabitants of the house—both children and adults—to peek into the outside world. Carefully designed details speak about the habits and rituals of the household: next to the entrance gate, there are "boxes for mail, milk, bread, meat, meters for gas, water, electricity."[66] The shelves in the dining room are made of marble. Play is not only for children: while they have their own playroom, another one, assumed to be for adults, is situated in proximity to the music room, the bar, and the living room. An opening strategically placed between the playroom and the bar makes one imagine drinks passed along in the leisurely

Figure 9. Bernard Rudofsky, Casa Virgilio Frontini, São Paulo, 1934–41, second floor plan, basement plan, and section. (© 2023 Artists Rights Society [ARS], New York / Bildrecht, Vienna)

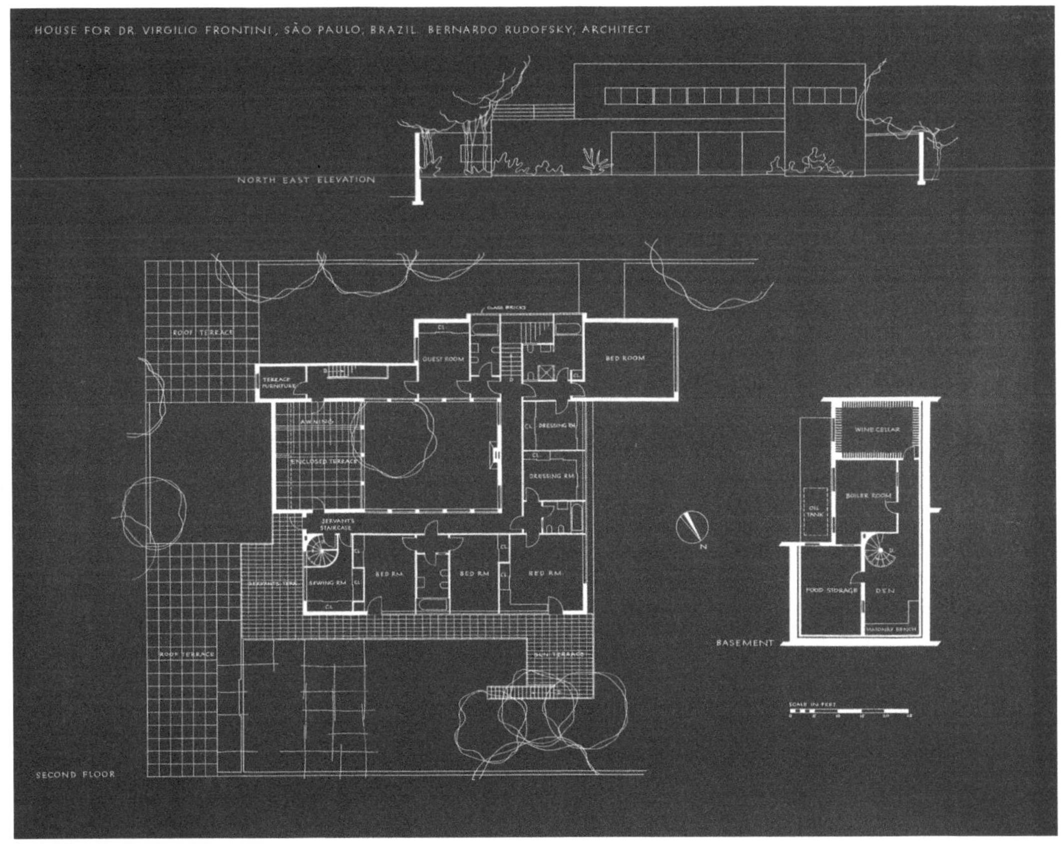

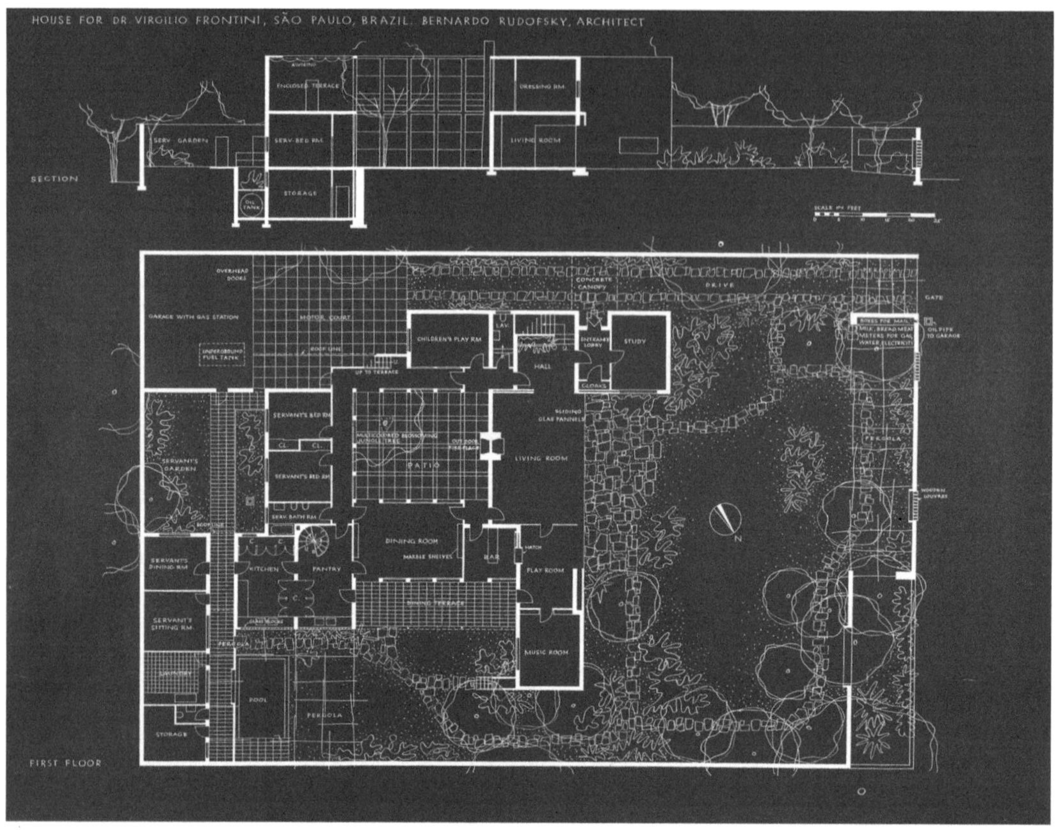

Figure 10. Bernard Rudofsky, Casa Virgilio Frontini, São Paulo, 1934–41, first floor plan and section. (© 2023 Artists Rights Society [ARS], New York / Bildrecht, Vienna)

hours of the evening. While the American "family room" is usually located in a dark basement apart from the life of the household (thus suggesting that leisure belongs to a time and place outside the main activities of the family), this room elevates the notion of play, positioning it among the most important practices of the family (fig. 10).[67]

The outdoor room is a recurrent motif in Rudofsky's designs and writings. If walls are often dematerialized in modern architecture as a way of blurring the boundaries between indoors and outdoors, Rudofsky achieves this relationship through other means. Elsewhere called "the bread of architecture," the wall is a mark in the landscape.[68] Its materiality is critical. Whether solid or made of sliding glass panels or glass blocks, the wall never fully vanishes, creating a total immersion into the landscape. Its presence announces the distinct natures of landscape and architecture but also their mutual connection. Landscape and architecture make each other visible. In Casa Frontini, a Janusian fireplace faces both the interior of the living room and the patio, offering multiple ways of inhabiting these rooms. Just as the house is nested within the perimeter of the outer wall, the patio—filled with a "multicolored blossoming jungle tree"—is nested within the house. It gives breathing space to the living room and dining room, both situated between the patio and the outer garden. Reversing the convention of outdoor spaces as transitions from exteriority to interiority, interior spaces become the thresholds between two exterior conditions (fig. 10).

The mood of the place comes to life through thoughtfully designed floors whose materiality and texture are chosen with much care and attention to detail: "The floor material of the duplex patio is gray and pale pink terrazzo with aluminum strips." Planted with trees, shrubs, and the "multicolored blossoming jungle tree," sprinkled with pebbles or paved with tiles, the ground plane creates a series of microenvironments within the confines of the precinct wall. While the use of native vegetation was not a common practice in Brazilian upper-class homes, a native tree, expected to blossom in white, pink, and violet at Christmas, grows in the patio. Other plants are strategically chosen to attract birds and butterflies, "the most precious ornaments of the house."[69]

A relentless critic of consumerism, Rudofsky foresees the commodification of architecture and proposes forms of resistance through design. Consumerism, modern leisure, and boredom—all closely related—threaten to corrupt the essence of the human being. Both the problem and its remedy begin at home:

> So far, people have been enraptured with the cornucopia of mechanical household appliances, or what we naively call, labor-saving devices. However, their attraction begins to pall because people really don't *know* what to do with the *time* they save. In the United States, the domestic euphoria is slowly giving way to disillusion with gadgetry, the blessings of mechanization. The result is *boredom, a poison* whose perilous nature we are only lately beginning to comprehend. In order to keep *our slender hold on sanity,* we must gain a better perspective of our priorities. The house has to become again what it was in the past: an *instrument* for living, instead of a *machine* for living.[70]

PART II

WAITING

ROBERT VENTURI AND
DENISE SCOTT BROWN

Boredom to me consists in a kind of insufficiency, or inadequacy, or lack of reality.

—ALBERTO MORAVIA, *BOREDOM*

Robert Venturi's 1966 treatise *Complexity and Contradiction in Architecture* begins with "a gentle manifesto" that includes the first references to boredom. Archival documents reveal that a particular fragment has gone through multiple iterations, from manuscript draft to final publication. Thus, an early version reads: "I like elements which are hybrid rather than 'pure,' compromising rather than 'clean,' distorted rather than 'straightforward,' ambiguous rather than 'articulated,' perverse rather than impersonal, accommodating rather than excluding, redundant rather than simple, vestigial as well as innovating, inconsistent and equivocal rather than direct and clear."[1]

To this sequence, Venturi adds—in a handwritten note at the bottom of the page (fig. 11)—"boring as well as 'interesting,' conventional rather than 'designed.'"[2] The final version from 1966 includes the intentional addition of *boring* and *interesting:* "I like elements which are hybrid rather than 'pure,' compromising rather than 'clean,' distorted rather than 'straightforward,' ambiguous rather than 'articulated,' perverse as well as impersonal, boring as well as 'interesting,' conventional rather than 'designed,' accommodating rather than excluding, redundant rather than simple, vestigial as well as innovating, inconsistent and equivocal rather than direct and clear."[3]

Perusing *Complexity and Contradiction in Architecture* uncovers further references to boredom that together constitute the beginning of a consistent, yet over-

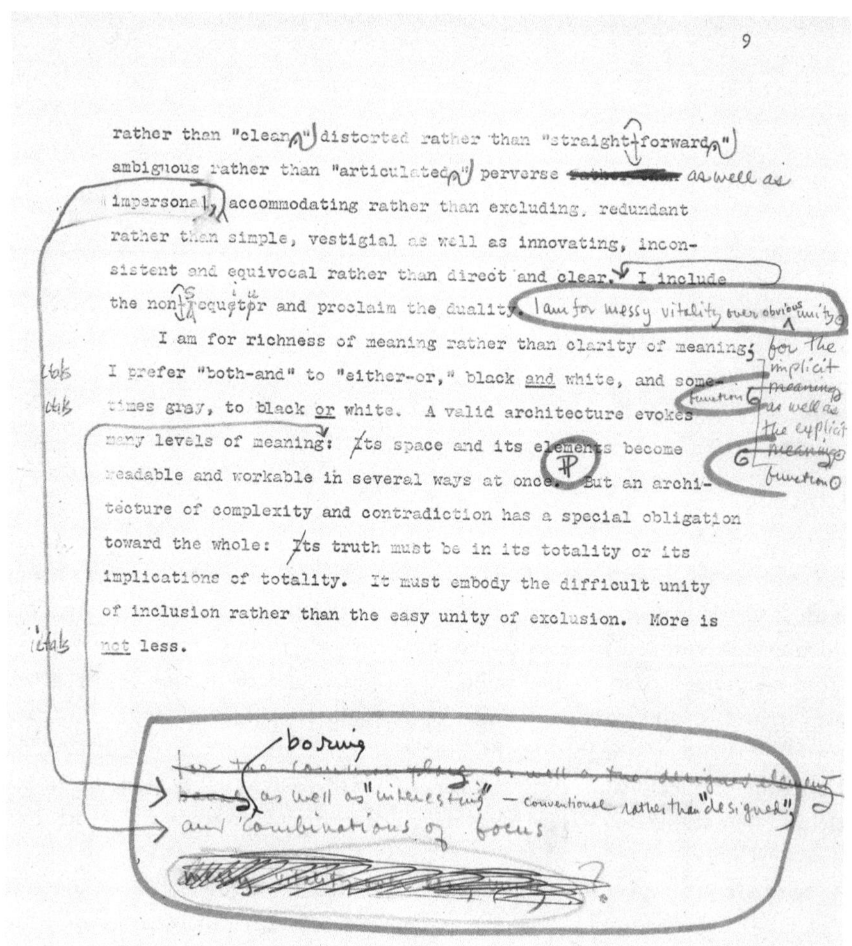
9

rather than "clean," distorted rather than "straightforward,"
ambiguous rather than "articulated," perverse as well as
impersonal, accommodating rather than excluding, redundant
rather than simple, vestigial as well as innovating, inconsistent and equivocal rather than direct and clear. I include
the non sequitur and proclaim the duality.

I am for richness of meaning rather than clarity of meaning;
I prefer "both-and" to "either-or," black and white, and sometimes gray, to black or white. A valid architecture evokes
many levels of meaning: its space and its elements become
readable and workable in several ways at once. But an architecture of complexity and contradiction has a special obligation
toward the whole: its truth must be in its totality or its
implications of totality. It must embody the difficult unity
of inclusion rather than the easy unity of exclusion. More is
not less.

Figure 11. Annotated page from the manuscript of *Complexity and Contradiction in Architecture* by Robert Venturi. (© The Architectural Archives, University of Pennsylvania, by the gift of Robert Venturi and Denise Scott Brown)

looked, discourse on tedium and architecture. While Venturi criticizes modern architecture for its formalist turn, he is also appropriating boredom as a way of subverting Modernism from within.

On the one hand, Venturi embraces boredom as an architectural language of silence, stillness, and simplicity, a direction present in some of the radical artistic movements of the time, such as Conceptual Art or Pop Art. This form of quiet boredom is inspired, I argue, by a biographical detail largely overlooked in architectural scholarship: Venturi's upbringing as a Quaker in the context not only of Quaker Philadelphia but also of his immediate family. His mother, Vanna Venturi, initiated the conversion of the entire family to Quakerism, and so the three of them began to attend Quaker meetings on Sunday. On the other hand, Venturi recognizes that midcentury alienation emerges from a collective discontent with social structures, conformity, and consumerism. This underlying boredom signals the need for changes and transformations in both architecture and public life. Venturi's civic projects designed (but never built) in the mid-1960s directly address the theme of boredom and draw upon the writings of the author and political activist August Heckscher. By de-emphasizing individualism, Quaker doctrine and Heckscher's writings situate community and public responsibility at the foreground of a meaningful life.

Critical to unpacking boredom is its temporal aspect. Design strategies for waiting, tarrying, and lengthening time transform a deadening tedium into a mental and physical space appropriate for reflection. Chapter 4 relates the genealogies of boredom in Venturi's work to his Quaker upbringing. The Quaker aesthetics of stillness tacitly informs Venturi's designs, such as his thesis project for the Episcopal Academy Chapel and the Guild House in Philadelphia. Chapter 5 examines how Venturi addresses the question of modern alienation in the built environment. Drawing on the writings of August Heckscher, an author frequently cited in *Complexity and Contradiction in Architecture,* the chapter looks at two early projects for public spaces: three buildings for the downtown of North Canton, Ohio, and the entry for the Boston Copley Square competition. Chapter 6 examines ideas about time as duration through the dialectic of the *boring* and the *interesting* (used extensively by Venturi and Scott Brown in *Learning from Las Vegas*) and concludes by repositioning Scott Brown's concept of *deferred judgment* in a contemporary context. I propose that through waiting and deferring judgment, one makes space for reflection, thus finding the resources to withstand boredom.

4

GENEALOGIES OF BOREDOM

Learning from the Quakers

"Less is a bore" and "the decorated shed" are arguably two of the most significant contributions that Robert Venturi (later in partnership with Denise Scott Brown) makes to architectural theory. Published six years apart, in 1966 and 1972, these two propositions contain the seeds of a curious paradox. The former, responding to Ludwig Mies van der Rohe's dictum "Less is more," is a direct critique of modernist architectural language and implies a revalorization of the excess and surplus carefully shunned by modern architects. The latter, while reducing a building to a structure with applied decoration, is both *more* and *less: more* ornament and *less* architecture.

Venturi embraces ideas about paradox even in his early projects, where he programmatically employs flat and plain surfaces while stating that "the examples chosen reflect my partiality for certain eras: Mannerist, Baroque and Rococo especially."[1] The numerous precedents in *Complexity and Contradiction in Architecture* support his position. On the one hand, he champions flat surfaces, but on the other, he turns toward an architecture of complex and convoluted surfaces. How are we to explain this paradox? How are we to understand this apparent inconsistency of thought? Is the paradox of *both/and* first articulated as a theoretical position in the "gentle manifesto," a rhetorical device meant to validate a certain arbitrariness, or does it suggest a more meaningful position?

The appeal of both Venturi's and Mies's quips, which have become commonplaces in architectural vocabulary, lies in their brevity and ambiguity, which to this day continue to generate rich interpretations and paraphrases. On closer inspection, however, their opposition is not that clear. "Less is more" implies simplification: stripping off ornamentation, minimizing costs through prefabrication and standardization, exposing the structure and the nature of materials, streamlining design. "Less is a bore" suggests a simplification of a different order: while arguing against what he sees as modernist "simpleness," Venturi proposes to reduce architecture to form—and form to symbol. He distinguishes between *simplicity* and *simpleness* (or *simplification*), criticizing the latter for its dearth of meaning: "Where simplicity cannot work, simpleness results. Blatant simplification means bland architecture. Less is a bore."[2] Venturi's quip does not exist in a vacuum, nor does it suddenly manifest a new and unusual interest in boredom. Rather, it brings together ideas and concerns already present in the ethos of the time.

"IN THE WORLD, BUT NOT OF IT": QUAKER ARCHITECTURE AND ART

Largely overlooked, Venturi's upbringing as a Quaker accounts for his understanding of paradox, of a world in which seemingly conflicting positions coexist in the same space. Within this framework, the theory of *both/and* presented in his "gentle manifesto" is not only legitimate but also, and more importantly, resourceful. Extrapolating from this position, one can see how a Mannerist or Baroque aesthetics is compatible with the use of flat and simple surfaces. From this particular perspective, flat surfaces have depth; *less* and *more* are not contradictory concepts; and a remedy to modernist boredom may emerge, in fact, from plain planes, which are cut, reshaped, and reassembled.

With a few exceptions, critics have largely disregarded the influence of Quaker beliefs and aesthetics on Venturi's work. Reading more deeply into his personal and artistic genealogy, Esther McCoy, Venturi's longtime friend, proposes that his ties with the Quakers offer possible clues to his "strict code of ethics and his love of simplicity." McCoy observes that the floor plans of the Vanna Venturi House, the Guild House, and the North Penn Visiting Nurses Association challenge the modernist space, a challenge she locates in Venturi's Italian roots and Quaker education. She interprets the plan of the Vanna Venturi House as a "safe and sound Quaker letter in second person singular."[3]

Another exception is architectural critic Inga Saffron's reading of a later project by Venturi and Scott Brown. She notices an intriguing affinity between their design for the Benjamin Franklin House in Philadelphia and the work of the early Quaker artist Edward Hicks: "The steel Ghost House, the colonial fence posts, the arbor and the spreading mulberry tree" evoke Edward Hicks's *Peaceable Kingdom* paintings.[4]

The Quakers (or The Society of Friends) are a significant, though discreet, presence in Venturi's life. Although he never clarifies any particular influence they might have had on his thinking, it would be unlikely for a Friend to be outspoken on faith issues. Nonetheless, in several interviews given over the years, he unassumingly and almost casually mentions his affiliation with the Friends, defining himself as an "Italian-American Quaker."[5] Describing his upbringing, Venturi explains his parents' conversion as a deliberate decision to offer him a religious affiliation. A pacifist and anti-violence activist herself, Vanna Venturi sees the Friends as the appropriate choice given their anti-war stance and overall ethical position.[6] Venturi also receives a Quaker education as a student at the Lansdowne Friends School. Archival documents substantiate his commitment to the cause of the Friends, indicating that toward the end of his architectural studies, for instance, he was planning to join the American Friends Service.[7] Perhaps part of a local tradition (but perhaps also related to the Venturi family's religious affiliation), the newlyweds Venturi and Scott Brown receive a catalogue of Quaker publications after their July 1967 wedding.[8] Scott Brown recognizes her South African upbringing and the Quakerism in the Venturi family as the main sources of the partnership's commitment to social justice and gives credit to her mother-in-law for Venturi's interest in social issues.[9]

Venturi's architectural theory of *both/and,* his admiration for "elements which are hybrid rather than 'pure,' compromising rather than 'clean,' distorted rather than 'straightforward,' ambiguous rather than 'articulated,' boring as well as 'interesting' . . . redundant rather than simple . . . inconsistent and equivocal rather than direct and clear," builds upon a tension inherent in Quaker doctrine.[10] Manifested at different levels, this tension exists between the spiritual and material worlds, between inclusion and exclusion, revelation and concealment. While the Quakers embrace an ethos of inclusivity, diversity, and nonjudgment, they set themselves apart from the world as a separate group.[11] The contradictory nature of being "in the world, but not of it" complicates the relationship between the physical and the metaphysical where the latter is not manifested in the former.[12] In what may appear to the untrained eye as boring, extended pauses, the participants in a Quaker ritual wait for and receive revelation in a physical world devoid of spiritual qualities. There are no corporeal mediators between the divine and the human; one has direct access to the heavenly through the grace of the Inner Light, the key concept in Quaker theology, rather than one's own will.

This act of patient waiting is in tune with what Scott Brown will term *deferred judgment.* However, the very same act could result in a boredom that emerges from the Quakers' disengagement with the physical realm and the distance they keep from the world. Venturi's early exposure to Quaker practices is echoed in his attitude toward material culture. His focus on architectural surfaces, his interest in iconology (expressed through words and letters), his emphasis on deciphering signs and symbols along with the collective dimension of a message shared and understood by the entire community: these are fundamental aspects of the Quaker mode of being in the world.

If Quaker aesthetics favors simplicity, starkness, and lack of ornamentation, qualities also dear to architectural Modernism, then why does Venturi move away from modernist tenets?[13] Discovering the richness of his Italian heritage, he is fascinated with the exuberance of Mannerist and Baroque architectures fundamentally opposed to the Quakers' visual asceticism. Moving between Quaker minimalism and Mannerist excess, how does he reconcile the two types of aesthetics?

Tying together professional and personal narratives, Venturi portrays himself as an outsider. His early childhood years spent in private schools distance him from the neighborhood children; as an architect, he feels relegated to the frontier of the profession due to his unconventional views, opposed to mainstream architectural movements. However, he assumes (and at the same time relishes) this supposedly fringe condition along with his wife and partner, Denise Scott Brown, herself an émigré, uprooted from her native South Africa to London and later Philadelphia.[14] These personal stories parallel the Quakers' history of persecution, marginality, and silent resistance. For the young architect, this heritage sustains the idea that standing up to convention is a necessary moral act.

The Quaker doctrine derived and at the same time distanced itself from the tenets of the Puritan Revolution of mid-seventeenth-century England. Disappointed in the teachings and practices of the Church of England, George Fox, the son of a Puritan churchwarden, began to seek salvation outside the official church and founded the Religious Society of Friends, spending his life traveling and preaching throughout Britain, Europe, and America. American Quakerism began with the English-born Quaker William Penn, who came to North America in 1682 and later founded the province of Pennsylvania and the city of Philadelphia. In 1963, historian Nathaniel

Burt describes the city as a wonderful paradox, a negotiation between plain Quakers and fancy Episcopalians, an enigma for outsiders, a place "devoted to moderation but fond of good living," where the myth of a joyless population coexists with that of a snobbish but pleasure-oriented "fox-hunting aristocracy."[15] At its core, Quakerism embraces and lives with paradoxes: "The paradoxical elements in Quaker thought and activities have often led to a misunderstanding of the Friends.... Quakers could be intellectuals and yet anti-intellectual, social activists and mystics, evangelical and quietist, complacent and insecure, intent on making money and anxious to avoid being wealthy, dogmatic and nontheological, tolerant and strict."[16]

Quaker aesthetics originates in broader Protestant views on "plain style," born in the seventeenth century in reaction to the Catholic Baroque. Historian Susan Garfinkel argues that "Quaker theology has within it a fundamental crisis of representation. All expressive behaviors, whether spoken, enacted, or built, function as embodiments of this conflict."[17] This paradox has been at the core of Quaker material culture. While the physical world is stripped of metaphysical content, craftsmanship is highly valued; while meetinghouses (the Quaker places of communal worship) are not sacred spaces, they have always acted as repositories of historical and cultural genealogies. The paradox of being "in the world but not of it," a simultaneous condition of inclusion and exclusion, has shaped Friends' attitudes toward all the manifestations of material culture, from exterior garb to architecture. Quaker dress from the seventeenth century, for instance, removed the ornamentation characteristic of the age of the Stuart kings, but that same simplification made the Friends more conspicuous.[18]

The four main principles, or "testimonies," guiding Quaker life are *community, equality, simplicity,* and *harmony.* What distinguishes the Quakers from other religious practices using silence as a form of worship (such as Zen meditation) is the idea of *community.* The act of recognizing the "still, small voice" is of crucial importance in Quaker worship, but there are no "guidelines" or "tests" to ensure its correct interpretation.[19] A tension thus emerges between silent reflection and the need for communication.[20] The presence of the community is critical in offering the individual the reassuring support of a safe haven. Of the four tenets, *simplicity* is the most contested. The general understanding is that it reflects the absence of the unnecessary, of the superfluous, of those things that clutter life. Rather than an exterior expression, it is a form of sincerity and genuineness.[21] It began as a form of resistance to other religious traditions that preferred sensorial pleasures to spiritual joys, but its interpretation has changed over time.[22]

Defined as "the absence of superfluity," simplicity was originally an outward expression (manifested in dress, speech, and the absence of distractions such as art and music), but it eventually became a spiritual quality rather than a material attribute.[23] Historically, simplicity has acted not only as a form of distinctiveness but also as one of recognition, enabling members of the same community to identify one another through their exterior appearance, built structures, and artifacts. A shift from "sober" to "plain" occurred in the last decades of the seventeenth century, when Quaker meetings began to reference "plainness."[24] For the next two hundred years, the goal of the "plain style" in speech, dress, architecture, and furniture was to distinguish Quakers from non-Quakers and keep them separated from the world.

It was only at the turn of the twentieth century that the attitude toward plainness started to change. Quaker historian and theologian Rufus Jones proposes that plainness, in fact, devalued nature, and that the Friends had to move beyond the paradigm of the plain style in order to be able to value the presence of God in fine arts and music. He replaces "plainness" with "simplicity," suggesting that the latter was a "quality of the soul."[25] By 1961, *Faith and Practice,* an annual publication issued by the Philadelphia Yearly Meeting, defines "simplicity" not as an attitude requiring standardization or uniformity but as a moral and ethical stance.[26] Since 1997, *Faith and Practice* has associated simplicity with "stewardship," where the latter is the "coming together" of Friends' major testimonies and expresses one of the main virtues of the Quaker way of being in the world and within the family.[27] Concepts such as "right sharing" or "walking gently on the Earth" further reinforce the emphasis on the ethical dimension of simplicity.[28]

Venturi's approach to an architecture that is simultaneously flat and complex—architecture that is a part of its context yet apart from it, simple in nature but elaborate in form—builds upon the paradox central to Quaker doctrine. Manifested in the spirituality of the Friends as well as in their material culture, the paradox of being "in the world, but not of it" finds its expression in Venturi's architecture, which also aims to accomplish two important Quaker directives: to recognize the signs and to tell the Truth. According to Quaker doctrine, the former is a mystical event experienced not as a sudden exposure but as a "gradual and progressive awareness."[29] In Venturi's architecture, the act of recognizing the signs is often a literal process of identifying the function and genealogy of a certain building. A form of simplicity, genuineness, and sincerity, telling the Truth is a moral and spiritual act that Venturi aims to translate into an architectural principle: once the truth—spiritual or architectural—is exposed, it does not require any further explanations or justifications and accomplishes its mission through its inner power. A look at Quaker architecture and art offers insights into the nature of the visual culture that Venturi experienced in his youth. Additionally, it shows the role of the community and their shared spaces, another theme that Venturi will explore in his designs.

The Quakers come together in meetinghouses. While the buildings' nature is neither sacred nor transcendental, they keep personal and collective histories alive. Paradox is inherent to worship spaces: though not valued as spiritual artifacts, they are maintained, reused, and rebuilt in order to preserve the community's integrity and continuity. Ingenious ways of recycling and repurposing building parts and materials from meetinghouses that are no longer in use reflect concerns for resources and economy of means as aspects of simplicity, but they also reinforce ideas about continuity, genealogy, and legacy.[30] Repurposing old meetinghouses for other uses and incorporating materials from the old structures into new ones are common practices in Quaker communities.[31]

The Quaker artistic tradition is built upon a certain tension between words and images. Silent worship requires a patient waiting, which is sometimes followed by a message that an individual hears, recognizes, understands, verbalizes, and then communicates to the community. Words become signs that carry the message of revelation, and recognizing them *as* signs is a form of receiving and understanding the divine message. Abstract entities disembodied from the material world, words are discreet but powerful presences in the Quaker universe.

One of the core ideas in Venturi's theory and practice emphasizes the display of words on buildings (signs, names, or numbers) as an explicit means of communication. The *decorated shed* (exemplified in projects such as the Guild House, Grand's Restaurant, the National Football Hall of Fame, and later the famous sketch stating "I am a monument") is, fundamentally, a generic structure with an attached sign that unequivocally states its purpose and intent. This attitude might appear inconsistent with Venturi's plea for ambiguity and the richness of messages. While he attributes the use of signs and icons to his own interest in New Criticism and Pop Art, Quaker material culture offers cues for situating his position within a broader genealogy. Historic evidence, and particularly artworks, shows that the Quakers situate signs and icons at the core of their art and spirituality.

A contentious topic in Quaker culture, visual arts originally raised suspicion as vain representations of life, threatening to remove the faithful from the reality of life itself.[32] Their acceptance is gradually introduced in the first half of the nineteenth century with Edward Hicks's allegorical paintings. Around 1825, Hicks—a Quaker preacher trained as a professional sign and carriage painter—begins the *Peaceable Kingdom* series of paintings, in which he elaborates on Isaiah's prophecy of universal peace. The recurrent motif of the series is the allegory of concord and harmony among all the creatures on earth, represented by the serene cohabitation of the wolf and the lamb, the leopard and the kid, the calf and the young lion.[33]

Drawing on the practice of sign painting, Hicks includes written messages (usually biblical verses) to reinforce and explain the meaning of the allegorical images. In *The Peaceable Kingdom of the Branch,* for instance, the words are situated outside the pictorial space and construct the frame of the image both as a physical edge and, metaphorically, as a clarification. In *Peaceable Kingdoms with Quakers Bearing Banners,* an allegory of Christ and the apostles, the streamer descends from time through space and reaches down into the present world. The words occupy the space and, wrapped around the crowd, carry the divine message as they float above the people, from whom they remain detached. The paradox of Hicks's paintings is that they are simultaneously allegorical images and literal texts. The act of explaining the images to ensure clarity of content is essential in a group whose practices are based on truthfulness and honesty. Similarly, in his work Venturi relies on the shared understanding of a message through words displayed on billboard-like surfaces attached to or wrapped around the architectural body, such as Grand's Restaurant (fig. 12) or the Guild House.

The practice of visualizing words and numbers is present not only in Quaker paintings but also in their built structures. The domestic architecture of upper-class Quakers in the Delaware Valley has letters inscribed on its walls. The owners set into the brickwork their family names, initials, and construction years as a sign of "wealth, . . . authority, and monumentality," a gesture that also constructs a historical and spatial genealogy.[34] Architecture displays and memorializes family and community, past and present, world and faith: "The obvious paradox that emerges from this reading is the reconciliation of worldliness with Quaker life. The answer lies in part in our understanding that the issue for early eighteenth-century Quakers was not so much one of living in the world but one of how people properly lived in the world."[35]

From Venturi's early projects such as the Frug House, Grand's Restaurant, the Guild House, or the National Football Hall of Fame to the later works the Venturi and Scott Brown team qualified as *decorated sheds,* the display of inscriptions has been largely situated within the trend of visualizing words present in the artwork of the 1960s and 1970s. However, considering Venturi's early upbringing and expo-

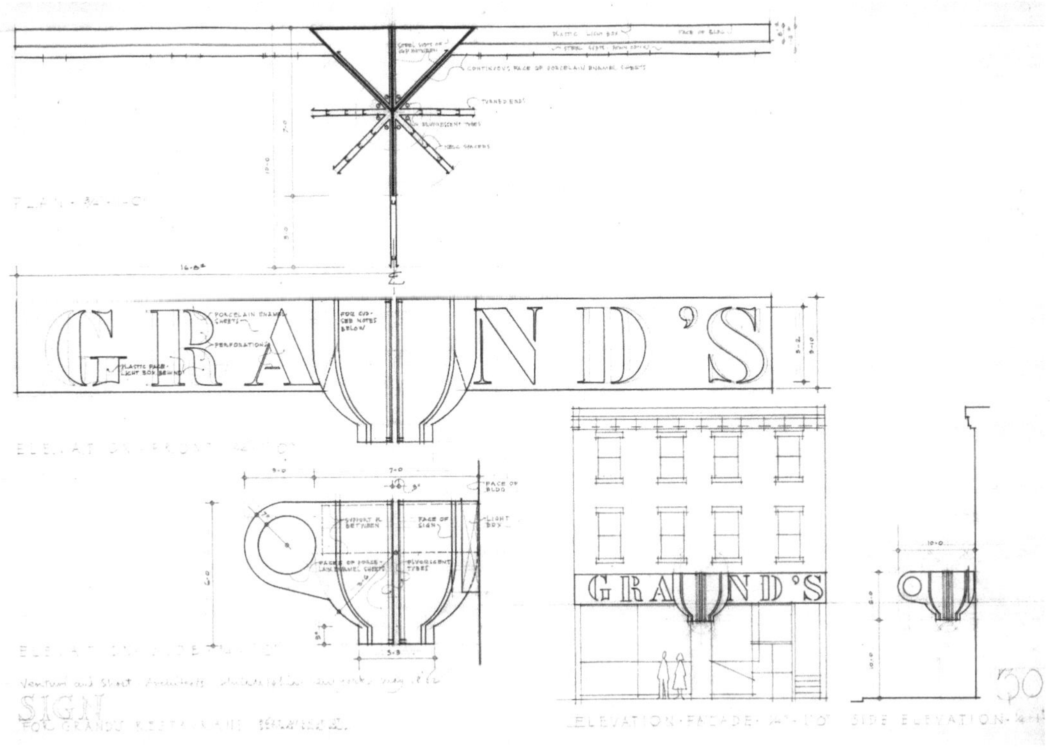

Figure 12. Venturi and Short Architects, sign for Grand's Restaurant, Philadelphia, 1962. (© The Architectural Archives, University of Pennsylvania, by the gift of Robert Venturi and Denise Scott Brown)

sure to Quaker doctrine and aesthetics, the theory of architecture as shelter with applied signs might be understood not only as the outcome of the partnership's interest in the commercial vernacular but also as an indirect nod to Quaker culture. While inscriptions communicate unambiguous messages, they also respond to basic human needs: the sense of belonging to a community and the ability to recognize the signs of its material culture give individuals a feeling of continuity and stability, one that modernity has radically altered. Venturi's critique of modern architecture is indirectly a critique of modern alienation and displacement. His own biography shows a constant search for personal and professional origins: while traveling the world, he never moves away from his native Philadelphia and always attempts to intertwine various cultural threads—from personal and architectural genealogies rooted in Italian culture to American vernacular and popular culture.

Although Quaker tradition appears to resist representation, it embraces, in fact, alternative dimensions of the artwork, often engaging with art forms that operate in a two-dimensional space and tend to flatten the three-dimensional world. In nineteenth-century Philadelphia, the Quakers privilege silhouettes over traditional oil paintings. A particular form of portraiture, silhouettes are either drawn freehand or traced directly from the outline of a head or a shadow with a physiognotrace. Made popular in the United States in the late eighteenth and early nineteenth centuries through the work of the Swiss theologian and philosopher Johann Kaspar Lavater, physiognomy emerges from the premise that people's facial traits reflect their character.[36] It is precisely the emphasis on *character* as the defining feature of an individual that appeals to the Quakers, who are searching for the essence of being and are willing to leave aside superfluous details. From a Quaker perspective, silhouettes could be construed as projections of the soul, made visible in the phenomenal world through the Inner Light, acting as the light source casting shadows. The invisible (the soul) thus turns visible through an ephemeral projection (the silhouette), itself a fleeting shadow.

Made of paper, the hollow-cut silhouettes are placed on pieces of fabric. By folding the piece of paper, one could create multiple silhouettes, which makes their production fairly easy and inexpensive. Thus, silhouettes fit Quaker conceptions about material life: plain, simple, and economical. Collected in albums, they bring together not only members of the same family but also friends, ancestors, and figures from the past, and they can be exchanged, mailed, and offered as gifts. At a larger scale, the albums also trace the lineage of the Quakers, thus legitimizing their position in history.[37] The silhouettes are simultaneously figurative and abstract, specific and universal: outlining the character of the sitters, the profiles give them an identity but also strip off the particular details that usually make the difference between an individual and a generic figure.

Since Venturi only obliquely references the presence of the Society of Friends in his life, the influence of silhouettes on his work invites productive speculations. Venturi and Scott Brown's design for the Knoll chairs, for instance, recalls the flatness of Quaker cut-out silhouettes and their play between universality and specificity (fig. 13). In a photograph of Venturi and Scott Brown posing with two of the Knoll chairs, Scott Brown is wearing a dress of the same pattern as the Queen Anne chair next to her. A tongue-in-cheek statement about the nature of the surface (also, perhaps, an ironic statement about two queens, Anne and Denise), the fabric of the dress and the fabric of the chair become autonomous and interchangeable.

Another example, Venturi's thesis project at Princeton—the Chapel for the

Figure 13. The Queen Anne chair (*left*); Denise Scott Brown and Robert Venturi at home (*right*). (© The Architectural Archives, University of Pennsylvania, by the gift of Robert Venturi and Denise Scott Brown)

Episcopal Academy (1953)—indicates a subtle but significant influence of Quaker aesthetics as an aesthetics of stillness, quietness, and patience. Historically, the Episcopal Church split from the Church of England after the American Revolution and more recently described itself as "Protestant, yet Catholic."[38] The chapel gives voice to both Roman Catholic and Quaker traditions. Volumetrically, the sequence of spaces specific to Roman Catholic churches creates a transition from the most profane to the most sacred: outdoors courtyard, narthex, nave with two aisles separated by a central circulation, and sanctuary. However, instead of facing the sanctuary, as is common in both Catholic and Episcopal worship spaces, the two aisles of pews face each other, a layout specific to Quaker meetinghouses (fig. 14). There, the Friends orient the benches toward each other as a way of building stronger communication between the members of the congregation, a configuration still preserved in contemporary architecture. This layout is an expression of the Quaker canon and its emphasis on community. The lack of ministry and priesthood is translated architecturally into a democratic distribution of the members of the community and the absence of a sanctuary or an altar.

The section drawings indicate a stepping up in two directions. Following the

Roman Catholic model, the first ascendant move follows the longitudinal axis from the narthex through the nave toward the sanctuary (fig. 14). The other stepping up unfolds within the nave itself (fig. 15). While the nave is spatially separated from the narthex and the sanctuary, the two aisles of pews within it are facing each other across the central horizontal circulation. This arrangement is not simply a matter of furniture layout but a deliberate decision to center the design on the congregation itself, echoing the Quaker meetinghouse tradition. Moreover, given the nature of the space as a school chapel, Venturi focuses on the shared space of the community rather than that of the sanctuary.

The section and the interior perspective give more clues on reading the Quaker signs (figs. 15 and 16). Structurally, the roof is defined by a series of trusses sitting on the lateral walls. Continuous along the length of the chapel, the roof reinforces the

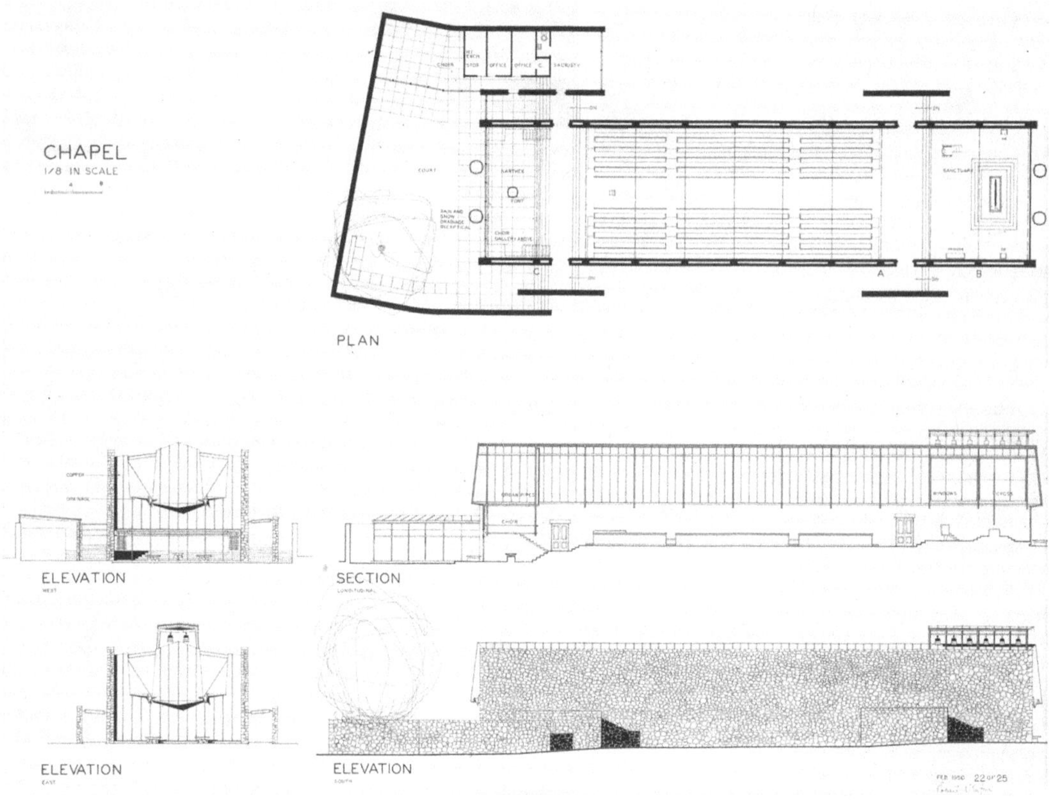

Figure 14. Robert Venturi, Thesis Project: Chapel for the Episcopal Academy, Princeton, 1953, plan, sections, elevations. (© The Architectural Archives, University of Pennsylvania, by the gift of Robert Venturi and Denise Scott Brown)

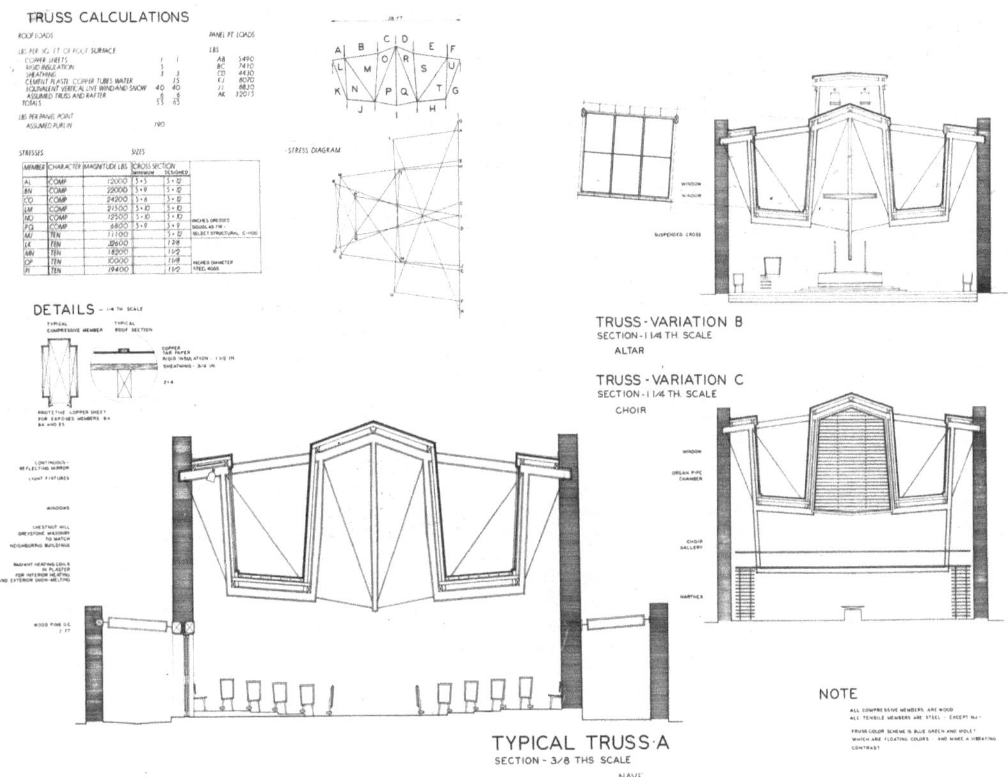

Figure 15. Robert Venturi, Thesis Project: Chapel for the Episcopal Academy, Princeton, 1953, details. (© The Architectural Archives, University of Pennsylvania, by the gift of Robert Venturi and Denise Scott Brown)

reading of the space as nonhierarchical. Venturi specifies that "all compressive members are wood. All tensile members are steel. Truss color scheme is blue, green and violet which are floating colors and make a vibrating contrast."[39] This color scheme might appear an unusual choice for a worship space, but it highlights the continuity of the truss, which visually and spatially connects the narthex, the nave, and the sanctuary (fig. 16). While the indirect light filtered down by the truss washes the lateral walls, the sanctuary, raised above the level of the nave, is flooded in light.

If the Inner Light constitutes the core of Quaker theology, the truss with its vibrating color contrast constitutes the spine of the chapel. Rather than directly drop the light through the dramatic central spine, the roof gently moves it toward the sidewalls. While these are relatively bright, the people sitting in the pews will be

Figure 16. Robert Venturi, Thesis Project: Chapel for the Episcopal Academy, Princeton, 1953, interior rendering. (© The Architectural Archives, University of Pennsylvania, by the gift of Robert Venturi and Denise Scott Brown)

backlit, appearing like silhouettes to their fellows sitting across the aisle. The Quaker cut-out silhouettes thus turn into a three-dimensional spatial experience, built on the tension between the seen and the unseen, light and matter, spiritual world and physical world.

Quaker meetinghouses continue to carry the tradition of stillness into contemporary architecture. A lifelong Quaker, artist James Turrell has been building his "skyspaces" throughout the world since the 1970s. Designed as enclosed spaces to observe the sky through a carefully controlled roof aperture, some of these installations are built specifically as meetinghouses for the Society of Friends; they open to the public at dusk to allow people to experience the changing sunset lights.[40] Sitting or lying back on benches and on the floor, people are invited to quietly look up at the sky in a lengthy process that gradually absorbs the individual into the vastness of the universe. It is perhaps in these moments that one gets a glimpse into time's material presence. The act of waiting becomes an act of contemplation, and we as humans begin to understand the power, beauty, and tragedy of our own finitude within the infinity of the world.

A(NOTHER) SPECULATIVE READING OF THE GUILD HOUSE (1963–1966)

The decades of the 1950s and 1960s see the rapid advancement of radio, X-ray, ultraviolet, and infrared technologies that attempt not only to make visible otherwise imperceptible signals but also to connect humans with outer space. Between 1963 and 1966, the television series *My Favorite Martian* brings to American households an anthropologist from Mars whose crashed airship lands him close to Los Angeles. Among many different skills, Uncle Martin, as his terrestrial friend Tim calls him, has the power to extend two retractable antennae from his head that immediately connect him to the network of waves present everywhere in his environment—but invisible to ordinary people. The twitching nose of the modern witch in *Bewitched* is perhaps also another sort of "antenna" sensitive to atmospheric changes.

It is in the context of exalted postwar consumerism, in a world awakening to its fascination with technological gadgets and invisible networks, that Venturi designs the Guild House (1963–66), a residence for the elderly that opens in Philadelphia in 1966. In a design decision amply discussed by scholars and architectural critics, on the rooftop of the building, centered on its axis, he places an antenna (fig. 17), a nonfunctional, purely decorative aerial carefully described in *Complexity and Contradiction in Architecture:* "The television antenna atop this axis and beyond the otherwise constant height line of the building strengthens this axis of scale-change in the zone of the central façade, and expresses a kind of monumentality similar to that at the entrance of Anet. The antenna, with its anodized gold surface, can be interpreted two ways: abstractly, as a sculpture in the manner of Lippold, and as a symbol of the aged, who spend so much time looking at T.V."[41]

How are we to interpret Venturi's brief references? How do they relate to each other, if at all? Is Venturi giving us clues about a larger, unseen topic at stake in his design?

At the official opening of the Guild House, Venturi presents "a small bouquet of fresh cut flowers to each occupant."[42] Completed with federal funding, the Guild House is the initiative of Francis Bosworth, the executive director of the Friends Neighborhood Guild, a nonprofit social welfare agency founded in 1879 and affili-

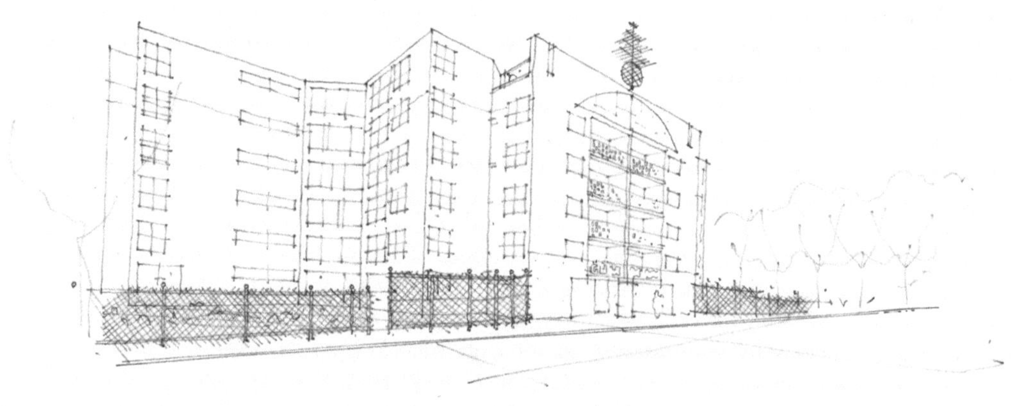

Figure 17. Venturi and Rauch, Cope and Lippincott, Guild House, Philadelphia, 1963–66, exterior view. (© The Architectural Archives, University of Pennsylvania, by the gift of Robert Venturi and Denise Scott Brown)

ated with the Quakers. For over a century, the Guild has been deeply engaged with issues of community development; racial, ethnic, and class integration; access to services; and affordable housing. In the 1950s, the Guild develops racially integrated cooperative housing at Eighth Street and Fairmount Avenue, and in the 1960s it builds the Guild House.[43] Close to his aging mother (his father had passed away in 1959), Venturi is sympathetic to the needs of the elderly. His project aims to provide the residents with the maximum degree of comfort and variety possible under the budgetary restrictions imposed by the Federal Housing and Home Finance Agency, whose guidelines, in keeping with the Quaker values of plainness and simplicity, require that the "building design must not be elaborate or ornate."[44]

The press release issued at the opening of the Guild House (originally drafted by Venturi himself) singles out the interior flexibility achieved through the structural system and the entertainment system as two of the building's main features: "Construction of the fireproof structure is flat plate reinforced concrete which permitted wide latitude in interior design to relieve monotony without undue increases in construction costs. A master TV antenna is included and air-conditioning is at the resident's option."[45]

From this unusual association of construction flexibility and entertainment, it appears that two of the important characteristics of the building are also the two major sources to "relieve monotony," or, in other words, to fight boredom: the structural system, which allows for variety in design, and television. A sign of progress and good care of the elderly, the antenna mentioned in the press release is different, however, from the one described in *Complexity and Contradiction in Architecture.* In fact, period photographs show several antennae placed on the roof behind the ornamental piece that occupies the foreground. Several "real" antennae, a "fake" one, a French château, and an American artist—how do they all converse with each other? And how are they in dialogue with the story and history of the Guild House?

GOLDEN HORNS. Venturi introduces the antenna by way of reference to the monumentality of Anet, a French château built by architect Philibert de l'Orme. Constructed between 1547 and 1552, Anet was a gift from King Henri II of France to his mistress Diane de Poitiers. After the French Revolution, its contents were auctioned, and some architectural elements were retrieved and displayed in the Musée des Monuments Français (Museum of French Monuments). Although partly demolished, the Anet castle would survive, thanks to subsequent owners who invested in its restoration.

The reference to the Anet castle has a twofold significance: built at a time when architecture was experiencing a shift toward Mannerism, the château illustrates Venturi's fondness for sixteenth-century architectural styles; at the same time, its troubled history suggests an inauspicious destiny that is often the fate of artworks that are either misunderstood or casualties of hostile historical circumstances.[46] Having constructed a public persona of a marginal, often misunderstood figure operating at the periphery of the profession, Venturi's reference to a "victimized" architecture suits his autobiographical profile. With parts of the castle located in the Musée des Monuments Français, itself situated inside the École des Beaux-Arts, Anet symbolizes classical art and its values. Whether Venturi is aware of this history is less relevant. Examining the Anet castle as a precedent opens up a speculative reading of the Guild House that situates the building in a larger cultural context of ideas, showing the often-invisible networks of significance within which we operate.

What exactly does Venturi see in the entrance of Anet that spawns his analogy between the French castle and his residence for the elderly in Philadelphia? The imposing statue of a stag with prominent antlers crowning the entrance gate to the castle most likely prompts Venturi's parallel between the antenna on the Guild House and the French château. The statue is a reference to Diane de Poitiers, the lady of the estate, and portrays her as Diana, the Roman goddess of the hunt. The correlation is based on more than the namesake: an unusually athletic woman for the time, de Poitiers swam, hunted, and rode horses every day, evoking the fearless goddess of hunting and wilderness.[47] Cold and ambitious, she placed a majestic statue of her likeness at the entrance of the palace, guarding the residence from above. Her château portrays not an architecture of pleasure but rather, in the image of its mistress, one of calculated schemes and strategies.[48]

A twist of fate reveals the invisible network of connections surrounding us. In Roman mythology, the goddess of the hunt had a fast, strong white stag with golden horns. As Diana herself came to be identified with the moon, the association of the sun (represented by the golden antlers of the stag) and the moon suggested the wholeness of the universe.[49] Twenty years older than her royal lover, de Poitiers embodies the complicated theme of age and aging, so appropriate in the context of a residence for the elderly. She passed away in 1566 at age sixty-six under unknown circumstances, but her remains were found only in 2008, in a common grave where her body was supposedly thrown after the revolutionaries opened her tomb in 1795. Forensic investigations have identified the presence of gold in her physical remains. Scientific evidence thus corroborates what was previously known from unverified period testimonies, namely, that de Poitiers was ingesting gold as an elixir for permanent youth. "We have identified Diane de Poitiers to a high degree of confidence," the specialists maintain. "We believe that she drank gold. . . . The high concentrations of gold in her hair indicate that she could have died of chronic intoxication with gold."[50] Passing from myth to reality and then into art, the gold went through an alchemical process of transmutation from the antlers of Diana's white stag into the body of Diane de Poitiers, settling into the horns of the Anet statue, and finally landing in the form of a gold-anodized antenna on the rooftop of a building in Philadelphia.

Etymologically, the word *antenna* derives from Greek (to stretch out or forth) and Latin (horns of insects or ends of sail yards).[51] Biological antennae are sensory organs that reach out to feel the environment, determine orientation, and make sense of the surroundings. The extensions of the legendary stag and those of the modern Guild House antenna perform similar functions: they situate and anchor the body that carries them in its particular setting, defining its context. The gold transgresses time and space and perhaps reveals the unspoken desire of the architect to relocate his "ugly and ordinary" building from Philadelphia into a mythical time.[52]

GOLDEN WIRES. Venturi remarks that the antenna on the Guild House can be interpreted abstractly "as a statue in the manner of Lippold."[53] An American artist who studied industrial design, Richard Lippold (1915–2002) contributes to a rebirth of the Constructivist tradition in the United States through his Constructivist-inspired wire sculptures.[54] He uses gold extensively in pieces such as *Variation with a Sphere, No. 10: The Sun* (1953–56), *Trinity Crucifix* at the Church of St. Gregory the Great in Rhode Island (1960), *Flight* (1960, the sculpture for the Vanderbilt Avenue lobby of the headquarters of Pan American World Airways in New York), *Ad Astra* (1976, the sculpture in front of the National Air and Space Museum in Washington, DC), and *Ex Stasis* (1988, on the campus of Marquette University in Milwaukee, Wisconsin).

When Venturi references Lippold's abstract sculptures, he tacitly engages not just their form but also their materiality. The antenna on the Guild House brings into the same horizon the golden horns of Diana's stag and the golden wires of Lippold's artwork—technology, mythology, and abstract art. These various devices sense and make sense of the environment while performing a balancing exercise through the anchoring or suspending of their own golden bodies.

GOLDEN BOREDOM. A television antenna captures the waves and translates them into images, and it is, in fact, what makes television (i.e., *remote vision*) work. Antennae are placed either indoors, on the television set, or outdoors, on a building, and they receive broadcast television signals that are then transferred to the television set. The office of Venturi and Rauch pays considerable attention to the nonfunctional "antenna" on the Guild House. Neither a catalogue item nor a conventional antenna, it is carefully designed in the office, based on precise specifications. Following Venturi's rule of *both/and,* it is *both* an interior *and* an exterior antenna that merges the two typologies, and thus in looking at it, one is *both* inside *and* outside the house. In a frontal view from afar, the circular piece at the bottom appears flat, just like the circular element of an indoor antenna. The design specifications indicate that this part is a "6' parabolic antenna 3090" with a convex section (fig. 18).[55] Metaphorically speaking, the Guild House becomes a giant television screen for the city, while passersby turn into spectators. As 5:4 was the proportion of the first rectangular television screens, this is roughly the proportion of the street elevation of the Guild House.

In his critique of the three forms of modern entertainment from the early decades of the twentieth century—advertisements, films, and radio—Siegfried Kracauer describes the constant exposure of modern humans to news and events from all around the world as a "species of antennal fate."[56] This constant background noise, Kracauer argues, which in itself can be utterly distracting and irrelevant, denies one

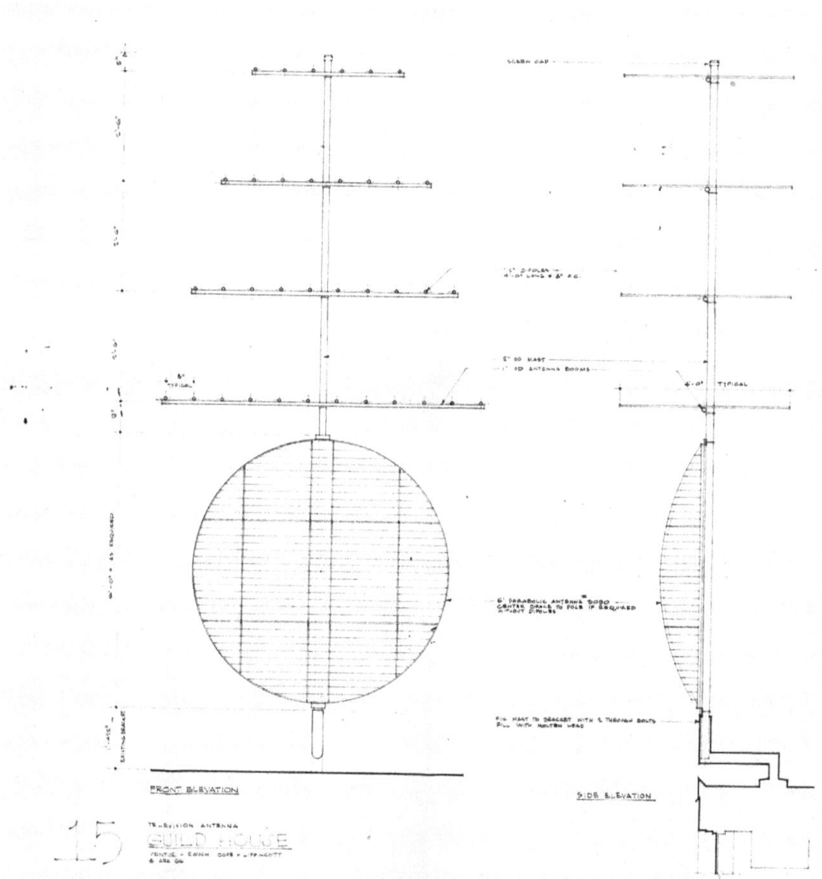

Figure 18. Venturi and Rauch, Cope and Lippincott, Guild House, Philadelphia, 1963–66, construction drawings for the decorative antenna. (© The Architectural Archives, University of Pennsylvania, by the gift of Robert Venturi and Denise Scott Brown)

the right to privacy and personal boredom.[57] The aerial on the Guild House foresees the "antennal destiny" of architecture, which in the coming decades will increasingly rely on the latest trends and most recent fashions.

Television, and by extension a television antenna, collapses time and distance, the essential and the irrelevant, the foreground and the background. Faraway events are brought in close proximity to one another and to the viewers themselves, who expect images to change, vary, and constantly move. In a state of perpetual expectation, people watch and wait, lured by the promise of more distraction. Crowned by the "fake" antenna, the flat façade reflects the superficiality of mass media. If the Quaker form of waiting has a spiritual dimension, waiting in front of the television screen epitomizes the boredom of the new age disguised under the constant noise of diversion and entertainment.

The aerial on the Guild House carries the promise of change at a time when television makes it possible for people to sit still, in their living rooms, while witnessing the world changing right in front of their eyes. To seniors, to the bedridden, to bored homemakers, television offers the potential of previously inaccessible distraction. When Venturi describes the antenna as a symbol of the elderly "who spend so much time looking at T.V.," he inadvertently reveals the latent discomfort of the age, not only of the aged, with slow pace and unhurried rhythms. As the press release proudly states, television and a flexible construction system offer the residents of the Guild House the tools "to relieve monotony." However, television builds a trap for a deeper and more profound boredom. If "real" antennae are receiving television signals, perhaps the "fake" ones capture the unseen waves of modern tedium.

Standing between the golden horns of Diana's stag and the golden wires of Lippold's sculptures, the golden antenna on the Guild House embodies the modern myth of escaping boredom through distraction. Horns, wires, or antennae, these "sensing devices," seize the invisible waves and networks of meaning present in our environment. If the movies and television series of the 1950s and 1960s are fascinated with the idea of the universe sending us signals, terrestrial architecture is gradually losing its depth—becoming instead a shallow, flat, and skin-deep screen.

5

CRITIQUES OF CONTEMPORARY TEDIUM

Bob before Denise

"Complexity and Contradiction vs. Simplification and Picturesqueness," the second chapter of *Complexity and Contradiction in Architecture,* launches into a critique of modern architects who have failed to recognize the complexity of the built environment.[1] Idealizing "primary forms" (like Le Corbusier) or "visions of simplicity" (like Frank Lloyd Wright), they have ignored rich ambiguities, "the diverse and the sophisticated."[2] Quoting from Christopher Alexander's *Notes on the Synthesis of Form* and August Heckscher's *The Public Happiness,* Venturi advocates for the need to embrace complexity in architecture.[3] While Alexander conceptualizes design as problem-solving in a world of complex systems and structures, Heckscher has different concerns; unlike Alexander's deterministic approach, Heckscher's humanist perspective centers on the collective well-being of communities. His book *The Public Happiness* shapes Venturi's interest in boredom. But who was August Heckscher, the most cited author in *Complexity and Contradiction in Architecture* after Venturi's favorite writer, T. S. Eliot?

AUGUST HECKSCHER'S *THE PUBLIC HAPPINESS*

Heckscher, one of Venturi's contemporaries, was an American liberal writer and political activist who served as the chairman of the New School for Social Research, the Woodrow Wilson Foundation, and the Parsons School of Design. The chief editorial writer at the *New York Herald Tribune* (1952–56) and a parks commissioner under New York mayor John V. Lindsay, he is the coordinator of cultural affairs at the White House in 1962 and also serves as a special consultant on the arts in the Kennedy administration. Heckscher is a trustee of the Twentieth Century Fund from 1951 until his death in 1991, and he serves as the director of the institution from 1956 to 1967.[4]

With a degree in government from Harvard University, at the time he publishes *The Public Happiness* Heckscher is a seasoned writer with several authored, co-authored, and edited books as well as dozens of articles on democracy, government, domestic and foreign policy, and—a constant and sustained topic—the role of the arts in the public sphere.[5] He writes *The Public Happiness* to signal that, in a world increasingly focused on the happiness of the individual, larger issues such as the happiness of the state and the very idea of citizenship are being neglected.[6] In the book, Heckscher expresses his gratitude to Sebastian de Grazia, the author of the comprehensive study *Of Time, Work, and Leisure,* with whom he "canvassed most of the problems of the modern period" (296).

Committed to and deeply engaged with civic matters, Heckscher acknowledges the great influence that Hannah Arendt's *The Human Condition* exercised on his book (45). His perspective on politics is founded on the classical Greek notion of the *polis,* where a good and meaningful life results from a good and meaningful connection between the individual and the community (vi). *The Public Happiness* is structured in three parts. The first diagnoses the alienation of the modern individual as an outcome of advanced capitalism. The second makes an argument for playfulness, irony, and resisting the tyranny of consumerism as appropriate responses to contemporary problems. The traditions of Puritanism and rationalism, Heckscher proposes, have repressed the spirit of play, which constitutes the origin of leisure as a creative pursuit—radically different from the contemporary sense of leisure as entertainment and distraction. The last part discusses possible ways to foster this particular approach to reality. The overarching proposition is that enlightened public policies that "stress the individuality of leadership as opposed to the anonymity of administrative rule" may eventually result in meaningful ways to find the "value of our existence." Heckscher's claim is not that the state can make people happy but that it plays a role in nurturing public happiness (viii–ix, 203). In this context, works in the public interest (from hospitals to parks and public art) are central in creating an environment that cultivates people's individual and collective well-being. The concluding chapters show how architecture, planning, and the arts are critical tools in shaping both citizenship and public happiness.

In the introduction to *The Public Happiness,* Heckscher recounts his personal awakening to the issue of boredom:

> In Copenhagen, an autumn ago, we were discussing some of the political and economic questions which habitually recur at international conferences. A young Dane got up in the back of the room. "It is very well to worry about satisfying the material needs of the people," he said in effect. "But these are not the real problems of our society. These real problems are deeper—*boredom, loneliness, alienation.* Unless the politics of our time can give relevant answers in this sphere, they will not engage the central interest of the citizen. They will cease being exciting, or even amusing, and become more and more the preoccupation of a small professional group." (v)

Heckscher situates the danger of collective boredom at the core of the civic responsibilities of the time. He discusses this topic at length throughout the book and dedicates an entire chapter to architectural and urban issues (253–74). Understanding the modern condition as increasingly abstract and remote from *things,* he proposes approaching the world through "an attitude essentially playful, ironical and detached" (viii). While the Puritanism and rationalism quintessential to the American character have muted people's "ironical" voice, Heckscher believes there is still room and hope for play in the contemporary world. He is no stranger to the larger discourse on the nature of leisure and its affinity with ideas about play. At the Twentieth Century Fund, he supports Sebastian de Grazia's extensive study on leisure, aligning himself with the Marxist critique of consumerism and the commodification of culture. Like Josef Pieper, he reclaims the higher notion of leisure—lost in the modern world—through the notion of play: "Leisure, if it is not to consist of mass orgies and mass boredom, must cultivate an attitude of play" (viii).

Many of Heckscher's arguments revolve around tedium. In the age of mass communication, the modern individual—assaulted by images and sounds—suffers from a debilitating boredom that emerges in response to a hostile world: "It is not the boredom of the haphazard or even involuntary kind; rather it is a deliberate boredom, a carefully contrived blank, a sublime disregard that might be thought worthy of the sage or seer. There is nothing that completely abolishes the world as boredom of this kind" (79). This boredom entails "a gray thought in a gray and milky shade," the desire for more entertainment, and a "search for new sensations" (79). The modern does not have access to an elevated state of boredom as contemplation because, Heckscher observes, he "is not satisfied with his own boredom" (9). He acknowledges that a main factor contributing to the modern individual's alienation is the built environment. Between the fear of overcrowding and that of emptiness, a generalized discontent produces "a psychological state where boredom succeeds to nervous agitation" (254).

A lover of classical Greece, Heckscher does not dismiss contemporary art and architecture; on the contrary, he believes in the relationship between high art and popular art and is open to artistic visions that embrace and reimagine trite everyday objects such as commercial signs and lights, which "carry within themselves the elements of a fresh creativeness" (284). He compares Times Square with a form of jazz and reads its "emphasis on drama, symbol and allusion" as the elements of a "new Baroque" expressed in modern architecture. Venturi's enthusiasm for Pop Art and the ambience of complex public places such as Times Square echoes Heckscher's position and places the two authors in a rich conversation.

Two particular chapters from Heckscher's book seem to have exercised an important influence on Venturi's thinking: "The Approach to Reality" and "Art and Politics." The former examines people's attitude toward modern life and boredom, identifying three groups of individuals. People in the first category "are not really bored" because they are in constant motion, following the trends and fads of their time (101). The second category includes those who make the best of the moment. The last category consists of "the true citizens of their time," who, without refraining from the pleasures of life, have liberated themselves from the constraints of consumerism and are thus able to find the deeper meaning of their existence. They are "not bored because even deceptions can be interesting to the enlightened, and not despairing because the only despair can be within themselves" (101).

What people in the third group all have in common, Heckscher believes, is a view of life as essentially complex, an attitude that embraces irony, playfulness, and a "feeling for paradox" (102). *Complexity, irony,* and *playfulness,* along with an understanding of modern boredom as the outcome of an existence remote from concrete things, are all ideas that will become central to Venturi's *Complexity and Contradiction in Architecture.*

THREE BUILDINGS FOR THE DOWNTOWN OF NORTH CANTON, OHIO (1965), AND THE BOSTON COPLEY SQUARE COMPETITION ENTRY (1966)

Heckscher's ideas about the role played by architecture and public spaces in shaping individual and collective identities find fertile ground in some of Venturi's early designs. The last chapter of *Complexity and Contradiction in Architecture* includes twelve projects designed by the office of Venturi and Rauch. Two of them, both interventions in the public realm, specifically address the question of boredom.

In 1965, Venturi and Rauch make a proposal for the downtown of North Canton, Ohio, the home of the Hoover appliances company. The intervention includes a town hall, a YMCA building, and the extension of the public library (fig. 19). Venturi compares the design of the town hall with that of a Roman temple. A freestanding partition—a "partially disengaged wall in front with its giant arched opening superimposed on the two-storied wall beyond"—replaces the classical giant columns and the pediment of the porch.[7] Several perspectival drawings indicate the prominence of this wall, which fulfills two functions: it constructs a façade toward the plaza and creates space for a secondary circulation path.

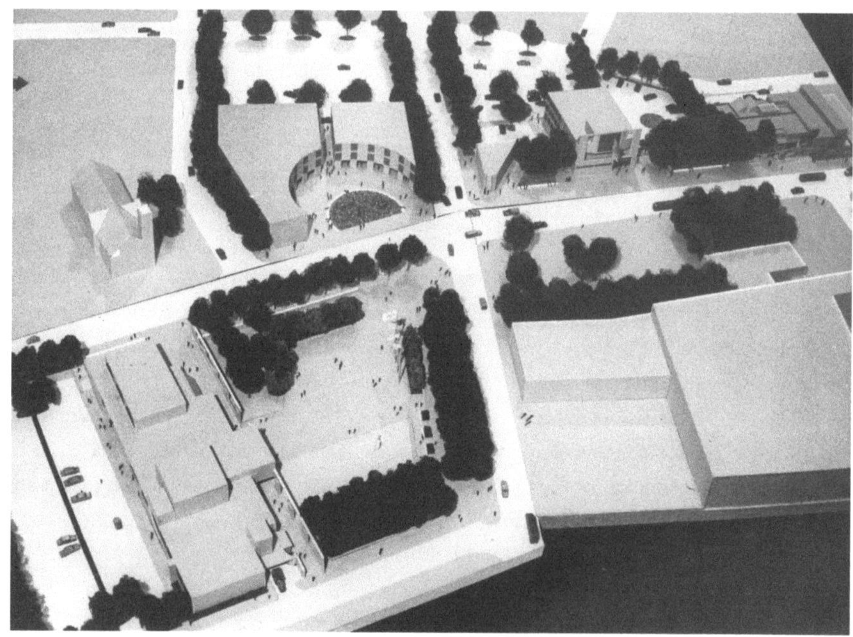

Figure 19. Venturi and Rauch, Three Buildings for the Downtown of North Canton, Ohio, 1965, model. (© The Architectural Archives, University of Pennsylvania, by the gift of Robert Venturi and Denise Scott Brown)

Figure 20. Venturi and Rauch, Three Buildings for the Downtown of North Canton, Ohio, 1965, exterior perspective. (© The Architectural Archives, University of Pennsylvania, by the gift of Robert Venturi and Denise Scott Brown)

The detached wall constitutes a common theme of the three buildings. The library addition is essentially a wall wrapped around the existing building. Through its openings, one gets a glimpse of the edifice behind. Sitting opposite the Hoover factory, the YMCA building has a false-front façade whose design is based on a play between different rhythms (fig. 20). With no beginning, middle, or end, "it is just one continuous thing resulting from the constant, even boring rhythm" of the large-scale openings: "The almost constant rhythm of grid-opening is played against the smaller and more irregular rhythms of the two-story building-proper behind. A contrapuntal juxtaposition contrasts the 'boredom' of the false façade with the 'chaos' of the back façade which reflects the interior circumstantial complexities" (fig. 20).[8]

While *boring* here describes the uniformity of monotonous formal rhythms, it also reflects a larger social condition: a certain ennui of the small town, the routines of factory work and mass-produced goods manufactured in the Hoover facility nearby. The dangerous tedium of repetitive jobs is rapidly turning into a serious problem, soon to be acknowledged in mass media. Under the headline "Bored on the Job: Industry Contends with Apathy and Anger on the Assembly Line," the cover of *Life* magazine's 1 September 1972 issue features an autoworker who installs a car fender every minute. Spread over several pages and lavishly illustrated, the main article looks at boredom as "the new industrial revolution." A major threat to people's well-being, sanity, and productivity, job monotony becomes a critical matter requiring the attention of labor unions and policymakers. Growing tensions between unions and the presidents of automotive plants underscore the need to implement major changes in manufacturing techniques.[9]

In Venturi's project, the freestanding walls act as stage sets where everyday life takes place. The theme of the detached (or seemingly detached) wall is a recurrent one in Venturi's early work. In the Pearson House, the Vanna Venturi House, and the entry for the National Football Hall of Fame competition, these walls both embody and critique the condition of modern architecture as a layer without depth. Eerily floating in front of buildings, they create a thick, multilayered space where various conditions of inhabitation can unfold. Neither completely solid nor fully transparent, these walls relate both to the building and to the public space, simultaneously separating and connecting the spatial and temporal. Concerned with the loss of character in modern architecture, in *The Public Happiness,* Heckscher envisions public spaces as "vast rooms on the outside," places where civic life can manifest itself (256). While the idea that outdoor public spaces are essential to a strong urban community is not new, Heckscher in his writings and Venturi in his design signal the danger of collective boredom emerging from bland, unengaging public spaces that lack life and character. The loss of the ordinary activities that constitute the fabric of public life would inevitably lead to alienation and estrangement.

A close examination of Venturi's working sketches for the North Canton project shows how imagined scenarios of everyday life unfold in the proposed spaces. In addition to the conventional silhouettes of people in motion, we see less predictable situations that were rarely rendered in architectural drawings at the time: people skating, a person in a wheelchair with a caregiver, toy boats floating on the artificial pond in the center of the plaza (fig. 21). The rhythms of the YMCA façade, as well as the rigor of the plans designed with practicality in mind, reveal the dullness of administrative duties. At the same time, they evoke the nature of the quotidian, which continues to follow its own course. Heckscher has argued that modern boredom is a consequence of individuals being increasingly exposed to *abstractions* rather than *things.* In this process, "what should be concrete in the environment becomes part of an eternal flux and vagueness" (vii). "The dissolution of things" and the loss of their meaning result from the excess of objects in consumer culture, where overabundance ultimately leads to indifference. The important question for Heckscher is how people can escape "from these fogs" and find their way toward a meaningful life. He finds a possible answer in the cultivation of a healthy community and public sphere. By turning toward the concreteness of the everyday, Venturi's project attempts to reconnect the individual with the community and its public

Figure 21. Venturi and Rauch, Three Buildings for the Downtown of North Canton, Ohio, 1965, detail of exterior perspective. (© The Architectural Archives, University of Pennsylvania, by the gift of Robert Venturi and Denise Scott Brown)

spaces. For both Venturi and Heckscher, boredom transcends its immediate reading as a formal composition made of repetitive elements and opens up larger questions about the nature of public life and human interactions in modern society.

The Pop artists whom Venturi admires embrace everyday life with objective detachment; architecturally speaking, this approach aims to translate life's tedious routines in built form. Just as an emotionless "boring painting" awakens in the viewer responses that are otherwise inaccessible, the façades' "boring rhythms" create a complicity with the inhabitants and their modes of life. In its careful orchestration of the tension between boredom and chaos, the North Canton project celebrates and makes room for public life. While Heckscher rightly recognizes the drama of the built environment that generates either boredom or "nervous agitation," Venturi proposes a public space that—paradoxically—builds upon yet overcomes modern boredom. The balance between a uniform field (both as a design background and as the fabric of life itself) and an accent (both as a break in the design pattern and an event in everyday life) constitutes a possible response to the question of boredom. This strategy will become clearer in the next project.

The twelfth and last project published in *Complexity and Contradiction in Architecture,* the Boston Copley Square Competition entry coauthored by Venturi and Rauch with Gerod Clark and Arthur Jones, revolves around two issues: play and boredom, themes that are also at the core of Heckscher's *The Public Happiness* (fig. 22).

The *boring/interesting* dichotomy describes the tension between the proposed grid and the existing buildings on site: "In the context of the 'boring' consistent grid

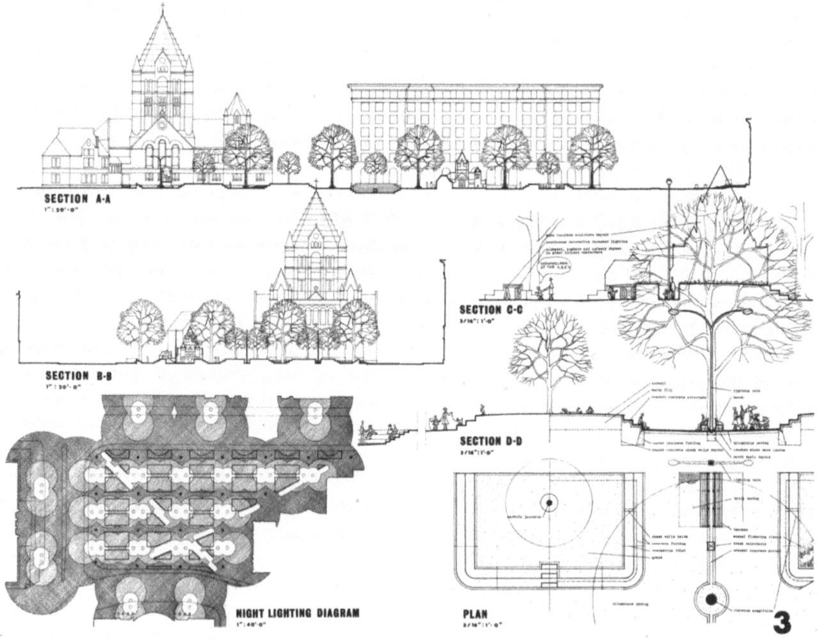

Figure 22. Venturi and Rauch, Boston Copley Square Competition entry, 1966, competition board. (© The Architectural Archives, University of Pennsylvania, by the gift of Robert Venturi and Denise Scott Brown)

inside the square the chaotic buildings to the north become 'interesting' and vital elements of the composition."[10] The "boring grid" provides the specific element that differentiates Times Square or the Piazza San Marco from roadtown (the ordinary architecture of convenience emerging along roads and highways): the ordered background. Venturi describes the project as a reflection, at a different scale, of Boston's gridiron street pattern.[11]

Throughout the first half of the twentieth century and well into the 1970s and 1980s, artists and architects use the grid as a distinct modern strategy. Art critic Rosalind Krauss interprets the use of the grid in modern art as an aversion to narrative and discourse, arguing that it declares "the modernity of modern art" on two levels: spatially, through its anti-natural and anti-real flatness, geometry, and order, and temporally, through its unique presence in the twentieth century.[12] Krauss finds the origins of the modern grid in nineteenth-century optics and observes how treatises on physiological optics were illustrated with grids. She notices that nineteenth-century painters extensively use grid-like windows in their art and that, becoming three-dimensional, the grid will provide a theoretical model for modern architecture.[13] Situating Venturi's use of the grid in this larger context offers a more nuanced understanding of his position that goes beyond the obvious formal attributes of the grid. Interested in perception himself, in how people *see* and *interpret* the information they receive, Venturi constructs a sophisticated structure that both comments on and transcends Modernism's use of the grid.

Venturi's proposed grid is meant to act at an empathetic level: intimately knowing the large scale of their city, Bostonians would understand the logic embodied by this smaller-scale design. This mode of thinking is manifested in different instances throughout the proposal, where design details echo one another at different scales: the movement through the square replicates the circulation at urban level; a miniature replica in cast concrete of the existing Trinity Church is placed in front of the actual Trinity Church; signs for adults turn into nursery rhymes for children, inscribed on walls at their own height (fig. 23).

The overall design strategy builds upon figure-ground relationships. Trinity Church remains an accent in the "three-dimensional repetitive pattern without a climax."[14] This pattern is the result of overlapping multiple layers: alleys, trees, lampposts, and street furniture. Different "accents" or "slight and violent exceptions" nuance the composition: the church and its miniature replica, inscriptions of nursery rhymes, variations in elevation.[15]

The *interesting,* the *vital,* and the *complex* emerge from productive ambiguities

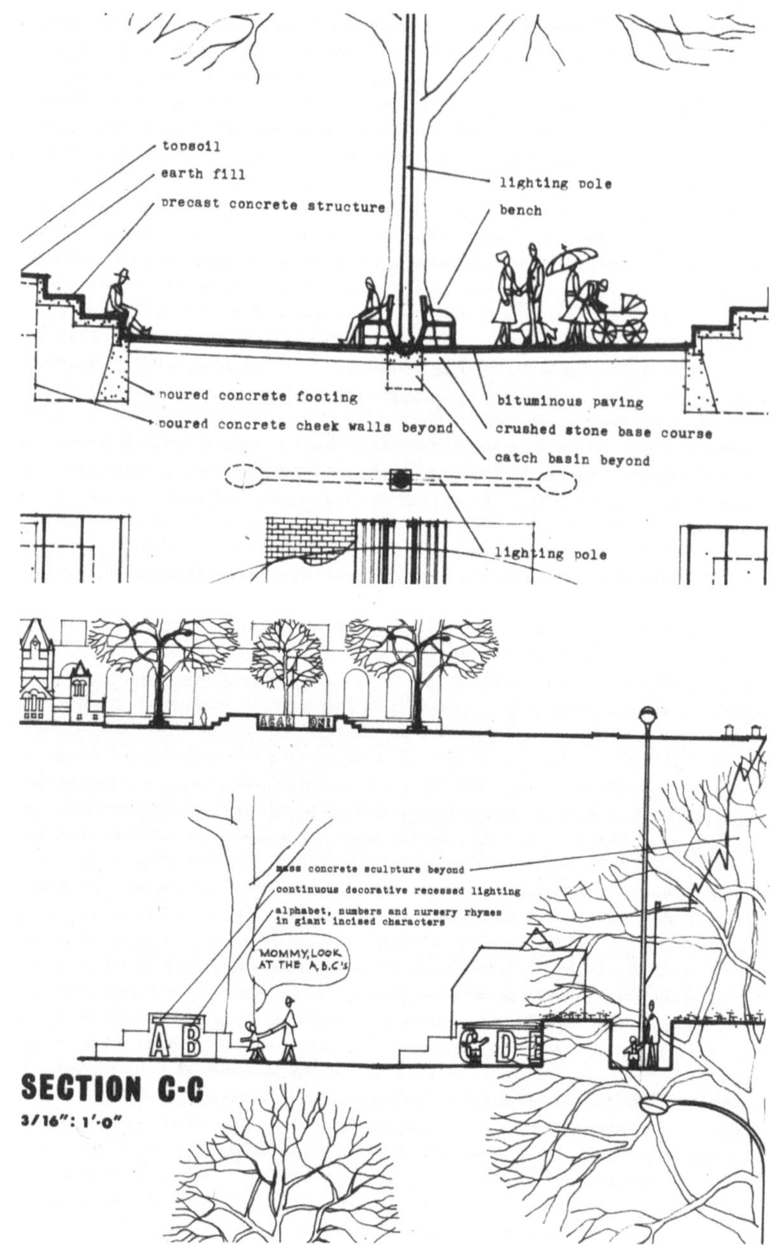

Figure 23. Venturi and Rauch, Boston Copley Square Competition entry, 1966, details. (© The Architectural Archives, University of Pennsylvania, by the gift of Robert Venturi and Denise Scott Brown)

such as blurring the boundaries between the different pieces constructing the whole. This design strategy recalls art historian Heinrich Wölfflin's analysis of the differences between Renaissance and Baroque architectures. Familiar with Wölfflin's writings, Venturi cites him in *Complexity and Contradiction in Architecture:* "This subordination of parts corresponds to Wölfflin's 'unified unity' of the Baroque—which he contrasts with the 'multiple unity' of the Renaissance."[16] Making the argument in *Principles of Art History* that between the sixteenth and seventeenth centuries a particular shift happens in the nature of artistic vision, Wölfflin formulates five pairs of principles that explain this shift: linear/painterly, planar/recessional, closed form/open form, multiplicity/unity, absolute clarity/relative clarity. In *Renaissance and Baroque,* he applies these ideas to distinguish between the two architectural styles.

The play between bringing things into focus and blurring their outlines, between close-up and distance, recalls Wölfflin's reading of Baroque architecture as the dissolution of lines and sharp contours, which Venturi makes use of in his design:

> There are more ways to see it [the grid]. It is like the intricate pattern of a plaid fabric. From a distance it is an overall repetitive pattern—from a great distance, indeed, it is a plain blur—but close-up it is intricate, varied and rich in pattern, texture, scale and color. . . . It is a question of focus: as one moves around and through the composition, he can focus on different things and relationships in different ways. . . . There is the opportunity for a variety of focuses, or rather for changing focus. . . . Violent juxtapositions of blurred and sharp focuses come from levels of relationships which relate more or less to the whole, or in complex compositions, to wholes within wholes.[17]

The design of the Copley Square proposal builds upon Venturi's use of Gestalt psychology, another field where his interests and Heckscher's converge. Heckscher reads the environment in Gestaltist terms of figure and background, structure and void (257). He praises the design of outdoor spaces as exterior rooms and the rich ambiguity of carefully orchestrated relationships between interiors and exteriors that enhance the meaning of a place. In the Copley Square design, Venturi attempts to create gradual levels of perception based on Gestalt perception theories: while the plaza is seen as a plain blur from a distance, its details, intricacies, and varieties in pattern, texture, scale, and color are perceived only as one moves closer.[18]

Venturi's treatise is based on the theory course he is teaching at the University of

Pennsylvania. His lecture notes indicate that he is thinking about boredom within the framework of Gestalt psychology. Specifically, the outline of the eleventh lecture (on composition, proportion, and unity) directly addresses these topics:

> Unity as the relationship of parts to form a whole.
> Perceptual basis: Gestalt psychology
> Necessity of balance of unity with variety; boredom vs. chaos; examples in housing too fragmental or too independent
> Varying relationships of the parts and the whole to create unity.[19]

Boredom and *chaos,* two extreme positions, have a double role in the Copley Square project. On the one hand, they describe the nature of the built environment, and on the other, they reflect the nature of life itself. Venturi emphasizes the distinction between European and American lifestyles: while Europeans spend time outdoors in the city in long *passeggiate,* Americans prefer to stay home watching television.[20] Therefore, he replaces the boring, empty, open plaza dear to modern architects with a thick plaid, "boring" only in name: "There are opportunities to see the same thing in different ways, the old thing in new ways. As there is not a single, constant accent—a fountain, reflecting pool nor the great church itself, for instance, neither is there a single static focus when you move within and around the square. There is the opportunity for a variety of focuses, or rather for changing focus. The main paradox of this design is that the boring pattern is interesting."[21]

This twist on boredom concludes Venturi's description of the Copley Square project. Heckscher decries the loss of a sense of place when "life is spread thinly, in an abstract pattern across the suburban space" (270). Venturi's response is to address the void—spatial and social—through the density of a "non-piazza" that offers a variety of experiences, perceptions, and relationships. His design echoes Heckscher's conviction that "the only real sense of space must come, paradoxically, from a willingness to accept the salutary crowdedness of true urban living. A man's independence comes not from his being falsely apart, but from being in a meaningful relation with others" (270).

Heckscher recommends that in a world gradually becoming thinner and more abstract, people must cultivate play and irony to resist the danger of modern boredom. Echoing him, Venturi's design embraces the notion of play: it allows children to engage with the park by reading nursery rhymes at their scale and offers adults a chance to experience the full-scale church and its miniature replica in a clever

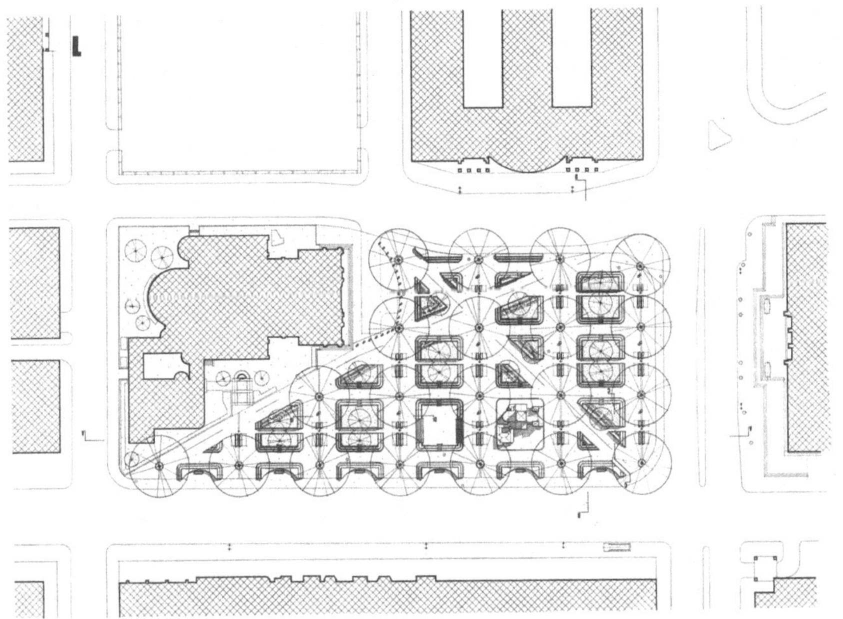

Figure 24. Venturi and Rauch, Boston Copley Square Competition entry, 1966, site plan. (© The Architectural Archives, University of Pennsylvania, by the gift of Robert Venturi and Denise Scott Brown)

and ironic dialogue (fig. 24). Play is at the core of the design process itself. Dozens of sketches on tracing paper with color markers fine-tune the various layers of the grid in what ultimately appears to be an act of pure design pleasure. The play with accents within the thick plaid of the grid relieves monotony and shows how the events of life are anchored in the firm fabric of the everyday.

Venturi employs boredom as a design strategy. Through repetitive rhythms, the public spaces thus created echo the cadences and tempos of ordinary lives that unfold in specific details: paper boats floating in a pool, nursery rhymes inscribed on the walls. While the design is not boring, a deliberate monotony invites the inhabitants to pause, examine, and reflect. The plaza thus creates a space for waiting. Whether a series of outdoor rooms (the redevelopment of downtown North Canton) or a thick plaid (the Copley Square project), the public space is designed with its inhabitants in mind. At a time when artists attempt to stimulate their audiences through an art that uses stimuli sparingly, Venturi challenges the potential occupants of these public spaces to ponder their own lives and environments. The play between the *boring* and the *interesting* suggests a temporal dimension of the work, where the inhabitant has a lengthy rather than immediate engagement with the project. Venturi uses modern language to criticize the modernist architectural paradigm. Boredom thus becomes a vehicle for introspection that creates the distance necessary to engage critically with the work.

Venturi's projects can be placed in dialogue with Heckscher's ideas. First, both of them recognize the threat of modern alienation resulting from consumerism and the atomization of society. Civic responsibilities lie at the core of being a well-rounded person, and healthy public spaces where people meet, share, and engage with each other constitute the primary tool to combat the modern individual's loneliness and estrangement. Second, Heckscher reclaims the notions of play and irony as creative strategies against the deadening tedium of modern life. Similarly, the accidents, reversals, double-functioning elements, and "contrapuntal juxtapositions" in Venturi's proposals for the two public spaces attempt to retrieve the complex architectural experiences that have been lost at the height of Modernism. Finally, Heckscher embraces the concept of paradox as another tactic against the flat line of boredom. Binary thinking and exclusions result in simplifications and, ultimately, lack of meaning. The dichotomies boring/interesting, conventional/designed, and ambiguous/clear will turn into the *both/and* approach theorized in Venturi's "gentle manifesto" as well as in the design of public spaces that accommodate and celebrate the imperfections and uncertainties of life itself.

With the fast pace of change in contemporary practices, the conversation about boredom continues to stay relevant in architectural discourse today. Confronted simultaneously with visual overload and scarcity of meaning, people feel alienated from themselves and their places. This sense of estrangement results from both dull and generic architectural production and the impersonal presence of iconic buildings. Looking back at the year 2020, it is, perhaps, opportune to reflect on the consequences and scale of the global COVID-19 pandemic. While physical distancing measures directly affected the lives of public spaces, they also brought to the foreground the notion of citizenship as a form of caring for the *other.* At the same time, as people were forced into isolation, boredom became unavoidable, either as a destructive mood or as a creative tool. An open conversation about contemporary ennui invites further explorations of moods, dispositions, and affects—all ambiguous yet essential characteristics of the built environment. At its worst, boredom is the malaise of the modern individual confronted with both excess and lack. At its best, it offers an unexpected potential for contemplation, reflection, and critical judgment.

6

TACTICS OF RESISTING ENNUI

Denise before Bob

Venturi's early design work and theoretical position emerging from *Complexity and Contradiction in Architecture* engage two forms of boredom. Under the influence of Quaker aesthetics and practices, boredom appears as a form of waiting, as stillness expressed through flat surfaces and economy of means. At the same time, the boredom of modern society is recognized as alienation from the built environment and, although it does constitute one of the underlying themes of the treatise, it is never addressed explicitly.

In *Learning from Las Vegas,* Venturi, Scott Brown, and Steven Izenour formulate a straightforward theory on the *boring/interesting* dialectic in architecture. Part 3, "Ugly and Ordinary Architecture, or the Decorated Shed," begins with a section titled "Some Definitions Using the Comparative Method," prefaced by Andy Warhol's aphorism "I like boring things." It concludes with a segment called "Is Boring Architecture Interesting?"[1] Intended as a rhetorical twist and illustrated through the famous comparison between Venturi's Guild House and Paul Rudolph's Crawford Manor, this dichotomy opens up critical questions about its own relevance for architecture.

Scholars employ these terms to evaluate Venturi and Scott Brown's work. Vincent Scully describes the Vanna Venturi House through the lens of the *interesting.*[2] Philip J. Finkelpearl, a Shakespeare scholar and university professor (and Venturi's lifelong friend from Princeton who introduced him to New Criticism), makes the argument that the "apparent oldness" of Venturi and Scott Brown's works is, in fact, their "true newness."[3] He suggests that the rhetorical game of *boring* and *interesting* involves a deliberate strategy of deception, where the *new* is disguised within the (apparently) *old.* He comments that Vincent Scully's answer to the question asked in *Learning from Las Vegas,* "Is boring architecture interesting?," is that their buildings are never boring "though they probably look that way—because they are truly new—to people who have been brought up on late International Style."[4]

For Karsten Harries, on the other hand, to evaluate architecture in terms of *boring/interesting* is to embrace the empty and dishonest aesthetic of Postmodernism. Harries argues, "This ['less is a bore'] suggests that postmodernism has its origin not as much in a humanistic (that is to say, in an ethical) as in a merely aesthetic response to modernism—more precisely, in the already mentioned response that, born of boredom, seeks relief in a cultivation of the interesting."[5]

How do we account for these distinct uses of the dichotomy *boring/interesting?* Can we move beyond the impasse of the aesthetic and the merely rhetorical? Can we revitalize our vocabulary not only to critique but, more importantly, to productively think with and about design? Cultural and literary theorist Sianne Ngai advances the idea that the *interesting* introduces a temporal dimension to the act of critical judgment, showing that it is both an aesthetic category and a tool of criticality. Building upon the temporal quality of the *interesting,* I argue that Scott Brown's notion of *deferred judgment,* rather than postmodern aesthetics, lies at the base of Venturi and Scott Brown's theory of the *boring* and the *interesting* in architecture. Last, I propose that *deferred judgment,* rather than the *interesting,* remains relevant and productive today in architectural theory.

LEARNING FROM THE BORING AND THE INTERESTING

Everyday language employs the terms *boring* and *interesting* rather loosely. Whereas the former is dismissive, the latter, frequently used as an antonym, is more elusive and often escapes clear meaning. It can indicate either a positive undertone ("This is an interesting book") or an ambiguous, noncommittal attitude ("Oh, that sounds interesting"). Certain critics (such as Mikhail Epstein) emphasize the marvel and excitement associated with the *interesting,* which "interlaces truth and wonder, the obvious and the incredible, the actual and the possible, increasing the intensity of their interrelationship."[6] Others, such as Harries, criticize the *interesting* as an indication of a superficial, aesthetic stance radically opposed to an ethical one.[7]

Ngai observes that one of the difficulties of tackling the concept of *interesting* is precisely its subjective, loose, and imprecise use.[8] Embedded in the etymology of the word, this elusiveness can be traced back to the Latin *inter esse,* which defines an in-between condition, the state of being in the interval. If the *Oxford English Dictionary* dates the first use of *interest* to 1450 in relation to a "legal concern *in* a thing," the *interesting* enters the English vocabulary with Lord Shaftesbury's 1711 *Characteristicks,* defined as something that concerns or touches; by the mid-eighteenth century, it designates a woman's state of being pregnant, a meaning that remains in use until the mid-twentieth century.[9] In this context, it is important to note that the word *boredom* is used in English starting in the 1850s, when Charles Dickens first employs it in *Bleak House.*[10] Ngai argues that the *interesting* emerges as a modern response to novelty and change, specifically to "novelty as it necessarily arises against a background of boredom."[11]

The multiple intertwining strands of the intellectual genealogy of the *interesting* tie together philosophy, aesthetics, social sciences, literary criticism, and visual arts. Like many of the commonly used terms that we employ today more or less unaware of their original meaning, the *interesting* is less a matter of language and more one of culture, society, and history.[12]

The study of *interest* and the *interesting* begins in the eighteenth century in the field of aesthetics in relation to judgments of taste and of beauty. With the advent of modernity, the *interesting* (along with other categories such as the *astonishing* or the *unusual*) begins to undermine strong categories such as the *beautiful,* the *true,* or the *good.* As traditional societies are disintegrating, the emphasis shifts from the values of the community to those of the individual. The rise of individualism, which gives legitimacy to every opinion, is also one of the main causes of the visibility of *boredom* in modernity. While focusing on fragments and particulars, the *interesting* validates arbitrariness and a multiplicity of tastes. Often discussed together, the *boring* and the *interesting* are brought into presence at a time when the inner experience of the individual becomes worthy of investigation, which happens simultaneously with the emergence of new aesthetic categories, such as the *ugly* or the *sublime.*[13] Several characteristics of the *interesting* as an aesthetic category, often in tension with ethical and moral standards, prevail throughout the eighteenth and nineteenth centuries.

The notions of deception and deceit are key to understanding the interrelationship of the *boring* and the *interesting.* Immanuel Kant demonstrates how the experience of time is subjective, depends on the activities unfolding during a certain interval, and is intimately connected to the experience of space. An excess of objects seen in the landscape (such as villages and houses) draws the deceptive conclusion that a large territory has been covered and therefore that a longer period of time has passed. Conversely, an empty landscape does not generate memories; it creates the illusion that fewer miles have been covered and that the time was shorter.[14] Thus time *appears* longer or shorter depending on the events taking place, and activities *appear* noteworthy based on their mere quantity rather than their significance. More objects, more entertainment, and more activities create the illusion of eliminating tedium while, in fact, they simply camouflage it. Similarly, Søren Kierkegaard associates the *interesting* with the aesthetic realm, where appearances are more important than the true nature of the self and where the consumption of the new and the original quickly turns into boredom.[15] In contrast, the ethical realm is one of critical reflection, moral responsibility, and accountability. The *interesting* creates the illusion of making the *boring* disappear, whereas in fact it only offers a temporary distraction. In his commentary on *Either/Or,* Harries remarks that the search for the *interesting* implies a rejection of the place and situation we currently find ourselves in: "The search for the interesting is essentially a flight from reality."[16] Kierkegaard's alternative is expressed in the metaphor of crop rotation: rather than constantly moving to new soil (in other words, constantly looking for change), one should commit to the same soil and, instead, vary the types of crops (in other words, understand and work within existing limitations). He writes, "The more a person limits himself, the more resourceful he becomes."[17] This intensive rather than extensive approach to boredom suggests that its remedy resides not in perpetual change but, instead, in thorough introspection. Finding resourceful ways to rediscover the world when one is subjected to mundane boredom is to transfigure and reinvent the banality of the everyday.

Another dimension of the interesting is excess, often associated with entertainment and distraction. Friedrich Schlegel observes that the loop of the *interesting* and the *boring,* where "the new becomes old; the unusual becomes common; the frisson of what is charming becomes dull," is the dead end of intellectual and artistic pursuits.[18] His definition of the *interesting* builds upon the opposition between subjective and universal values, between the stimulation of the senses and the stimulation of the intellect. Identifying the ontological and sublime dimensions of boredom, Arthur Schopenhauer remarks that what bridges the gap between the *boring* and the *sublime* is the act of contemplation, which enables the transfiguration of what might be perceived as tedious into an otherworldly experience. In contrast, the *interesting* resides in this search for empty distraction and excitement.[19]

In twentieth-century phenomenology, the *interesting* indicates something inessential, expendable, and disposable. Despite their shared etymology, *interest* is intimately connected to the essence of a thing, whereas the *interesting* resides at its periphery and belongs to "the ranks of what is indifferent and soon boring."[20] Situated in a continuous loop, the *boring* and the *interesting* constitute two sides of the same condition. Susan Sontag defines the *interesting* as "the commonplace, the inessential, the accidental, the minute, the transient," and Giorgio Agamben describes curiosity—directly related to the *interesting*—as the restless activity that builds upon "the constant availability of distraction."[21] If "philosophy begins in wonder," curiosity operates in the realm of the superfluous and the marginal.[22]

A radically different position situates the *interesting* (and its association with novelty) at the core of human progress, development, and creativity. Philosopher Lars Svendsen construes multiple readings of the *interesting.* As multiplicity and excess, it leads to the diminishing value of objects, which in time turn into disposable entities. However, as novelty and excitement, the *interesting* corresponds to the time of discovery, learning, and wonder that one experiences during childhood; adolescence, suspended between childhood and maturity, is the time of boredom.[23] Displacing the hegemony of truth as the subject matter of philosophy, Gilles Deleuze and Felix Guattari argue that today "it is categories like Interesting, Remarkable, or Important that determine success or failure."[24] The *interesting* is essential for understanding criticism as a creative endeavor.[25]

Midcentury artists are often quoted for their provocative statements on *boring* and *interesting* as weak categories that challenge long-established artistic values. Donald Judd famously argues that "a work needs only to be interesting." Ed Ruscha claims to be interested "in what is interesting." Andy Warhol declares, "I like boring things." And about conceptual art, Joseph Kosuth writes, "It is interesting or it isn't, just as one is informed or isn't."[26]

Implicit in these (and similar) propositions is a shift in the meaning of the *interesting* from an aesthetic category to a tool of both creativity and criticality. The *boring* and the *interesting* emerge as functions of the imagination. Philosopher Michael L. Raposa contends that boredom arises from one's inability to interpret the information received as meaningful or interesting. It is through the power of imagination, he proposes, that one discovers the infinitely *interesting* within the apparently *boring.*[27]

According to Ngai, the *interesting* bridges the gap between aesthetic and critical judgment. Examining the persistence of the term in both everyday language and critical writing, she asks a simple question: What does this say about the relationship between aesthetics and criticism?[28] She identifies a series of attributes of the *interesting:* semantic blankness (it lacks specific characteristics), a syntactic placeholder (it calls for a later return to the object), and low affect (it does not elicit strong emotions). Her main argument is that what distinguishes the *interesting* from stronger categories, such as the *beautiful,* is its temporal dimension. To qualify an object as interesting is to create an opportunity for elaborate explanations and dialogues around the object. The *interesting* "diverts our attention from judgments (quick) to justifications (slow)" and requests lengthy, public explanations. Ultimately, the *interesting* is a tool of criticality: "We tell people we find works interesting when we want to do criticism."[29]

The extensive comparison deployed in *Learning from Las Vegas* between Venturi's Guild House and Rudolph's Crawford Manor shows how the *interesting* opens an opportunity for architectural criticism. Based on highly curated photographs of the two buildings, Venturi's analysis aims to demonstrate how Crawford Manor (and by extension the *duck*) is deliberately built to *appear* interesting, whereas the Guild House (or *the decorated shed*) is honestly affirming its boringness. Bookended by the rhetorical question "Is Boring Architecture Interesting?," the chapter concludes with a comparative table synthesizing the differences between the *duck* and the *decorated shed.* "For all its commonness, is Guild House boring? For all its dramatic balconies, is Crawford Manor interesting? Is it not, perhaps, the other way around? Our criticism of Crawford Manor and the buildings it stands for is not moralistic, nor is it concerned with the so-called honesty in architecture or lack of correspondence between substance and image *per se;* Crawford Manor *is* ugly and ordinary while *looking* heroic and original."[30]

Venturi and Scott Brown's use of the *boring/interesting* dichotomy invites a more nuanced reading. While the *boring* and the *interesting* have been largely associated with the aesthetic and ethic-less concerns of Postmodernism (a legitimate position reinforced by the comparison above), I suggest that for them, the origin of this dialectic lies elsewhere. Specifically, Scott Brown's notion of *deferred judgment,* developed before she entered the partnership, introduces a temporal aspect to architectural criticism and practice akin to the temporal dimension of the *interest-*

ing. By deferring (a hasty) judgment, the architect is invited to provide deliberate justifications. The last section of this chapter examines Scott Brown's concept of *deferred judgment.*

WAITING: DEFERRED JUDGMENT

> Dear Bob, I have decided to go away this weekend so have stayed to finish your book. The attached are a group of specific comments, . . . I would like to see the devices you use for "expressive" purposes more integral & serving other functions as well—less like stage sets—tho' in the context of this having no other function the stage set quality is suitable. . . . But I think you use too many devices (always remembering that I don't approve of any of them) & will do till you get more work & can spread them fewer per building. None of this is insulting. I respect your work . . . but disagree with it—mainly because I think there are other constraints acting upon us today. I like the things you like, have learned from them what you have taught, but I would apply the lessons differently.[31]

It is Friday night, 12 July 1963. Denise Scott Brown finishes reading the draft of *Complexity and Contradiction in Architecture,* writes down her comments, and sends her feedback to Robert Venturi. Upon reading her letter, he writes in its margin, "You are *mean.*"[32]

Integrity. Function. Constraints. These are not yet fully developed ideas that Scott Brown will further elaborate on in her writings. Although scholars have begun to acknowledge and credit her critical contribution to the Venturi–Scott Brown partnership, little is known about her early career before the two become a team, when she is an active urban planner, educator, and critic. One of Scott Brown's most valuable contributions is the concept of *deferred judgment* (or *non-judgmental view*), usually situated at the origin of a postmodern direction in architecture and analyzed in light of the partnership's enthusiasm for the architecture of the Las Vegas Strip, commercial architecture, suburbia, and the non-architecture of signs and billboards. Shifting attention away from formal considerations, I propose an alternative reading of deferred judgment that unveils its temporal aspect. By postponing our "verdicts," we prudently introduce a time for reflection, which, in turn, opens up the space for critical debate.

DEFERRED JUDGMENT. In legal terminology, a *deferred* or *delayed* sentence is a deal in which the defendant pleads guilty to certain charges in exchange for meeting specific requirements within a determined period of time. Upon completing them, they may avoid a formal conviction. Critical to this notion is its temporal dimension: the practice essentially offers more time to the parties involved in the process. As time goes by, various changes might occur in the positions of different agents: there is hope and expectation that by fulfilling certain duties, the defendant will transform their behavior and that, subsequently, the court might show clemency and compassion.

To acknowledge the temporal dimension of deferred judgment in planning and architectural theory is to understand time as duration and extension rather than instantaneity. Instead of living exclusively in the present, in the immediacy of quick deliberations, one becomes aware of the passage of time, of the fluidity of past, present, and future, when multiple scenarios might unfold. To the succession of fleeting moments, deferred judgment proposes the alternative of living within time and experiencing history as lived presence. Situated in the space of the interval, the *inter esse* at the origin of the *interesting,* deferred judgment offers an invitation to linger, tarry, and ponder, to delay action and quick criticism. Sianne Ngai argues that the temporal dimension of the *interesting,* in conjunction with its semantic blankness, opens up the space for aesthetic judgment by returning to and examining the object qualified as interesting. Similarly, the temporal aspect of deferred judgment creates opportunities for conversing, clarifying, engaging, and, eventually, theorizing.

In her 1969 article "On Pop Art, Permissiveness, and Planning," Scott Brown explicitly articulates her position on deferred judgment. Illustrated with Ed Ruscha's photographs, the article summons architects and planners to set aside their modernist biases and, before designing and building, to take a closer and more sympathetic look at the environment, with its flawed and imperfect realities. Empathy and an appreciation for the different manifestations of life are among the most important attributes of contemporary designers: "For the best thing an architect or urban designer can offer a new society, apart from a good heart, is his own skill, used *for* the society, to develop a respectful understanding of its cultural artifacts and a loving strategy for their development to suit the felt needs and way of life of its people. This is a socially responsible activity."[33] Building on precedents from psychoanalysis, sociology, and linguistics to Pop Art, action painting, photography, and film, Scott Brown argues that while this sympathetic attitude has gained strength in most disciplines, it has not reached the fields of architecture and planning. To set aside judgments and preconceived ideas is to open up opportunities for unexpected discoveries. "This is not to abandon judgment," she asserts, "for planned action implies judgment. Judgment is merely deferred a while in order to make it more sensitive. Liking what you hate is exhilarating and liberating, but finally reaffirming for judgment."[34] It is important to note that nowhere in the article does she propose an aesthetic agenda.

However, one of the first instances in which she clearly addresses the notion of deferred judgment is the 1967 article "Teaching Architectural History," a review of the Architectural History and the Student Architect symposium organized in April 1967 at the annual conference of the Society of Architectural Historians. Architecture schools in the United States have always shared a common concern (though never a consensus) on the pedagogy and direction of architectural theory and history. In response to what is perceived as a crisis in architectural education, in 1967 the Society of Architectural Historians invites faculty from different schools to debate the state of the discipline.

Scott Brown focuses on the polemics between Peter Collins (McGill University) and Spiro Kostof (University of California, Berkeley). The former advocates teaching a "history of the theory of architecture," with the goal of developing students' critical thinking; the latter argues that architectural history should simply be a "broadening experience" for the student rather than a selection of critical perspectives curated by the teacher. Scott Brown proposes to bridge the gap between the two through a methodology that embraces history *and* theory thematically, rather than chronologically, by means of analysis and comparison. Such a course will turn students into broad, receptive people and, ultimately, will cultivate their creativity. She argues that from Kostof's position, "all buildings are worth examining and that the humblest buildings can be moving." Looking at history with an all-encompassing eye will "reduce prejudice, enhance sensitivity, and engender interest in a broad range of related fields." Scott Brown defines Kostof's approach as a "non-judgmental view."[35]

Three different, though intertwined, themes emerge from Scott Brown's early interest in "deferred judgment" (a term somewhat interchangeable with "non-judgmental view"). These themes, which might constitute today a fruitful opportunity for introspection, are *integrity, function,* and *constraints,* which her 1963 letter to Robert Venturi begins to articulate.

INTEGRITY. "I would like to see the devices you use for 'expressive' purposes more integral & serving other functions as well," comments Scott Brown on Venturi's manuscript.[36] While "integrity" usually indicates a sense of wholeness or an ethical and moral stance, an underlying theme in Scott Brown's early writings addresses the integrity of the profession and its current situation. Delaying a too-quick acceptance of established professional structures offers opportunities for questioning the status quo, an enterprise as important today as it was at midcentury. This awareness of integrity gives a presence to alternative voices and discourses otherwise ignored or kept silent, which Scott Brown begins to illuminate in her early essays.

She makes present those voices within the discipline that have been historically ignored: those of women, marginal countries, fringe publications. In the April 1967 issue of the *AIA Journal,* Scott Brown writes an article about ladies' rooms.[37] In a clever twist, she offers two readings: on the one hand, an amusing, almost entertaining, account of the shortcomings of women's restrooms (usually designed by male architects); on the other hand, and more importantly, a harsh and somber critique of a male-dominated profession and its gender-based biases. We truly understand that serious matters are at stake when we situate this essay in context: the featured theme of the issue is "Cities: What's the Matter?" and, while all the other contributors are male, Scott Brown, an urban planner and faculty member at UCLA, writes an article on powder rooms.

At a time when the architectural world is rarely looking outside the centers of power, Scott Brown gives agency to peripheral regions. In 1964, she publishes a thoroughly documented article on the planning of the South African province of Natal.[38] Based on primary sources from the region, her lengthy analysis both critiques planning decisions that reinforce apartheid policies and questions comparable segregation policies at home in the United States.

Scott Brown draws attention to people outside the discipline, those who actually inhabit the cities and buildings imagined by architects and planners—and whose needs and aspirations designers routinely ignore. Her review of the documentary *Form, Design, and the City* (1962) and the article "The Meaningful City" (1965) show her skepticism of the grandiose design ideas of visionary urban renewal plans, and she invites architects and planners to listen to the voices of everyday people, the "thousand designers."[39]

Lastly, there is the unique voice of Scott Brown herself, whose first-person writing style, sharp and sarcastic, erodes the dry conventions of academic jargon. She tacitly invites each of her interlocutors to find their own voice, a search she herself is pursuing. As a student at the University of Pennsylvania, she takes a course in 1960 with the German-born architect and urban planner Erwin Anton Gutkind—and instead of writing the expected paper to complete the course, she decides to send a letter. Her justification for this decision is threefold: first, she wants to convey her own ideas rather than those of her teachers and other authors; second, she explains that a letter offers a freedom lost in an academic paper whose basic aim is pedagogic; and third, simply put, she explains that a letter, unlike a paper, invites a reply.[40] The young architect is already trying to carve that space of dialogue and interaction that deferred judgment will later formalize. Pondering the integrity of the profession gives an agency to all these different voices that together construct a sense of wholeness. In this process of deferring judgment, we make space for ourselves and for the others.

FUNCTION. One of Scott Brown's main criticisms of Venturi's book addresses the notion of function.[41] The overall considerations on function in her early writings take two directions—a critique emerging from the often-misinterpreted reading of the modernist dictum "form follows function" and the role (or function) of architects and planners—thus offering opportunities to expand the world of architecture beyond buildings to include other artifacts.

In a brief, riddle-like manifesto from 1967, Scott Brown compellingly argues for a reconsideration of "form follows function": "What is the function of a table? I may eat off it, write at it; at a party, dance on it, or drink myself under it. A child may throw a cloth over it to make a house or turn it on end to make a boat. I am lord at its head, serf at its foot, equal if it is round, a humble supplicant if I kneel before it. What, then, is the meaning of the phrase 'form follows function'?"[42] Observing that the functions of a table, from the most banal to the most symbolic, may (and will) change over time while its form will remain unaltered, Scott Brown questions whether the same is true for other objects: a comb, a wallet, a staircase, or a superhighway. The reader is left somehow longing for a more elaborate argument, but her suggestion to dissociate form from function surfaces in other writings.

As early as 1960, in the letter-paper addressed to Gutkind, Scott Brown is exploring the relationship of function and urban form. She puts forward the idea that planners should not plan people's lives but rather offer provisions for various scenarios to unfold. She believes "not only that form follows function, but that form evokes function, and that function changes though form remains."[43] Understanding time as duration, she positions people, buildings, and cities in a historical perspective that stretches between past and future, from the medieval town to the American city, and in which the various modes of inhabitation change but continue to occupy the same physical forms.

Responding to a survey about the future of architectural education in the October 1970 issue of *Architectural Record,* Scott Brown advocates for customized learning experiences where students are given the opportunity to have office experience, research experience, or some other unforeseen combination.[44] She recognizes that the future architect will have to perform multiple roles and embrace different careers and that, consequently, architectural education will have to address these new challenges. "On Pop Art, Permissiveness, and Planning" includes references from outside the discipline (such as the visual arts, literature, film, and social sciences), and it suggests not only that architecture and planning should look at and learn from other fields but also that the outcomes of the discipline itself are changing as it begins to encompass "society's cultural artifacts."[45] The use of Ruscha's deadpan photographs signals not just "a new vision of the very imminent world around us" but perhaps the less obvious fact that the photographs themselves *are* architecture.[46]

Deferring assumptions about what does and does not belong to architecture and planning liberates the discipline from normative prescriptions and allows creative associations to occur, such as those between Ed Ruscha's *Thirtyfour Parking Lots,* Michelangelo Antonioni's *Red Desert,* and Herbert Gans's Levittown (all referenced in "On Pop Art, Permissiveness, and Planning") or those between a table, a comb, a staircase, and a highway (from "The Function of a Table").

CONSTRAINTS. "I respect your work . . . but disagree with it—mainly because I think there are other constraints acting upon us today." This is how Scott Brown wraps up her comments on Venturi's draft of *Complexity and Contradiction in Architecture.*[47] While the world is experiencing a profound turmoil, Venturi's book focuses exclusively on architectural form and never addresses social, ethical, or political issues, which Scott Brown situates at the core of the discipline. The awareness of the various constraints at work in the profession encourages speculative modes of thinking and practice and, at the same time, demonstrates the value of banal day-to-day operations.

At a time when architects tend to follow mainstream publications, Scott Brown dedicates an extensive article to "little magazines" published in Europe after World War II, describing them as "often scurrilous, irresponsible and subversive of the existing order, . . . hand-made and usually ill-kempt in appearance, but with a certain flair."[48] This apparent marginality disguises forms of radical thinking that suspend normative operations and offer potential strategies to disrupt the status quo in American planning.

While embracing speculative practices, Scott Brown also recognizes the presence of the constraints or forces that shape our urban environments. In the same letter to Gutkind, she invites architects and planners to "leave the theories for a while" and instead observe and understand the "new systems and structures trying to come through, to see if the cities are trying to tell us what they 'want to be.'"[49] She concludes "Form, Design and the City" (1962) by asking, rhetorically, "Where in our profession has there been deep thought and conclusion about the relation of city forces to city form?"[50]

Elsewhere, starting from the preservation efforts around Irving Gill's Walter L. Dodge House in West Hollywood, Scott Brown looks at both the forces of change and the forces of preservation at work in the city. In her view, planning efforts based on "conservative surgery," a term borrowed from Patrick Geddes to designate nondestructive interventions in the existing urban fabric, would provide a "strategy of love" ultimately conducive to the "maintenance of stable values, economic and otherwise."[51]

Scholarship in cultural studies has begun to interrogate the value that capitalism and the neoliberal economy place on innovation, novelty, and entrepreneurship. Bringing into focus the inconspicuous yet indispensable presence of maintenance and repair, scholars such as Andrew Russell and Lee Vinsel are reevaluating the relevance of upkeep and support structures for the functioning of our world.[52] Their concern with technological infrastructure, as opposed to technological innovation, resonates with our architectural practices that routinely have to engage the banal and the ordinary. The exercise of deferring judgment in our love story with the extraordinary and the exceptional acknowledges the critical role of "conservative surgeries" and other unglamorous maintenance modes that do not "make history" but exist within and sustain it. Tactical rather than strategic in nature, deferred judgment offers the promise of deferred gratification as it makes space for free associations as well as critical theory to unfold.

Scott Brown's midcentury suggestion might restore an almost extinct perception of time as duration in our hurried world, where we make rushed design decisions and hastily pass judgments. Sprinting through the day, we experience a compressed time that constantly escapes us. By deferring judgment, we create space for finding interest (*inter esse*) between our daily chores and choose to resist fast modes of being, thus living within rather than outside history. There is a chance that we might become more reflective and less reactive.

PART III

WONDERING

SAUL STEINBERG

To that friend who tells me he is bored because he cannot work, I answer that boredom is a higher *state, and that we debase it by relating it to the notion of work.*

—EMIL CIORAN, *DRAWN AND QUARTERED*

"Why do you work? To chase boredom, the boredom that is the great foe." This is how Saul Steinberg summarizes his personal motivation to work in a 1966 interview for the French journal *La quinzaine littéraire.*[1] Irony? Sarcasm? Candor? Perhaps a dash of all of these, but certainly not something to be easily dismissed or taken lightly. Indeed, in numerous instances, Steinberg returns to boredom as the foundation of his creative work and continues to elaborate, both visually and verbally, on this mood so ubiquitous in modern society.

Steinberg cherishes his freelancer status, which allows him the freedom to work, rest, and travel at his own pace and, equally important, gives him the freedom of choice. Establishing the boundaries between production and leisure, he identifies boredom as the tipping point between the time of doing nothing and the joy of work: "I enjoy the privilege of being unemployed. That's the pleasant part of my job. I work for a while and then I read, sleep, travel. It is important to know when to stop working. My best work springs out of boredom and trying to amuse myself."[2]

If, for Steinberg, boredom is the state of mind that both moves his work forward and stimulates invention, then how is it expressed in his art? More importantly, what does it tell us about architecture and one's place in the world?

Chapter 7 contextualizes Steinberg's genealogies of boredom through two lenses: first, the midcentury artistic milieu, with its particular interest in ideas about boredom, and second, his personal life. Based on his firsthand experience of post–

World War I Romanian anti-Semitism, Italian fascism, and American immigration struggles, Steinberg relates boredom to the government machine that levels out and deadens any form of life. Expressed in rubber-stamp drawings, faux-script diplomas, and graphic representations of totalitarian architectures, the boredom of the political apparatus emerges as the invisible force that governs people's lives and personal experiences.

Chapter 8 examines a series of specific drawings published over the span of fifteen years, between 1953 and 1968, where Steinberg takes note of contemporary manifestations of boredom: International Style graph-paper skyscrapers, false-front façades, cookie-cutter architectures, suburban boxes, and the commodification of daily routines and practices. The years between 1953 and 1968 are particularly rich in works that examine ennui in the built environment and everyday life. In 1958, Steinberg designs several architecture-themed murals for the American Pavilion at the Brussels World's Fair, curated by his friend Bernard Rudofsky. The same year, he contributes a mural to *An Exhibition for Modern Living* at the Detroit Institute of Arts, which displays interiors designed by some of the most famous architects of the moment, such as Ray and Charles Eames and Alvar Aalto.[3] In 1961, the *Journal of the American Institute of Planners* features a selection of Steinberg's architecture-related drawings published over the years.[4] The two books he publishes during this time, *The Labyrinth* (1960) and *The New World* (1965), summarize much of his work on the boredom of the built environment.

Finally, chapter 9 looks at Steinberg's visual tactics of resisting ennui by folding the dread of boredom into daydreaming. Laying out on paper often unremarkable and largely overlooked everyday human experiences, he uses architecture as the common ground between his audience and himself. He describes the relationship between the architect-artist and his audience as a shared complicity built upon a common understanding of culture and history.[5]

7

GENEALOGIES OF BOREDOM

"A Difference of Altitude"

The period between 1953 and 1968 is bookended by two rare instances in which Saul Steinberg expresses his thoughts about architecture not only through drawing but also in writing. In 1953, *ARTnews* publishes Steinberg's article "Built in U.S.A.," a critique of the eponymous exhibition at the Museum of Modern Art that celebrates American Modernism. In 1968, *Look* magazine features "Our False-Front Culture," a summary of Steinberg's take on tedium in the built environment. At the core of both pieces lies the critique of a commodified architecture and culture that engender the existential boredom so pervasive at midcentury. During the fifteen years between these articles, Steinberg unpacks the often-elusive relationship between the atmosphere of the built environment and people's own moods and dispositions. Through different manifestations of boredom, "le grand ennemi," humanity reveals its limitations, possibilities, and desires, all bounded by its inescapable finitude.

Not only are these years a period of artistic explorations in various media—from murals to drawings, collages, advertising, and paper-bag masks—but they also bring significant changes in Steinberg's personal life. He loses his parents, permanently separates from his wife, the Romanian-born American artist Hedda Sterne, and meets Sigrid Spaeth, a German design and photography student working in New York who will remain his partner until her death in 1996. In 1959, at the recommendation of his friend Costantino (Tino) Nivola, an Italian-born sculptor, he purchases the house across the street from the Nivolas' house in Amagansett, Long

Island, which will remain his personal and artistic refuge, bringing him in proximity to rising artists and art critics of the time, many of whom become his friends. Between 1968 and 1973, he rents studio space in the same building in New York where Andy Warhol operates his Factory. Personal experiences trickle down into Steinberg's work, which always makes present the fluid territory between subjective attachment and objective distance.

ARTISTIC JOURNEYS AND PERSONAL HISTORIES

During the middle decades of the twentieth century, boredom gains visibility among artists and art critics as a common subject, frequently up for debate. On the one hand, it is appropriated as a catalyst for change and new creative avenues; on the other, critics continue to disagree over the true meaning of boredom in art.

Artists discover that capitalizing on the audience's purposeful disengagement and lack of affect in relation to an artwork proves to be an effective creative tool. A "dead-pan disenchantment" emerges in midcentury visual arts as a conscious approach to liberate them from the subjectivity of emotions.[1] Sam Hunter describes this as "the aesthetics of boredom" that invites viewers to go beyond an intentionally banal appearance and engage more deeply with the work "at a time when there is too facile an appreciation of culture."[2] Susan Sontag, another critic active in this conversation, offers a similar designation, "the aesthetics of silence," which forms the title of an essay in *Styles of Radical Will*.[3] John Cage introduces silences and dissonances as new forms of music, famously stating, "If something is boring after two minutes, try it for four. If still boring, then eight. Then sixteen. Then thirty-two. Eventually one discovers that it is not boring at all."[4] Merce Cunningham, Cage's life partner and artistic collaborator, revolutionizes dance with his objective and highly structured choreographies.

Andy Warhol's focus on the repetitive and the ordinary and Donald Judd's straightforward, matter-of-fact Minimalism, although different in nature, share the same intention: to elicit a response from the audience through an artwork completely devoid of emotions and feelings.[5] The subject matter of Agnes Martin's paintings is repetition as a spiritual practice. Working in a standard format (six-by-six-foot canvases), she draws laborious grids that would be dull if they did not capture a glimpse of infinity. Boredom spreads to other artistic fields. The films of Michelangelo Antonioni and Jean-Luc Godard, or Alain Robbe-Grillet's novels, involve methodical and slow descriptions that invite reflection and scrutiny through what otherwise appears rather tedious and unengaging.

Alberto Moravia, known to his friends as a perpetual victim of boredom, publishes in 1960 the novel *La Noia,* originally translated into English as *The Empty Canvas,* most likely out of fear that a direct translation—*Boredom*—would not appeal to an English-speaking audience. Dino, a painter disenchanted with life, develops a neurotic love for Cecilia, a girl whom he fails to know beyond their sexual encounters. His feelings grow along with his indifference to, and disengagement with, himself and the world. In an interview titled "L'Occidente s'annoia" (The West is getting bored), originally published in *L'Espresso* in November 1960, Moravia defines boredom as "the product of a form of alienation. Or suspending the relationship between the individual and reality and therefore, between the artist and matter itself, or if you prefer, between the subject and the object."[6]

"We are bored in the city," declares Ivan Chtcheglov (writing under the pseudonym Gilles Ivain), a precursor to the Situationists in 1953.[7] "What currently marks our public life, is boredom. The French are bored," writes the journalist Pierre Viansson-Ponté in *Le Monde* on 15 March 1968. In his 1964 "Dream Song 14," John Berryman summarizes the state of mind of an entire generation: "Life, friends, is boring."[8]

In 1965, Barbara Rose warns the art world that if viewers feel bored while looking at some contemporary art, this is precisely the artist's intention: to test the public's commitment to the artistic experience. This point of view, however, remains contentious. Hilton Kramer suggests that the conversation around boredom is irrelevant because once a "boring" artwork raises one's interest, it is no longer boring. Lucy Lippard contends that the effort needed to take the experience of boredom to a level of enjoyment is time-consuming and, ultimately, unfulfilling. Sontag argues that boredom does not really exist; it is simply a form of frustration that results from the inability of educated people to understand the new artistic languages of the time.[9] These arguments extend beyond midcentury—in the 1980s and 1990s, a series of articles continues to debate the value of boring art.[10] More recently, writing about Warhol and Judd, Jonathan Flatley proposes that both artists, by different means, seek to produce affect without representing it, thus reversing the approach embraced by Abstract Expressionism and, more broadly, Modernism. By focusing on "interesting" (Judd) and "liking" (Warhol), the two artists "replace the dialectic between interest and disinterest with the one between interest and boredom."[11]

In this space of silence, devoid of affects and emotions, lies the opportunity for wonder, new forms of criticism, and new forms of engagement with the work. Steinberg's explorations take place against this background, where boredom becomes a deliberate strategy of contemplation and critical judgment. His approach, however, is different. Unlike most of his contemporaries, he performs the role of both artist and critic, deploying unique forms of architectural criticism.

It is a well-established argument that Steinberg acts as a "critic without words" through his graphic representations of architecture. Rather than reiterate this position, I propose that the primary function of Steinberg's word-less architectural criticism is not to split but—to borrow from Bruno Latour—to bring matters together in an assembly and, furthermore, to elicit the sense of wonder that criticism often neglects. Following Latour's proposition that the responsibility of the critic (and, implicitly, *critique*) is not to divide but rather to create spaces of convergence and interaction, Steinberg's work understands architectural criticism as having a generative and creative role.

When asked how they begin to write fiction, many authors disclose that they start with what they know best. Similarly, Steinberg, who consistently defines himself as a writer rather than an artist, begins with what he knows best: his own life. His visual storytelling draws on personal experiences that constantly inform his worldview, emerging from careful observations of people, places, and events. His imagination is rooted in an unmediated relationship with the world.

Born in 1914 to a Jewish family in the small Romanian town of Râmnicu Sărat (which, he muses in an interview, was invented for his birth), Steinberg grows up in the capital city, Bucharest, on Strada Palas (Palas Street), "a little street completely apart from traffic" that he describes as his "homeland."[12] He studies philosophy for a year at the University of Bucharest; although he is interested in art, he knows his family would never support this career choice, so he decides to study architecture instead. In 1933, Steinberg begins his studies at the Regio Politecnico in Milan, where he earns his degree in architecture in 1940. In his inimitable tongue-in-cheek style, he will later observe that "the study of architecture is a marvelous training for anything but architecture. The frightening thought that what you draw may become a building makes for reasoned lines."[13] It is at the Politecnico that he meets Aldo Buzzi, a future writer, who will remain his closest and most cherished friend for the rest of his life.

In Milan, Steinberg "labors" in an architecture office, but only for a short time because he is quickly disenchanted with the practical aspects of the profession:

constant networking, lack of independence, and reliance on other people's money. "It's a horrible thing to be an architect," he concludes after his brief experience in practice.[14] At the same time, he is fascinated with the aura of the métier and secretly longs for the recognition that accomplished architects receive. When his alma mater invites him in 1987 to contribute a poster to an exhibition of work done by famous alumni, he is elated, writing, "the fact that the School recognizes my fame gives me a true and innocent pleasure."[15] Throughout his life, he contributes drawings to architectural journals and maintains friendships with famous architects of the time, among them Le Corbusier, Bernard Rudofsky, and Peter Blake.

To support himself in architecture school and later upon completing his studies, Steinberg publishes drawings in *Bertoldo,* an Italian humor newspaper that welcomes young artists and writers. His work is immediately successful, and he quickly builds a reputation as a cartoonist, even receiving fan mail. In a troubled political climate, with fascism on the rise all over Europe, humor, through its subversive nature, is his way of telling the truth.[16]

Beginning in 1938, Steinberg is subjected to Mussolini's anti-Semitic racial laws, and by 1941, he is sought by the police as a stateless foreign Jew with no right to remain in Italy. Upon turning himself in, he is taken to the Italian internment camp of Tortoreto in the Abruzzi; after six weeks, he manages to obtain the necessary visas to fly to Lisbon, and he then boards a ship to New York in transit to the Dominican Republic, for which he has a residency visa. He spends a year in Ciudad Trujillo before securing an American visa. In the United States, he settles in New York City, marries fellow Romanian artist Hedda Sterne, and only returns to Romania once, in 1944.[17]

Never a practicing architect, Steinberg nonetheless remains an architect his entire career. Although known mainly for his contributions to the *New Yorker* magazine, he has many gallery and museum exhibitions and his work covers a variety of media, from drawing, photography, collages, and installations to murals, textiles, and advertising art. Like Rudofsky and Venturi, he challenges and expands the boundaries of the discipline in a midcentury professional landscape that sees intersections, transgressions, and collaborations among architecture, visual arts, literature, and film. Although classified as a visual artist, Steinberg's work resists easy categorization. Moreover, he engages in forms of criticism that require an eye trained in architecture. Unlike conventional architectural criticism, which is often either too simplistic or too inaccessible, Steinberg's criticism acts as a bridge between the different forces shaping the built environment: designers, the establishment, and everyday people.

Despite his disinterest in the *profession* of architecture, the *field* of architecture constitutes the foundation of Steinberg's art. "I came out of architecture," he acknowledges, and he credits his education for the main features of his own art: "A big influence on me has been the study and the discipline of architecture—the combination of precision, draftsmanship and reason. Architecture is the most noble, difficult and philosophical branch of the arts."[18] He explores the motif of the drafting table and the drafting tools—historically, the trademark of the profession—through drawings, collages, reliefs, and installations. His artwork reveals another dimension of the drafting table, which, beyond its practical uses, becomes the birthplace of a philosophical worldview, the highest form of exercising the profession. Later in life, somewhat surprised and puzzled by his own feelings, he confesses this inexplicable longing for the tools of the trade: "Working now, I've done oil paintings on paper and many wooden objects—rulers, triangles, T-squares—in short, many nostalgic things from architecture school and in general from the drawing table. I don't quite know the reason for this passion."[19]

Steinberg sees and understands people and their worlds through architecture. In a letter to Aldo Buzzi, he sheds light on his view of architecture as an allegory of life itself: "If my life, or yours or others were translated into architecture, who knows what incredible constructions, lack of logic, waste of materials, miraculous equilibrium, wrong locations."[20] Buzzi, in turn, knows that his friend is first and foremost an architect:

> Architecture (who does not see it?) entered his blood and filled his drawings, and he looks at it from a perspective that also belongs to a technician. Architecture: that is, the constructive force of the sign; perspective, which Steinberg has pushed to its limits. . . . Architecture: that is, the styles, the fashions, the polemics, the exaggerations, the *montessorian* manias of certain architects. . . . The mysteries of the *modern,* the *monumental,* the *rational,* the *organic.* In this sense, his architectures are precise to the minutest details. Steinberg could be a great architect, but I am sure he will never work as one. He hates hassles.[21]

Writing Steinberg's obituary in the journal *Architecture,* Blake unequivocally describes him as "by far the most brilliant architecture critic in the United States in the past half century" who foresaw the emergence of all-glass skyscrapers, Venturi's decorated sheds, and Renzo Piano and Richard Rogers's nuts-and-bolts architecture.[22]

Situating Steinberg's work in the context of architectural representation as a tool of the imagination, architectural critic and historian Marco Frascari qualifies it as architectural production. The tension between gravity (both as seriousness and as physical weight) and humor constitutes for Frascari one of the key characteristics of architectural design.[23] Steinberg's drawings are architectural drawings because they fight gravity and construct specific time/place relationships through habits and social practices.[24]

Steinberg will befriend Le Corbusier, whose North Africa sketches inspired him as a student,[25] and the two will spend time together in New York, Paris, and at Tino Nivola's Amagansett house (where Le Corbusier draws a mural on the kitchen wall, which to this day is preserved in perfect condition). Upon receiving Steinberg's book *The Labyrinth* (1960), Le Corbusier writes back: "You draw like a king. The dignity that cloaks your trenchant jokes makes you unique."[26] Enthusiastic about Steinberg's art, Le Corbusier recognizes its architectural essence: "I can't help but tell you that you are a great artist. I revisit with infinite joy your 'Passports.' You have the gifts of grandeur and style that belong to a great character. Your passing through architecture gave you a vision and a quality of construction and simplification that will allow you, the day you decide to start, to make magnificent paintings. And by paintings I think mostly of murals."[27]

BOREDOM AS THE NATURE OF INVENTION

Steinberg arrives at "construction and simplification," the main qualities of a meaningful architectural work, by observing, recognizing, and describing what Pierre Bourdieu calls *habitus*. For Steinberg, the embodied *habitus* shows the creative potential underlying the mood of boredom that surfaces, on the one hand, from the repetition of simple, domestic acts, and, on the other, from the stifling machine of the political apparatus trickling down into people's lives. Boredom accounts for Steinberg's understanding of the nature of invention.

Bourdieu constructs the notion of *habitus* from his ethnographic studies of the Kabylian house. Central to his concept is the *body*—the *physical* body of each individual occupying the house, the *ritualistic* body of the inhabitants—which situates the house in relation to a larger social ordering system and the *collective* body of the community. The relationship of the body to the world is a circular one that Bourdieu defines as "the em-bodying of the structures of the world, that is, the appropriating by the world of a body thus enabled to appropriate the world."[28] Opposed to behavioral determinism as a cause-and-effect explanation for how individual and collective habits and skills are generated in a community, Bourdieu observes that the structures producing practices assign limits to the *habitus*'s operations of invention.[29]

In other words, *habitus* does not generate novelty, nor does it endlessly repeat itself. Rather, it accounts for innovation as the outcome of embodied practices, specific worldviews, and cultural and historic structures. Steinberg's work aligns with this position, born from an intimate understanding of the practices of everyday life. Not unlike contemporary Pop artists, his inspiration comes not from the extraordinary but from the obvious, mundane, and overlooked details of the ordinary. Unlike the Pop artists, however, Steinberg introduces the phenomenal experience of the world.

Unpublished archival materials reveal Steinberg's most intimate notes in the form of journal entries, scribbles, and quick jottings. Constantly reflecting on (and interrogating) his own condition as an artist and an individual, he returns to the question of his deep motivation for work. In his notes, Steinberg confesses that the "important motor" of his life is not to astonish others but something far more frank and human: "money, success, boredom, vendetta."[30] Having moved from country to country and place to place, Steinberg spent years living an unstable and insecure life. His attitude toward money is complex and ambivalent: it secures financial stability, but it also stands for what he describes as the eastern fear of materialism, which threatens to taint high artistic ideals.[31] Similarly, "success" and "vendetta" seem to vindicate his social and artistic status. In this sequence, "boredom" constitutes the moment of awareness that elicits a fresh look at the work: "Boredom will make me eventually return to work . . . work that derives from work (and not from an experience). This may not be true, because the acummulated [*sic*] experience stored in the mind will eventually come out and boredom is ~~the instrument for this consolation~~ as good a ~~motive~~ reason. In this dept. of boredom goes the sense of duty."[32]

What Steinberg describes as "accumulated experience" resonates with Bourdieu's notion of embodied *habitus,* which he strives to make present in his work. Boredom plays a key role in continuously redefining the limits and terms of his pursuits, as he states in a 1967 interview with a German television station when he reiterates the idea that tedium drives his creativity forward. Equally important, he implicitly questions the assumption that work and leisure are inherently dialectic, advancing two important ideas. First, in response to social constraints, work could (might?

should?) offer joy and pleasure. Second, boredom calls attention to the exhaustion of current possibilities and signals the necessity of change.

> Now, working every day and this necessity of working will come to me suddenly and easily. On the contrary as a young man I wanted to avoid all the time working. Work is difficult. Even now I avoid it in a way, but still I do it because I find that the work besides giving this test and this reassurance about myself it provides the highest form of entertainment. In the end what we want to avoid is boredom. Boredom can be what society can provide you. . . . Is it I get slightly bored with my work, I don't find the excitement, real excitement, now this boredom tells me something, it's a message, it means that I grow up and that what used to be entertainment, what used to be excitement once, it's no more so, and I have to find to invent new things, more difficult may be, more subtle, new anyway that will certainly interest me.[33]

While the emergence of tedium does imply a certain fatigue, the change it prompts is different from superficial and empty novelties, like the ones Kierkegaard critiques in his account of an aesthete's life. Creativity in Steinberg's work is different. Change does not happen for its own sake; rather, it is part of a larger growth, which the artist visualizes as a spiral, a motif to which he returns often in his artwork. Life tends to organize itself in a circle, Steinberg observes, where events eventually repeat themselves and one returns, comfortably, to the same beaten tracks. Alternatively, to conceive of one's path as a spiral is to add height—and implicitly depth—to one's life. "I consider this evolution more like a spiral that keeps going the way, it's a conical spiral, a spiral that goes in three dimensions. It starts and it keeps going, going, going. As you go up the circle becomes more and more restricted, smaller but higher. The difference is the difference of altitude, of height."[34]

Considering this statement, the "construction and simplification" that Le Corbusier observes in Steinberg's work might be interpreted as a process of revisiting the same familiar territories, but from a different perspective and in a new light each time. In the process, he gradually eliminates the superfluous and the excess, offering a tighter and deeper perspective. Creativity does not imply novelty but requires, instead, a disciplined exercise in defining limitations and restrictions, in seeking individual practices that speak simultaneously about personal and collective histories, and in finding those particulars that reveal the nature of the whole.

Boredom does not signal the need for superficial change, instead prompting another, closer look. Sianne Ngai interprets the concept of *interesting* as a category of critical judgment. Similarly, for Steinberg *boredom* elicits a form of critical engagement with the world, which is then translated into his artwork. A mood, a state of the soul akin to nostalgia, boredom is for Steinberg a form of introspection. Its temporal dimension plays a key role in his slow appropriation of the world and the wonder he finds in constantly rediscovering it.

One of the earliest documented instances when boredom stimulates Steinberg's creative impulse is the time he spends in Ciudad Trujillo (today Santo Domingo in the Dominican Republic) in 1941–42, waiting for a visa to the United States. His journal entries are filled with the desperation and doubt of someone not only afraid of losing track of the people he cares about but also afraid of losing his own identity. The constant worries over not receiving news from his family or from Ada (Adina) Ongari, his former lover from Milan, reveal the fear of being forgotten and left behind. *Jale,* he writes at the end of a note regarding Ada.[35] A Romanian word that conveys mourning, deep sadness, grief, and despair, *jale* captures his struggles and sense of intense loss.

Each period of Steinberg's life seems to be associated with a particular language, as if memories can only be thought of and constructed in the language of the original event. While his 1941–42 Ciudad Trujillo diary is largely written in Italian, *mama* (mother) and *tăticu* (daddy) are always written (and remembered) in Romanian. Homesick and bedridden, he finds pleasure in writing down the Romanian names of the places he has visited with his friends Campus and Fronescu from Bucharest. Alternatively, perhaps the simple act of recording the names of Romanian popular tourist destinations brings him the joy of remembering his previously carefree life.[36]

The uncertainty of his immigration status hovers over the excruciating boredom of everyday life spent waiting for a visa to secure his exit from Italy. His journal begins in Italy in December 1940 and extends to Ciudad Trujillo (where he arrives in June 1941) and the United States (in 1942). The tedium of daily routines turns into an introspective state, and he thus begins to recollect and record habits, situations, and people from his earlier years. His sketches are simultaneously personal stories and descriptions of certain types of *habitus* shared at a larger scale by the residents of early twentieth-century Bucharest. His longing and nostalgia emerge when he is suddenly confronted with the absence of *habitus,* finding himself outside his *habitus.* The experience of boredom as a creative state weaves together details of his current everyday life (letters, daily routines, number of cigarettes smoked) with memories from his past life (lovers, friends, family, places). Architectural critic Georges Teyssot writes that the act of habitation comprises routines that both organize everyday life and create the framework needed to adapt to unfamiliar circumstances.[37] The boredom spawned from repetitive actions performed out of necessity and constraint engenders memories of, and longing for, another form of languid torpor, that of the familiar practices, *habitus,* and customs from a past life.

A diary entry from Monday, 9 February 1941, records on three columns what seems to be the dull timetable of a regular day:

Siren 7 am—newspaper	1 I think of Adina	6 we eat
Siren 8 am—I wake up	siren at a quarter to 2	7:30 1 cinema
8:30—9:00 correspondence	3 cracker / cookie	9:30 2 cinema
12 we eat	4–5 correspondence	11–12 going to bed[38]

Written mostly in Italian—his adopted language, fondly appropriated during the years spent in Italy—his diary is filled with entries that record the tedium and uncertainty of every day, along with the recollections of people dear to him. He spends his days eating, drawing, writing, and worrying about himself (fearing real and imaginary ailments, as a lifelong hypochondriac) and about his loved ones. Adina, his longtime lover, is left behind *col marito e cane* (with husband and dog). He records on 10 February 1941 that a watch he has received as a gift from her stops working, but then the following day it inexplicably starts ticking again.[39] His family is still in Bucharest, where the rise of anti-Semitic fascism threatens the lives of his relatives and friends. The agonizing boredom makes even insignificant events become little wonders worth registering: on Monday, 20 October 1941, in Ciudad Trujillo, "at 7 in the evening I threw away a cigarette butt and it landed upright," followed by a tiny sketch of a burning cigarette butt standing up.[40] On 22 October 1941, he remembers his friend Campus giving an onion to a dog, which eats it.[41]

Along with the experience of tedious routines and embodied habits, another type of tedium nurtures Steinberg's imagination: the boredom of the bureaucratic machine, which has multiple ways of trickling down into everyday life. Manifested physically, it is built through totalitarian architectures, the dull, repetitive houses of suburbia, the impersonal International Style skyscrapers, and the monotony of roadside architecture. Expressed through illegible paperwork, diplomas, and certificates, boredom insinuates itself in the institutions of power that control people's credentials, civil liberties, and, eventually, their right to live or die.

8

CRITIQUES OF CONTEMPORARY TEDIUM

A Fair Position

That Steinberg's work is a form of architectural criticism is not a new argument. The drawings and diagrams of this "critic without words" have been interpreted as "instruments of architectural critique, matching writing in authority and significance."[1] Not unlike Thorstein Veblen, David Riesman, or H. L. Mencken, who challenge accepted dogmas and doctrines only to reveal the possibilities of a better world, Steinberg "has reminded us of all the sham that marks our urban design and our ceremonial pomp."[2] While criticism is typically associated with divisive positions, dichotomies, and conflicting arguments, it also has another, often overlooked, function: not to split but, as Bruno Latour contends, to bring people and matters together in a common arena. Acting as a resource of architectural imagination rather than a post-factum interpretation, Steinberg's architectural critique has a generative role camouflaged under a seemingly disengaged position.

Steinberg employs boredom as an instrument of architectural critique that operates on multiple levels: as a catalyst for reinventing the artistic work; as the stultifying mindset of political and bureaucratic establishments and their built expressions; and last, going full circle, as an introspective mood akin to daydreaming. Exposed to and confronted with each and all of these manifestations of boredom, the viewer discovers a horizon of contemplation. Critique, like philosophy, begins in wonder.

Latour argues that "the critical mind, if it is to renew itself and be relevant again, is to be found in the cultivation of a *stubbornly realist attitude*," a realism dealing with what he calls "*matters of concern,* not *matters of fact.*"[3] Following the Heideggerian distinction between *things* (such as handmade jugs) and *objects* (such as industrially produced Coke cans), he proposes to collapse the two notions and transform *objects* into *things,* or in other words, bring together the *matters of fact* (the cans) and the *matters of concern* (the jugs). Latour describes the two contradictory positions prevalent in contemporary criticism as the *fairy* and the *fact.*[4] From the *fairy* position, critics show that material entities do nothing by themselves. Rather, people project their own desires onto them. On the other hand, from the *fact* position, the same critics show that people's behaviors are determined by exterior forces, or matters of fact. Latour distances himself from the phenomenological position, which would only further reinforce the rift between objects and things; instead, he advocates for what he calls a *fair* position, in which "the critic is not the one who debunks, but the one who assembles."[5] Assuming this position, Steinberg brings forth the creative role of criticism.

"BUILT IN U.S.A." (1953) AND *THE LABYRINTH* (1960)

Steinberg almost never writes explicitly about architecture. Two exceptions constitute the bookends between which this chapter unfolds. The first is his response to the exhibition *Built in USA: Post-war Architecture,* which is organized at the Museum of Modern Art in New York in 1953. The second exception, which will close this chapter, is the article "Our False-Front Culture," which he publishes in *Look* magazine in 1968.

In the eponymous publication catalogue for the MoMA exhibition, Philip Johnson concludes his preface with a celebratory statement: "With the mid-century modern architecture has come of age."[6] The exhibition is, indeed, a collection of mature modern and modernist buildings, ranging from Frank Lloyd Wright's Fallingwater to Richard Neutra's Experimental School in Los Angeles and Ludwig Mies van der Rohe's Illinois Institute of Technology buildings. But beyond its intended purpose, the catalogue discloses an understanding of architecture as a codified language, showcasing a contrived perspective on a built environment that is far more diverse and nuanced than the exhibition suggests. Steinberg reacts in the February 1953 issue of *ARTnews* with a brief statement and a series of drawings (fig. 25), criticizing the exhibition for presenting an artificial perspective of a much more complicated environment. He unveils a reality where the obsession with grandeur coexists with the slums of the disenfranchised, the disappearance of craftsmanship,

52 (2/53)

By Saul Steinberg

Text not written by ST – or probably heavily edited/rewritten by someone at Art.

BUILT IN U.S.A.

Postwar architecture, 1945-52

The major exhibition opening at the Museum of Modern Art, titled *Built in U.S.A.* and accompanied by a book of the same name, is an optimistic survey of a few handsome works selected from an enormous field of nonsense—thus a narcissistic view which leaves the impression that things are doing splendidly.

In architecture, for obvious reasons, faults are more important than virtues. The overwhelming presence of bad architecture cannot be ignored, and praising a few cases of honesty (or talent) never stopped a crime wave.

Not seen in the Museum's exhibition are the latest and most significant developments in the underworld of postwar architecture, such as:

Giantism . . . the marble cottage (and its city cousin, the ivory basement) . . . the new slums . . . mannerism . . . the primitive modern in skyscrapers and official buildings . . . the disappearance of the craftsman . . . the new role of the architect as interior decorator or lay-analyst to affluent families . . . easel architecture . . . city planning made to impress airplane passengers . . . photogenics. . . .
Some unphotogenic views are presented on this and the following three pages.

Figure 25. Saul Steinberg, "Built in U.S.A.: Post-War Architecture, 1945–52," *ARTnews,* February 1953. FIRST PAGE: *Untitled,* 1950–52 (*top*), ink on paper, Beinecke Rare Book and Manuscript Library, Yale University; *Untitled* (*bottom*), ink on paper, whereabouts unknown. SECOND PAGE: *Untitled,* ca. 1950–52 (*top left*), ink on paper, whereabouts unknown; *Untitled,* 1950 (*top right*), ink on paper, 14½ × 11½ in., Beinecke Rare Book and Manuscript Library, Yale University; *Untitled,* 1950 (*middle right*), ink on paper, whereabouts unknown; *Untitled,* ca. 1950–52 (*bottom*), ink on paper, whereabouts unknown. THIRD PAGE: *Untitled,* ca. 1950–52 (*top*), ink on paper, whereabouts unknown; *Untitled,* ca. 1950–52, detail (*bottom*), ink on paper, whereabouts unknown. (© The Saul Steinberg Foundation / Artists Rights Society [ARS], New York)

the reduction of the architect to an interior decorator, top-down city planning that ignores the real needs of people, and the overall interest that lies in appearance rather than substance, form rather than content.[7]

Steinberg's critique begins with a verbal and visual pun: a photo shoot whose protagonist is an architectural, rather than a human, model (in this case, Wright's Fallingwater). Staged and unnatural, the setting calls attention to the highly artificial nature of our perception of reality (abetted by the painting of the sky held up by an assistant at the back), which is determined and controlled by mass media. On the next page, cookie-cutter houses emerge in a dull suburban development built on either side of a highway, where bumper-to-bumper cars move at a slow, painful pace. In the city (the drawing below), crammed rooftops and crowds of indifferent people parallel the agglomeration of cars, suggesting a congestion similar to the one caused by car exhaust pollution in suburban developments. Random forms and repetitive shapes make houses hard to distinguish from cars. The "city planning made to

impress airplane passengers" is a critique of irrational design strategies that do not make sense in practice and are remote from people's everyday lives.

Questioning the paradigmatic and often misused modernist motto "form follows function," Steinberg asks rhetorically at the end of the article: "Which function for what form?"[8] Skeptical of the success of modern architecture celebrated in the MoMA exhibition, he puts next to each other two photo artifacts from Orlinda, Brazil: an ordinary water tower, disguised behind a pierced concrete wall, and a creative contraption made of a light bulb and a primitive oil lamp. While the exterior shape of the banal water tank gives the appearance of a building with a more sophisticated program, the ingenious lighting assemblage has the refreshing honesty of a work that is both genuine in form and practical in function. Where modernist abstractions fail, invention is born from the concrete matter and *habitus* of the everyday.

By confronting the two images—the banal *disguised* as extraordinary and the ordinary simply *being* ordinary—Steinberg exposes the dullness of the perforated concrete wall, one of the tropes of modernist architecture, and by extension, the travesty of claiming the universal victory of Modernism. The viewers reach these conclusions following their own creative processes through visual associations rather than through a moralizing story. The suburban tedium and the urban chaos are concrete experiences, common to all viewers, and their representation engages the audience in a tacit partnership.

Throughout his career, Steinberg publishes several compilations of drawings assembled from recent works (some already published, others not). Related neither to an exhibition nor to a volume edited by a critic, these compilations represent a rather unusual genre, where the artist has a direct voice in the selection, layout, overall structure, content, and title of the book. *The Labyrinth,* Steinberg's fourth book published in fifteen years, includes drawings that most clearly touch on the topic of boredom in the built environment. To Buzzi, Steinberg explains that the book "contains a great variety of Minotaurs, Heroes, Ariadnes, thread, etc.," hence the title.[9] One of the important aspects of Steinberg's artwork is the omission of captions, which shifts his drawing out of the cartoon world, where he is often mistakenly placed. The drawings neither explain nor clarify matters; rather, they encourage readers to create their own stories through a sense of shared meaning. For *The Labyrinth* in particular, he acknowledges the temptation to add commentaries, like a "key to dreams," in order to make the drawings more accessible.[10] Fortunately, he eventually refrains from doing so, and thus "the labyrinth" offers a constellation of interpretations and meanings.

For Steinberg, the experience of the labyrinth, described as a "troubled spiral," is not unlike that of boredom—a condition of being in crisis, of being "in trouble."[11] Historically an allegory of search and discovery, the labyrinth has, for Steinberg, a different purpose: not to find the center but to deliberately get lost, to look for and accept the unsettling circumstance of the crossroad.[12] Similarly, boredom prompts, as we saw earlier in this chapter, the imperative of an invention that draws on embodied practices and situates the work in an ever-growing spiral, where the same things are revisited yet again, though always from a different altitude. Just as being bored is a necessary condition for the imagination, so is the labyrinth a necessary state of creative discomfort.

Steinberg explores the theme of the labyrinth at various scales and in various media. In 1954, Italian architect Ernesto Rogers from the architectural partnership BBPR invites him to design the *sgraffito* murals for the Children's Labyrinth at the

Tenth Milan Triennale, an experience Steinberg recalls fondly as a half-mile-long mural, executed peripatetically, in hand-drawing (or rather handwriting).[13] Associated with human figures, other labyrinths indicate modes of speaking inherent to the subject, as specific to one's character as their fingerprints. And, surprisingly, the shortest distance between two points is not the straight line but the labyrinthine thread. The last drawings in the book are arabesque paths between two points (fig. 26). (Steinberg's friend Ennio Flaiano, an Italian writer, will write in an essay published thirteen years later, "In Italy, the shortest distance between two points is the arabesque. We live in a network of arabesques.")[14]

The Labyrinth tells a series of intertwined narratives. Lacking page numbers (like most of Steinberg's books), it elicits both a linear reading and a thematic one. To locate or go back to a particular drawing, the reader is required to leaf through other pages first and thus inevitably has to make mental notes, associations, and references.

Figure 26. Saul Steinberg, *A to B*, 1960. Ink and collage on paper, 14½ × 23 in. Private collection. Published in *The Labyrinth* (1960), [251]. (© The Saul Steinberg Foundation / Artists Rights Society [ARS], New York)

Perhaps unexpectedly, *The Labyrinth* opens with a straight line. Originating in a self-portrait of the artist, *The Line*—a variation on the drawings for the 1954 Children's Labyrinth mural in Milan—is a prologue, a system of reference, and Ariadne's thread. Unlike the Cartesian coordinates that locate the position of an object in space, Steinberg's own system of reference is situated at the intersection of multiple worlds that reflect, mirror, and illuminate each other. The straight horizon line brings together perspectives and viewpoints, delineates and joins, hides and clarifies, only to end—ironically—in elaborate arabesques. The simple line is the most complex labyrinth. Like Ariadne's thread, the line ties together the different sections of the book. Of the many storylines one could follow in *The Labyrinth,* several indicate the sources of modern alienation giving rise to individual and collective boredom: the failure of language, the car culture, and the built environment.

THE FAILURE OF LANGUAGE. In an interview from 1960, Steinberg expresses his admiration for people's ability to understand each other using few words, "through the briefest amount of communication."[15] His drawings perform precisely this kind of wordless communication that surpasses the boundaries of language. Language and architecture share the same mythological roots. In his foundational treatise on architecture, Vitruvius situates the origins of architecture in the shared act of people conversing around a fire. In Kierkegaard's version of Genesis, boredom sits at the foundation of the world, which gods create to alleviate their tedium, and ever since it has been consistently present in the history of humankind.[16] Eve is born out of Adam's boredom, and then, together with Cain and Abel, they are bored as a family—a condition that extends to the entire human race. "To amuse themselves," people decide to build a structure to reach the sky: "This notion is just as boring as the tower was high and is a terrible demonstration of how boredom has gained the upper hand."[17] Going along with the architectural collapse, the failure of language condemns people to a state of permanent miscommunication, a condition that Steinberg's labyrinthine speech bubbles make present.

For Steinberg, the broken experience of language is also a personal one: "I speak six languages, none of them well. The line—let's call it graphology—is my real language."[18] People live inside their own heads, and language is rarely a shared medium. Less reliable as a system of communication than one might assume, language is nevertheless a truthful indication of one's character. Not only do people speak the way they think but they also look the way they talk: flowery, sharp, ornate, strict, flirtatious, bubbly, incomprehensible, or sloppy (fig. 27).

Akin to fake diplomas and illegible writing, language estranges people. Although

ubiquitous, it is often meaningless. People talk without truly understanding each other, hence the sense of alienation and solitude. In Steinberg's labyrinthine conversations, there are no dialogues, just self-centered monologues. Each individual lives inside their own (speech) bubble.

Figure 27. Saul Steinberg, *Untitled*, 1957 (*left*), ink on paper, 20 × 24 in., Beinecke Rare Book and Manuscript Library, Yale University; Saul Steinberg, *Untitled*, 1957 (*right*), ink on paper, whereabouts unknown. Both originally published in the *New Yorker*, 1 June 1957; both republished in *The Labyrinth* (1960), [9], [11]. (© The Saul Steinberg Foundation / Artists Rights Society [ARS], New York)

THE CAR CULTURE. From the endless roads traveling the vast American landscape to the indistinct chaos of suburbia and the flat façades of International Style skyscrapers, boredom is present everywhere. August Heckscher describes the mid-century American city and its suburbs as a disquieting space where bareness and crowdedness alternate, "producing a psychological state where boredom succeeds to nervous agitation."[19] Similarly, Robert Venturi contends, "it is our fate now to be faced with either the endless inconsistencies of roadtown, which is chaos, or the infinite consistency of Levittown . . . , which is boredom."[20] Grounded in the reality of the American rural and urban landscape, the drawings in *The Labyrinth* evoke with precision and lucidity the unsettling play between order and disorder, void and excess, boredom and chaos.

Anticipating Jean Baudrillard's observation that driving through America will tell one more about the society than all of academia could ever do, Steinberg learns firsthand about the American landscape through systematic road trips that he takes throughout his entire life, either by himself or in the company of partners and friends.[21] Fascinated with its role in everyday life, Baudrillard situates the car at the center of the American world, along with the most ordinary suburb and the latest fast-food outlet, which in their banality are more relevant than any cultural event in old Europe. Driving, he remarks, creates not only a new experience of the space but also a new experience of the social system.[22] Steinberg's work makes present the boredom emerging from this new reality, which Baudrillard describes as a paradoxical condition: "Whatever the boredom, the hellish tedium of the everyday in the US or anywhere else, American banality will always be a thousand times more interesting than the European—and especially the French—variety. Perhaps because banality here is born of extreme distances, of the monotony of wide-open spaces and the radical absence of culture."[23]

An inevitable accessory of American life, the car operates as a prosthesis, an extension of the human body that becomes invisible because of its ubiquity. The body occupies and becomes one with the car, which in turn moves on limitless roads, along with similar creatures. A society of people-cars travels in solidarity and solitude through space. Steinberg's drawings (fig. 28) capture the two opposite scales of this experience: on the one hand, close-ups of the human body and the car merge into one entity, and on the other hand, a mass of cars is often indistinguishable from the vastness of suburban developments. One drawing depicts hands on the wheel, the view ahead mirroring the one in the rearview mirror—where the driver's eye is also reflected—and the driver, car, and road become one with the expanse of the landscape in an endless set of reflections. In another sketch, a line of bumper-

Figure 28. Saul Steinberg, *Untitled*, 1957 (*left*), ink on paper, whereabouts unknown (originally published in the *New Yorker*, 11 January 1958); Saul Steinberg, *Untitled*, 1958 (*right*), ink on paper, whereabouts unknown. Both republished in *The Labyrinth* (1960), [110], [123]. (© The Saul Steinberg Foundation / Artists Rights Society [ARS], New York)

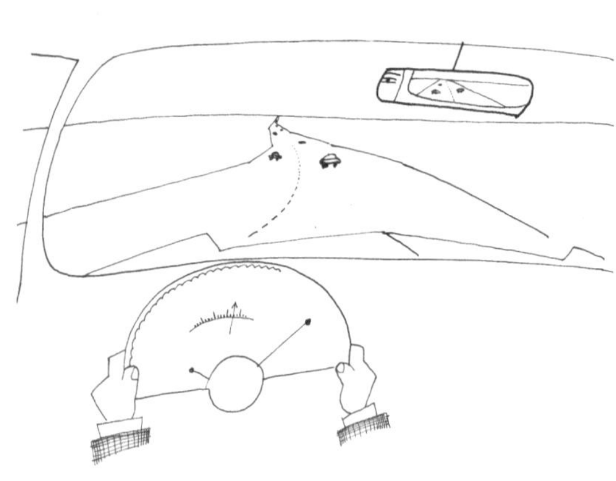

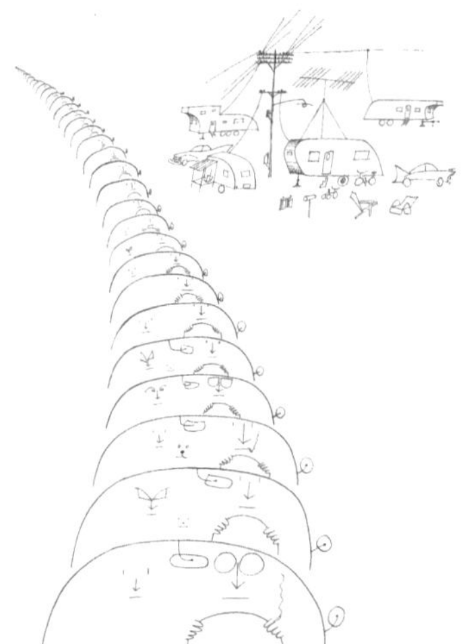

Figure 29. Saul Steinberg, *Motels and Highway*, 1959. Ink and crayon on paper, $22\frac{1}{16} \times 30\frac{1}{16}$ in. Art Institute of Chicago; Gift of The Saul Steinberg Foundation. Republished in *The Labyrinth* (1960), [129]. (© The Saul Steinberg Foundation / Artists Rights Society [ARS], New York)

to-bumper, identical cars, of which we see only the windshields, becomes a row of bored, featureless faces (fig. 28).

Insect-like cars buzz along suburban roads lined with endless motels and diners (fig. 29). Resembling random doodles, repetitive marks on the paper define a vast territory expanding to the horizon line, where the only legible signs read "motel," "cars," and "used cars." Undifferentiated lines fill up the page just as boredom fills up the spaces and regions where buildings, cars, and people blend and merge in a form of automatic writing at geological scale (fig. 30).

The puzzling experience of the labyrinth results not from convoluted geometries but quite the opposite, from an equally incomprehensible uniformity and monotony. The indistinct chaos of suburbia generates both unintelligible noise and deadening silence. Neither small town nor suburb, the peripheries sprawling outside urban centers offer the same standardized facilities no matter where they are

Figure 30. Saul Steinberg, *Untitled*, 1957–60 (*left*), ink and colored pencil on paper, 13⅝ × 17 in., Beinecke Rare Book and Manuscript Library, Yale University; Saul Steinberg, *Untitled*, 1957–60 (*right*), ink on paper, whereabouts unknown. Both republished in *The Labyrinth* (1960), [114–15]. (© The Saul Steinberg Foundation / Artists Rights Society [ARS], New York)

located: all the motels are called "Magnolia" and there is no vacancy in any of them. In an unsettling drawing titled "Aspera" (Latin for "rough"), in a large empty space carved out from a crammed development, lonely people roam around aimlessly, as if through an invisible labyrinth—perhaps one of the most accurate renditions of everyday life in modern America, where the individual remains isolated in the middle of a busy crowd (fig. 31).

THE BUILT ENVIRONMENT. Main Street as a concept and a physical space is the common denominator between the American metropolis and the American small town. The site of the main commercial activities, Main Street builds the cultural and social frameworks that shape one's character and personality, the defining traits one carries throughout life.[24] Steinberg's small-town Main Streets are drive-through spaces that begin and end nowhere. Cardboard-like buildings stand next to one another in a hodgepodge of eclectic styles. Deserted downtowns and false-front façades have the stage-set quality of a theatrical performance or the unsettling atmosphere of a forensic scene. In a chilling rendition of a main street, ominous window frames resemble hanging bodies, perhaps an allusion to the history of slavery and systemic racial persecution in the American South, which Steinberg witnesses firsthand during his travels. In July 1958, Steinberg drives through the South (Virginia, West Virginia, North Carolina, South Carolina, Georgia, Tennessee) and witnesses the segregation and racism embedded in the fabric of everyday life. He records these experiences in his travel sketchbooks and writes to Aldo Buzzi, "I've seen poor coal-mining local-

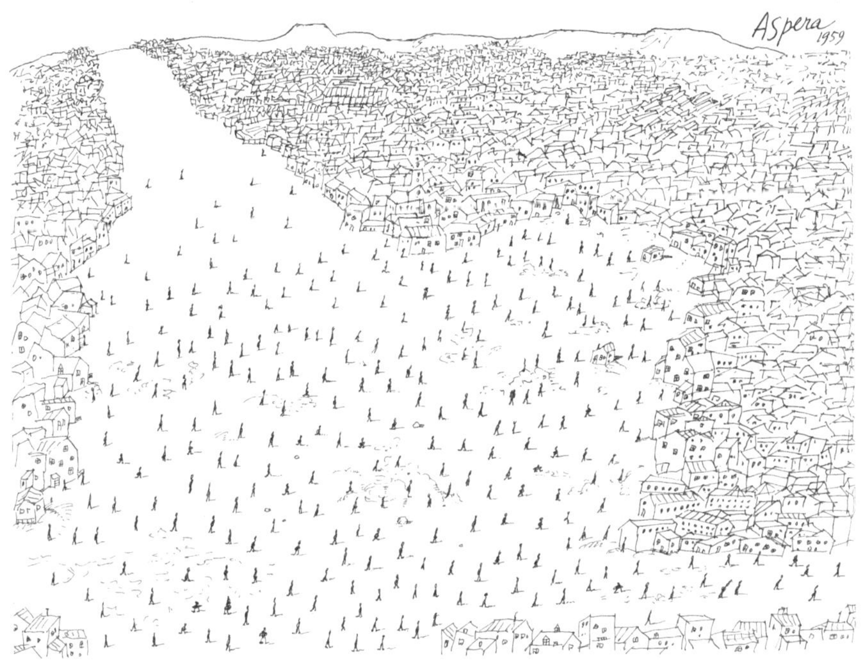

Figure 31. Saul Steinberg, *Aspera,* 1959. Ink on board, 20 1/16 × 30 1/8 in. Art Institute of Chicago; Gift of The Saul Steinberg Foundation. Republished in *The Labyrinth* (1960), [228]. (© The Saul Steinberg Foundation / Artists Rights Society [ARS], New York)

ities in Kentucky and West Virginia. An old America, religion, violence, horrible landscapes, miners living in African villages"[25] (fig. 32).

If a small-town Main Street reflects the dullness of a place where nothing happens, Main Street in a metropolis is equally daunting, though for different reasons. In the congested traffic, cars no longer look like cars but become gigantic insects swarming the streets in a dark cloud of pollution and noise (fig. 33).

In Steinberg's architectural vocabulary, the "false front" typical of American cities, big and small, disguises either chaos or emptiness. Invisible from the eye-height of the pedestrian, what happens behind the screen (and scene) can be revealed only from the omniscient perspective of an on-high view, the same vantage point that allows one to comprehend the vastness of the landscape stretching to the horizon. In a seamless process of disguise and dissimulation, people emulate their environment: "People

Figure 32. Saul Steinberg, *Untitled*, 1957. Ink on paper, 12⁵/₈ × 22³/₄ in. Nelson-Atkins Museum of Art, Kansas City, Missouri; Gift of The Saul Steinberg Foundation. Republished in *The Labyrinth* (1960), [113]. (© The Saul Steinberg Foundation / Artists Rights Society [ARS], New York)

are disguised in costumes, as are the buildings. If we look at the Chrysler Building and the Empire State Building, as well as the skyscrapers of New York, or Kansas City, any town that has skyscrapers, they are costumed buildings."[26] Identical square faces collected together walk and move like an indistinct mass (fig. 34). Not surprisingly, this drawing immediately follows the monotonous renditions of urban centers, a sad acknowledgment of the ways in which dull environments shape people's lives.

Two-dimensional and paper-thin, skyscrapers are drawn either with one continuous line (fig. 35), which makes them appear both daunting and vulnerable, or as grotesque out-of-scale decorations, giant presences dwarfing everything around and casting ominous shadows over the neighboring buildings. Tall buildings, and specifically International Style skyscrapers, are recurrent themes in Steinberg's work. Anticipating Marshall McLuhan's much-quoted quip "The medium is the message," Steinberg often employs graph paper in his representations of tall buildings.[27] A master of disguise, he performs several roles simultaneously: the modernist architect trained to design architecture at the drafting table, the architectural critic voicing concern with exhausted modernist language, and the advocate of laypeople subjected to the tedium of uniformity and repetition.

Steinberg's variations on the unchanging modernist grid address not only archi-

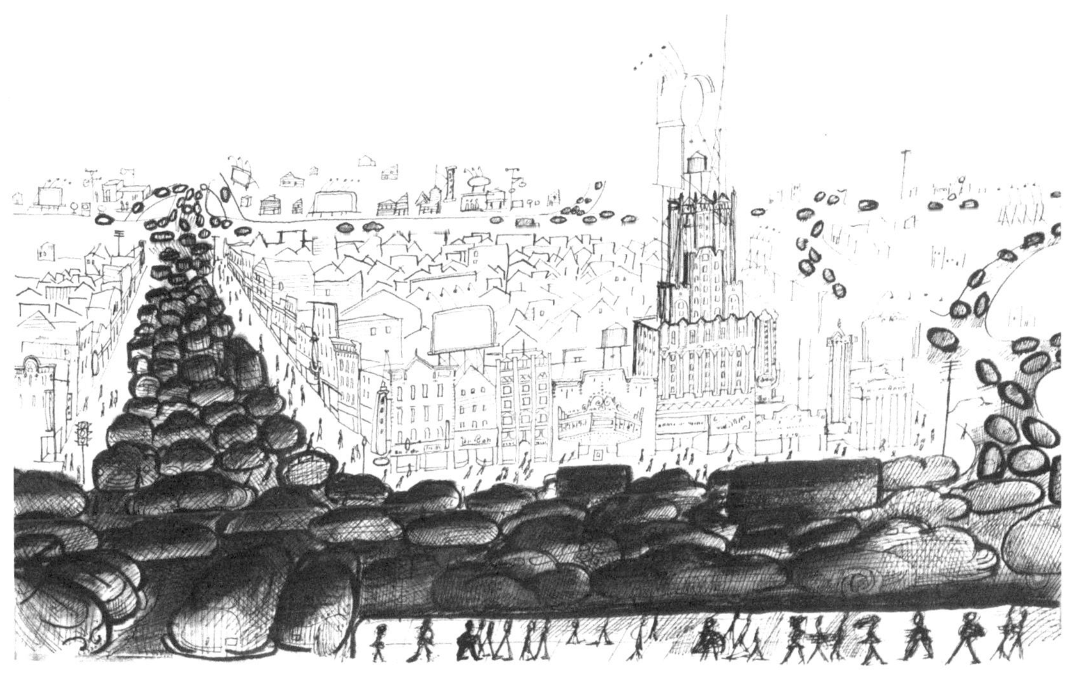

tecture but society at large. Critic Will Norman writes that in Steinberg's work, "the grid becomes more than a method for organizing the visual field—it is also recognized as a form of spatial discipline with concrete social effects."[28] Steinberg observes the tyranny of the grid in work that goes back to the early 1950s. In a *sui generis* recapitulation of the history of architecture, one of his murals for the Children's Labyrinth (Milan, 1954) begins with the primitive hut and a lacustrine house and ends with a flat International Style skyscraper. In between, past medieval castles, warriors' tents, minarets, and bulb-shaped domes, begins the (architectural) history of America. The log cabin morphs into "neo-" (Classical or Romanesque), only to become midcentury California-style modern. Based on the proportions of a Mondrian painting, the modernist grid governs both the plan and the elevation, generating "architettura da chevalet" (easel architecture), removed from real life and concerned only with lifeless aesthetics. (Steinberg advises those who will trace his

Figure 33. Saul Steinberg, *Untitled,* 1949–54. Ink on paper. Whereabouts unknown. Republished in *The Labyrinth* (1960), [125]. (© The Saul Steinberg Foundation / Artists Rights Society [ARS], New York)

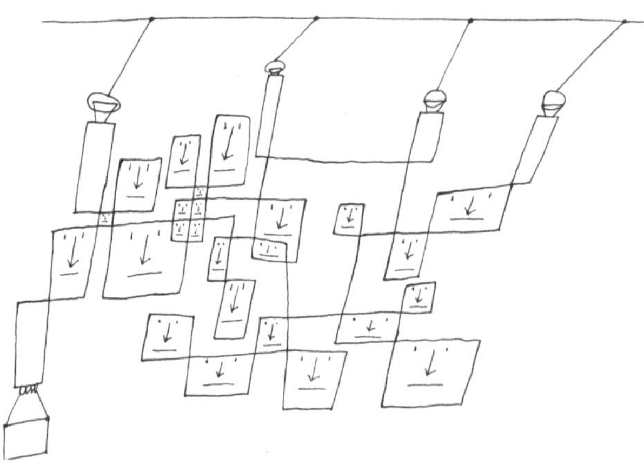

Figure 34. Saul Steinberg, *Subway,* 1958. Ink on paper, 11½ × 14½ in. Beinecke Rare Book and Manuscript Library, Yale University. Republished in *The Labyrinth* (1960), [142]. (© The Saul Steinberg Foundation / Artists Rights Society [ARS], New York)

Figure 35. Saul Steinberg, *Untitled,* 1957. Ink on paper. Whereabouts unknown. Originally published in the *New Yorker,* 13 April 1957. Republished in *The Labyrinth* (1960). (© The Saul Steinberg Foundation / Artists Rights Society [ARS], New York)

drawings on the wall to slightly change Mondrian's proportions.) On a different scale, massive apartment buildings orchestrate and contain people's quotidian boredom. "Case popolari—architettura che deriva dagli strumenti da disegno" (social housing—architecture derived from drawing tools) turns the normative modernist grid into a system of social regimentation.[29]

The outcome of the grid as an emblem of architectural and social control is, paradoxically, similar to the effect of chaos and disorder, as they both engender the boredom inflicted on midcentury society. Whether manifested in a totalitarian or a democratic regime, the effects of the grid are the same. Humans—trapped either in the labyrinth of the uniform networks of American cities or the incoherent maze of unplanned developments—are left to experience and negotiate everyday tedium on their own. Talking without communicating in labyrinthine speech bubbles, they become reflections of the environment, moving along as lonely figures in indistinct crowds.

"OUR FALSE-FRONT CULTURE" (1968)

This chapter starts in 1953, with one of Steinberg's few written critiques on contemporary architecture, and ends fifteen years later with another rare instance where he carefully crafts the comments accompanying his drawings. Published in *Look* magazine, "Our False-Front Culture" includes a series of drawings and commentaries that directly confront the issue of boredom in architecture. With the sharpness and effectiveness of speech balloons, Steinberg's words echo the brevity and clarity of architectural manifestoes rather than the lengthy demonstrations of architectural criticism. He identifies three intertwined conditions of the built environment born out of, but also generating, the boredom of a commodified culture: false-front, package, and rubber-stamp architecture. Together, they construct a drama in three acts telling the story of contemporary ennui. Key to his narrative is the use of rubber stamps as a subversive drawing medium evoking the tedium of standardized values forced upon consumer culture.

On one side of a street, a few modest cardboard-like buildings labeled "bar," "café," and "saloon" stand against a hillside (fig. 36). On the other side of the street, a white, modern-looking wall pierced by three arches is almost magically freestanding, without any support or connections. In between, six cowboys' silhouettes suggest a downtown main street, somewhere in the far west, stretching in an empty landscape under an ominous, troubled sky. Steinberg writes, "Most of the new cultural-center architecture is in this tradition, which is very much an American tradition, symbolic of optimism and progress (also suggesting the pleasant complicity of people living in a stage set). In its current revival, a sort of magic is attempted: build the false front, and somehow content will fill up the inviting empty shell."[30]

Recalling Giorgio de Chirico's daunting plazas, the scene also brings to mind

Figure 36. Saul Steinberg, "Our False-Front Culture," *Look,* 9 January 1968. (© The Saul Steinberg Foundation / Artists Rights Society [ARS], New York)

Tantalizing caricatures of some cultural foibles —and rare words of explanation by the artist

OUR FALSE-FRONT CULTURE BY SAUL STEINBERG

Most of the new cultural-center architecture is in this tradition, which is very much an American tradition, symbolic of optimism and progress (also suggesting the pleasant complicity of people living in a stage set).
In its current revival, a sort of magic is being attempted: Build the false front, and somehow content will fill up the inviting empty shell.

continued

LOOK 1-9-68 47

Figure 36 (*cont.*) Saul Steinberg, "Our False-Front Culture," *Look*, 9 January 1968. (© The Saul Steinberg Foundation / Artists Rights Society [ARS], New York)

The Package The content that, in the hopeful native view, will bring the false front alive is The Package. These Unidentified Flying Objects are cultural packages, traveling from one Center to another. They contain a lab-tested mixture of art and entertainment that unifies the culture standards of the nation.

Rubber-stamp architecture Government, charity and bureaucracy live here, where boredom stands for dignity and symmetry equals beauty. This architecture is also the mark of the Totalitarians—it is amazing that it should flourish here.

48 LOOK 1-9-68

Figure 36 (*cont.*) Saul Steinberg, "Our False-Front Culture," *Look*, 9 January 1968. (© The Saul Steinberg Foundation / Artists Rights Society [ARS], New York)

Figure 36 (*cont.*) Saul Steinberg, "Our False-Front Culture," *Look*, 9 January 1968. (© The Saul Steinberg Foundation / Artists Rights Society [ARS], New York)

Venturi's sketches for the civic buildings in downtown North Canton, Ohio, discussed elsewhere in this book, where freestanding walls create layers of spaces around buildings. Here, however, Steinberg exposes the absurdity of contentless forms, of which exhausted modernist architecture is a perfect illustration. What he defines as the "false front" is another type of mask that disguises the—quite literal—void behind. What is left of the original aspirations of modern architecture is the bare white wall.

That Steinberg talks not only about "cultural centers" but also about "centers of culture," which distribute the information from a centralized structure to the periphery, becomes clearer in the second act of his story. A flying contraption is about to descend upon an isolated house, awaited by a couple eager to receive the controlled information coming from the center (fig. 36). "The content that, in the hopeful native view, will bring the false front alive is The Package," Steinberg writes. "These Unidentified Flying Objects are cultural packages, traveling from one Center to another. They contain a lab-tested mixture of art and entertainment that unifies the culture standards of the nation."[31]

Steinberg echoes Rudofsky's critique of a commodified society that not only encourages consumerism but ultimately promotes uniformity and standardization. People buy the same products, live in identical houses, live similar lifestyles, and take everything for granted, without any questions or doubts. New forms of mass media, among which television emerges as the most powerful, deliver carefully controlled bits of information, art, and entertainment, ready to be ingested in prescribed doses. Similarly, in a 1962 article problematizing recent trends in architecture, Lewis Mumford recognizes the shortcomings of Modernism and the failure of its faith in technological progress, suggesting that the fall of the machine has brought the advent of the package. In other words, consumerism has replaced reliance on industrialization.[32] Decrying the architectural equivalents of contemporary advertising, Mumford mocks the package-like buildings, devoid of content, indifferent to their physical environment as well as to people's desires and aspirations: "The result is the characterless package, which has become the main hallmark of fashionable architecture for the last decade" or the "dazzling Christmas packages that have no relation to contents."[33]

Building upon the two previous scenes, the third and final act of Steinberg's story reveals the disquieting similarities between seemingly different political establishments whose (common) goal is ultimately to control their subjects. While totalitarian regimes openly resort to brutality and repression, democracies use the soft power of consumerism, which turns action and resistance into a soporific state of mind: "Government, charity and bureaucracy live here, where boredom stands for dignity and symmetry equals beauty. This architecture is also the mark of the Totalitarians—it is amazing that it should flourish here."[34]

Rubber-stamp people, objects, and architectures unfold in parallel parades that construct a uniform world without distinctions or specificity. Nothing situates this scene in a particular political setting, as the only differences are not between the objectives of each society but rather between the means to achieve them. Capitalism and its consumer culture offer the *appearance* of freedom of choice while exercising control from within. Authoritarian regimes openly impose restrictions and normative behaviors under the *appearance* of higher ideals, uncontaminated by materialistic desires. In the end, both societies fail to nurture the sense of self, personal aspirations, or collective dreams. Writing decades later, Joseph Rykwert will likewise observe that the architecture of capitalist cities, determined by profitability and economic interests, is no different from that of the communist centers, imposed by the strict rules of party propaganda.[35] The message might be different, but the billboards and advertising techniques are the same: "One of the complaints about the 'boredom' of East European centers under communist regimes arose from the absence of just such variegated and conflicting appeals from city walls—the buildings were, of course, no more exhilarating than those of the capitalists. Dirigist authorities had learnt how to emulate advertising, but substituted politically exhortative billboards in its place. Their message was uniformly bland and conformist, even if their formal effect on the urban scene was not all that different from that in the 'free world.'"[36]

Steinberg has long explored the use of rubber stamps as an expressive drawing medium. Invented in the 1860s and consistently employed in post offices as well as banking and administrative institutions, they are ubiquitous in our world and, in addition to the obvious associations with bureaucracy, they provide popular and inexpensive forms of printing for sign making, business forms, or personal stationery.[37] Steinberg has always acknowledged his early exposure to his father's box-making business as one of the main influences on his art. His artistic use of rubber stamps could be traced back to popular forms of economical printing that he most likely witnessed as a child.

Readily available throughout the twentieth century, rubber stamps have been used outside their intended context, and their originally limited vocabulary of words and numbers has been constantly expanding with a variety of images ranging from figurative representations (of inanimate objects and human figures) to nonfigurative renditions (such as Steinberg's abstract compositions of lines). Often employed as a sign of resistance against the very institutions they represent, low-tech rubber stamps offer a middle ground between handmade and fully mechanized tools, which is why they appeal to artists such as Andy Warhol.[38] They offer a somewhat limited vocabulary of forms, which forces an artist to push the boundaries of their creativity. When asked why he uses rubber stamps, Steinberg responds playfully: "They help me avoid the narcissistic pleasure of hand work. Work is a trap that keeps people from thinking—it's therapy. I avoid it by making these simple elements and then arranging them. With about fifty stamps I can do everything necessary to render space, nature, technology. It's a computerized form of art."[39]

The last page in Steinberg's 1968 *Look* magazine article exemplifies his long interest in rubber stamps as a graphic medium. Beginning in the late 1940s, he uses commercially available rubber stamps, and in the mid-1960s he begins to order stamps of his own design.[40] He calls his collection of custom-made rubber stamps his "personal postal service, a glorious dream come true, a sheer luxury."[41]

In the 3 December 1966 issue of the *New Yorker,* Steinberg publishes a portfolio whose title ("Rubber Stamps") seems to innocently draw attention to the medium rather than the content, while, in fact, the drawings reveal a more engaged political position. The viewer moves from parades of identical people and cars to troubling scenes of crowds prompted to "Rush" and consequently precipitating into an abyss, only to dwell at the end in the drowsy tranquility of a commodified culture. It is this last idea that Steinberg develops at length in the *Look* magazine portfolio.

Critical of the assumption that "boredom stands for dignity and symmetry equals beauty," Steinberg constructs images of monumental architectures in a hybrid language of Cubism and Neoclassicism, the latter often associated around the world with institutions of power. Boredom is instrumentalized on the one hand as a vocabulary of dry and oppressive architectural forms and, on the other, as repetitive acts assuming a fabricated authority. The drawing is built as a sequence of parallel parades of people, cars, and architectures, distributed from the bottom to the top of the page. The commodification of art allows everyone to call him- or herself an artist and produce, in unison, similar works. One needs only the right artistic pose in front of the easel to claim the status of a legitimate artist. The drawing exposes the precarious nature of contemporary culture, whether in a democratic or a totalitarian regime, which needs the endorsement of an institutional system to recognize and accept value—an endorsement Steinberg generously offers at the very top of the page. Mocking each other, the "Certified" and "Duplicate" stamps crown the central architectural image, framing the less visible "Made in U.S.A." In a world that celebrates highbrow art and architecture, the cliché of the rubber stamp makes manifest the "boredom inflicted by the state."

9

TACTICS OF RESISTING ENNUI

Folding Boredom into Daydreaming

Steinberg's *The New World,* published in 1965, is not a book about America. The title, the artist admits in his tongue-in-cheek manner, says nothing.[1] A collection of drawings from the *New Yorker* and other sources, it includes intimations of imaginary worlds that one fantasizes about in daydreams. Claiming a more personal rapport with the work, Steinberg was planning to title it *Confessions* but changed his mind, apparently for marketing purposes.[2] In a lengthy article published in *Life* magazine, he attempts to "explain" some of the drawings, but his explanations end up, not surprisingly, having the same mysterious quality as his work.[3] Visually and verbally, Steinberg plays with riddles, fables, and allegories that change, flip, and shuffle meanings and conventions.

Focusing mainly on *The New World* and *The Labyrinth,* this chapter will delve into Steinberg's techniques of folding ordinary boredom into the state of daydreaming that opens a horizon of contemplation and wonder. Through his work, he implicitly questions the nature of architectural drawings. Modernity and, with it, architectural representation largely appear to represent clarity and straightforward answers, where riddles are resolved and there is no room for allegorical or metaphorical thinking. The modernist machine devours and turns any deviation from the norm into a straight line (fig. 37).

Building Information Modeling, Computer Aided Design, and Revit drawings and models aspire to produce efficient, accurate, and precise documents. Despite

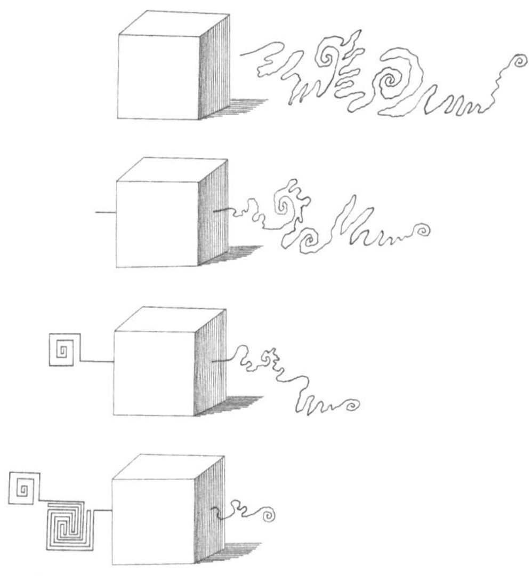

Figure 37. Saul Steinberg, *Untitled*, 1958. Ink and collage of four drawings affixed to paper, 20 × 23½ in. overall. Beinecke Rare Book and Manuscript Library, Yale University. Originally published in the *New Yorker*, 21 May 1960. Republished in *The Labyrinth* (1960). (© The Saul Steinberg Foundation / Artists Rights Society [ARS], New York)

such claims of absolute clarity, architectural representation, far from clear and unambiguous, achieves its full potential in the world of conundrums and mysteries. Trained at the height of Modernism, Steinberg resists its normative processes and proposes a different logic—of ambiguity, multiple meanings, open endings, gratuitous pursuits, and unresolved mysteries. His work operates in the territory of riddles.

RIDDLES AND INVERSIONS

Riddles exist everywhere. In tales, legends, and myths, young men have to decipher riddles as part of their necessary rites of passage; a suitor has to answer various riddles before the girl is entrusted to him in marriage; crossing boundaries and thresholds on their last journey, the deceased often find riddles that place them in the appropriate realm of the afterlife. From time immemorial, all cultures have employed riddles as cognitive operations[4] that describe the indescribable through metaphors. "The very nature indeed of a riddle is this, to describe a fact in an impossible combination of words (which cannot be done with the real names for things, but can be with their metaphorical substitutes)," writes Aristotle in *The Poetics.*[5] Around the middle of the twentieth century, linguistics and folklore studies, under the umbrella of structuralism, advance another definition: "A riddle is a traditional verbal expression which contains one or more descriptive elements, a pair of which may be in opposition; the referent of the elements is to be guessed."[6] A more nuanced approach states that "riddles play with boundaries, but ultimately to affirm them (like a child playing with mud to find and define the boundaries of his body). Shared characteristics between categories are a threat to the distinctiveness of the categories; riddles examine those things that are shared and pinpoint those that divide."[7]

The Labyrinth includes a series of embodied drawings, where words become living creatures and the letters composing them express the meaning of the word. Before Ed Ruscha started his word paintings in the 1960s, Steinberg was already visualizing the relationship of form and content in verbal language. Falling off a cliff into the sea and punctuated with an exclamation mark, "HELP" conveys a desperate cry to be saved. "SWINDLE" begins with an overly decorated majuscule and ends with the *L,* while the *E* is deceptively hiding inside the *D.* Weakened and emaciated, "SICK" is lying in bed.

The letters in "RIDDLE" construct an artificial landscape, comprehensible only when seen from above by an observer, resembling the artist himself, who stands on the floating *R* (fig. 38).

The omniscient bird's-eye view seems to shed light on the riddle unfolding at the artist's feet, as if revealing its full meaning. The *I* is strongly anchored into the ground. The *D* reveals the negative of its shape in its underground double. From the specific vantage point of the on-high observer, the *L* actually resembles an *I.* Last, camouflaged into the thickness of the *L,* the *E* disguises its presence and thus escapes the scrutiny of the viewer. Things are not what they appear, and the search for perfect clarity is a futile pursuit. The riddle has no answer and dwells in the space of ambiguity and ambivalence.

Inversion, like Steinberg's double *D* shown through the relationship of positive and negative spaces, is a central tactic in the process of riddling, folding two apparently conflicting realities into each other. In this process, both shared and specific properties are intentionally shuffled and mingled, only to fully disclose themselves in what is usually a dramatic revelation. Inversions call into question facile dichotomies. It is in the course of this operation and within this thick space that fruitful and unexpected associations come to life.

Figure 38. Saul Steinberg, *Riddle,* 1960. Library of Congress, Washington, DC, Prints and Photographs Division. Originally published in the *New Yorker,* 20 August 1960. Republished in *The Labyrinth* (1960). (© The Saul Steinberg Foundation / Artists Rights Society [ARS], New York)

Boredom and daydreaming are two ostensibly opposed moods. While the former has negative connotations overall, associated with destructive emotions and the stifling of creativity, the latter has positive undertones, enjoys a higher status, and inspires creativity. Although the concept of boredom has emerged and been intertwined with modernity, its reception and interpretation have varied. The "empty longing for a new desire" (Schopenhauer), "the root of all evil" (Kierkegaard), or a pathological condition, boredom is also a mood conducive to philosophy (Heidegger), "the apogee of physical relaxation" (Benjamin), and the patient gateway toward great passion (Kracauer).[8]

Daydreaming, on the other hand, has positive connotations. Defined as a "series of thoughts or yearnings that pleasantly distract one's attention, an idle fantasy or a vain hope," daydreaming, like contemplation or reverie, fosters creativity and imagination.[9] A sense of impracticality underlies the act of daydreaming, which implies the subject's distance from "real" problems or "real" solutions. Daydreaming activates the subject's imagination and transports them to another time or place.[10]

Perhaps unexpectedly, daydreaming and boredom share a sense of disengagement from the present, a certain absent-mindedness, a welcomed idleness, as well as aspirations for impractical pursuits. While in a state of daydreaming or a state of boredom, one is never in the present and keeps longing for what is not there. Before becoming oppressive, the sense of discontent that boredom engenders moves one into a state of reverie, where possibilities open up and imagination wanders.

On the one hand, as we have seen in the previous chapter, Steinberg's drawings are critiques of the boredom embedded in commodified architectures. On the other, as we will see in this chapter, they build upon the common territory between two seemingly opposed moods, playing out the folding of boredom into daydreaming.[11] Inverting these subjective states, these drawings propose spatial riddles, which, unlike verbal riddles that have a precise answer, construct, instead, a thick space of ambiguity. As shown earlier, Steinberg's drawings are architectural not because they foreground architectural spaces but because they invite viewers to inhabit those (real or imaginary) spaces and construct their own worldviews. Commenting on his own drawings from *The New World,* Steinberg discloses his personal understanding of the relationship between the architect-artist and the audience: "I appeal to the complicity of my reader who will transform this line into meaning by using our common background of culture, history, poetry. Contemporaneity in this sense is a complicity."[12]

Acedia, boredom's ancestor, has a genealogy that goes back to ancient Greece. In its original sense, it means listlessness, apathy, and, quite literally, a non-caring state.[13] Christianity appropriates the term to illustrate negative psychological states (such as laziness or apathy) and give them moral dimensions: acedia indicates a moral failing and becomes a deadly sin, commonly translated as "sloth."[14] Medieval monks fear it as the "demon of noontide," threatening to surreptitiously undermine their vigilance and alertness in the lazy hours of midday, the time of stillness without shadows. Indifference gives rise to negligence and carelessness, a mode of being oblivious to the present and the immediate world, driving one into the abyss of emptiness. Acedia is manifested through aversion to both manual work and prayer—in other words, a disinterest in both material and spiritual matters. Keeping the monk away from his important pursuit, the love of God, acedia stands in opposition to spiritual joy.

The concept reemerges in modern times, but its connotations change, leaving behind binary classifications. Analyzing ennui in Western literature, literary critic Reinhard Kuhn notes that when the demon of noontide does not stifle creativity, paradoxically, it "can and often does induce efforts to fill the void that it hollows out."[15] Boredom, ennui, or *Langeweile* sometimes inverts itself into the pleasant mood of daydreaming. Steinberg's drawings present the imprecise territory between boredom and daydreaming, questioning the dichotomy between the two conditions and operating, instead, at their intersection (figs. 39–44).

Activating the realm of imagination, the inversion of boredom and daydreaming is anchored in mundane realities and elicits the sense of wonder one experiences when looking closely at the ordinary world. In the eighteenth century, Xavier de Maistre, a French army officer better known as a writer, is confined to a forty-two-day arrest in his room in the aftermath of a duel. The outcome of his unintended sojourn is the 1794 book *Voyage autour de ma chambre* (*A Journey around My Room*), a small volume describing the imaginary travels spawned by the domestic objects in his room. A parody of the eighteenth-century fashionable Grand Tour, during which young European aristocrats discover the wonders of the ancient world, the book inverts the grandiose narratives of extraordinary adventures with the more modest, but no less engaging, stories of the everyday. Constrained by physical boundaries, de Maistre turns his boredom into contemplation: "A nice fire, books, pens; how many resources there are against boredom! And what a pleasure it is, too, to forget your books and your pens, and instead poke your fire, succumbing to a gentle contemplation or arranging a few rhymes to amuse your friends."[16] Like de Maistre, Steinberg transforms boredom into contemplation by paying close attention to the unremarkable things around him, to the matter and stuff of the world.

In the early decades of the twentieth century, Siegfried Kracauer recognizes the modern separation between work and leisure as one of the main sources of boredom. This division splits people's time into active and passive hours and so, under the pressure of a commodified culture and fearing the void of having nothing to do, individuals resort to facile forms of entertainment. Quiet Sunday afternoons—when everything, even entertainment, slows down—engender a stifling boredom reflected in the eerie stillness of decorative miniature glass figures, frozen in their porcelain silhouettes. "If, however, one has the patience," Kracauer writes, "the sort of patience specific to legitimate boredom, then one experiences a kind of bliss that is almost unearthly. A landscape appears in which colorful peacocks strut about, and images of people suffused with soul come into view. And look—your own soul is likewise swelling, and in ecstasy you name what you have always lacked: the great *passion.*"[17]

For children who have not yet appropriated the normative categories of the adult world, boredom and daydreaming often act as catalysts of the imagination. Writing about one's memory of their childhood home, French philosopher Gaston Bachelard describes children's relationship with the two moods: "What special depth there is in a child's daydream! And how happy the child who really possesses his moments of solitude! It is a good thing, it is even salutary, for a child to have periods of boredom, for him to learn to know the dialectics of exaggerated play and causeless, pure boredom."[18] Further and further away from our childhood homes, we continue to reconstruct them in our memory in a process that collapses boredom and daydreaming: "Centers of boredom, centers of solitude, centers of daydream group together to constitute the oneiric house which is more lasting than the scattered memories of our birthplace."[19]

The drawings examined here (primarily from *The Labyrinth* and *The New World*) occupy the temporal and spatial interval described by de Maistre, Kracauer, and Bachelard, where boredom inverts itself into daydreaming, generating unforeseen associations. To fabricate these riddles, Steinberg resorts to specific techniques. Individuals are placed in particular bodily postures that welcome the state of reverie (the way de Maistre lounges in his armchair). Mundane, inanimate objects come to life, becoming characters with dreams and desires (like Kracauer's glass figurines) that reveal the drama of human finitude. Detailed, close-up views (as opposed to distant, bird's-eye perspectives) bring into focus memories and recollections of times past and create an intimate connection between the viewing subject and the objects examined (just as the child learns and invents their world by closely looking at it). If the "RIDDLE" resists revealing itself to the omniscient figure hovering above, it might slowly open up to the more sympathetic reading at a personal scale.

WONDERING: THE WORLD ANEW

SITTING AND RECLINING. Recounting the (real and imaginary) geography of his room, which he discovers with fresh eyes during his travel around his chamber, Xavier de Maistre describes the two pieces of furniture where one experiences both tedium and daydreaming. The armchair, "an excellent piece of furniture . . . , highly useful for every man inclined to meditation," invites him to spread out, extend his body, and succumb to gentle contemplation.[20] At the other end of the room, placed in the most pleasant spot, washed by the first rays of the sun, the bed offers another locus for meditation and dreaming: "Is there any theater which arouses the imagination more, or awakens more tender ideas, than this piece of furniture in which I sometimes lose myself?"[21] Mind and body are both engaged in getting away from the present, either by actively dreaming or by passively getting bored. The armchair and the bed, where one sits, reclines, or lies down, are the intimate places of anticipation and limbo that Steinberg seizes in his drawings.

The bored, as well as the contemplative, never live in the present, longing either for an idealized past or for an imagined future. The couple in Walter Sickert's painting *Ennui* is bored—or perhaps contemplative? The woman is looking to the left, as if she were nostalgic for a past unbeknownst to the viewer, while the man is looking to the right, as if he were yearning for a hopeful future. Disengaged from each other and from the spectator, both characters in the painting look away and dream of being elsewhere. The bored and the contemplative never look their interlocutors in the eyes, which makes it hard to distinguish between them and decipher the riddle of their thoughts.

In *ennui,* as in daydreaming, the head is heavy with the weight of thoughts or, on the contrary, as light as the void inside. The bored and the contemplative abandon their bodies to loose postures. Both boredom and daydreaming claim domestic, familiar spaces, where bodies relax and lose the tightness of the upright posture: "Ennui, it has been said, is a 'domestic demon.'"[22] The tedium of everyday life induces the uniform, the shapeless, but also the multiform, the excess—of ornament, of color, of objects, of furniture.[23] Boredom and contemplation are inward-looking, private moods. They belong to an inner world, often depicted as the space between an interior and an exterior seen through a window or reflected, as inversion, through a mirror.

An entire section of *The Labyrinth* registers moments of limbo when bodies are sitting or reclining. Examining the nature of the seated position, Joseph Rykwert remarks that the standing and sitting postures complement each other, building the expectation for the other one to emerge.[24] Looking (up) at the upright position, Bernard Rudofsky observes that it "demands magisterial poise of the kind not seen any more outside of courtrooms."[25] Rykwert notes the affinity between standing up and the primordial stretching of the body at birth. The act of sitting is both a form of surrendering to fatigue and a coming-closer to the earth. As a social norm, it often indicates a form of privilege clearly expressed in relation to others, who are standing.[26] Reclining offers different readings. Neither standing (as if ready for action) nor sitting (as if resting, but still alert), the passive posture of reclining allows a range of different events or nonevents to unfold: boredom, (day)dreaming, laziness, apathy, awakening, sickness, or even death are all possible. Unpredictably, the protagonist might sit up, stand up, move, or simply fall asleep.

Steinberg's drawings capture these languid positions in full-body attitudes or glimpses of bodily details. The looseness of a limb or the position of a head, a finger, an elbow, or a neck intimates that particular moment when the tedium of the day turns into daydreaming. Lost in their thoughts, people absent-mindedly smoke, swing in rocking chairs, or read the newspaper. Smoking with her head resting on her palm, a woman keeps her eyes closed as her body vanishes—too much or perhaps not enough in the tedium of indifference from which expectations arise (fig. 39).

A woman seated in an armchair is nervously tapping her foot and hand while her eyes speak of both past desires and anticipation. If armchairs invite a contemplative mood, rocking chairs revert one back to a childhood stage and a state of reverie,

Figure 39. FIRST PAGE: Saul Steinberg, *Untitled*, 1956 (*top right*), ink on paper, private collection; Saul Steinberg, *Untitled*, 1956 (*bottom left*), ink on paper, 11⅞ × 8⅞ in., Beinecke Rare Book and Manuscript Library, Yale University; Saul Steinberg, *Untitled*, 1956 (*bottom right*), ink on paper, 12 × 8½ in., Beinecke Rare Book and Manuscript Library, Yale University. All originally published in "Fumez-Vous?," *Femina–Illustration*, May 1956. SECOND PAGE: Saul Steinberg, *Untitled*, ca. 1956–58, ink on paper, private collection (originally published in the *New Yorker*, 18 January 1958). Republished in *The Labyrinth* (1960), [102–3]. (© The Saul Steinberg Foundation / Artists Rights Society [ARS], New York)

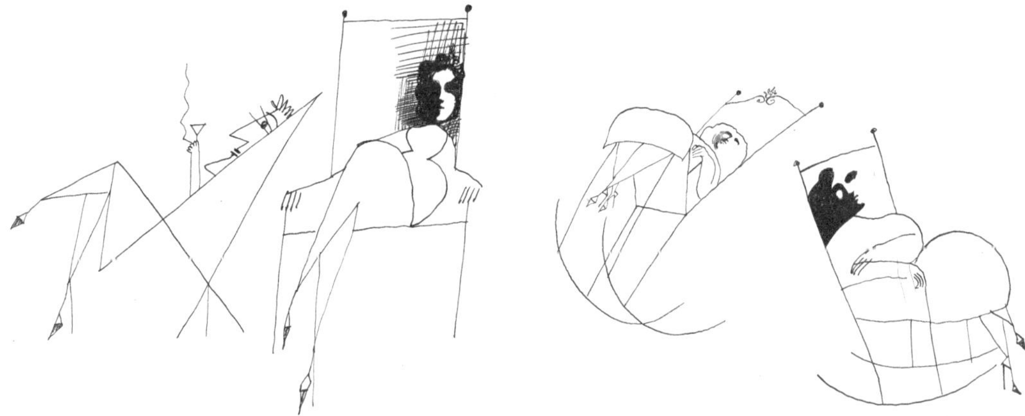

Figure 40. FIRST PAGE: Saul Steinberg, *Untitled,* 1956–57 (*left*), ink on paper, 14½ × 11½ in., Beinecke Rare Book and Manuscript Library, Yale University (originally published in the *New Yorker,* 26 January 1957); Saul Steinberg, *Untitled,* 1958 (*right*), ink on paper, 11½ × 5½ in., Beinecke Rare Book and Manuscript Library, Yale University (originally published in the *New Yorker,* 15 February 1958). SECOND PAGE: Saul Steinberg, *Untitled,* 1956–58 (*left*), ink on paper, 14½ × 11⅜ in., Beinecke Rare Book and Manuscript Library, Yale University (originally published in the *New Yorker,* 1 February 1958); Saul Steinberg, *Untitled,* 1956–58 (*right*), ink on paper, whereabouts unknown. Republished in *The Labyrinth* (1960), [106–7]. (© The Saul Steinberg Foundation / Artists Rights Society [ARS], New York)

between reality and imagination. Neither here nor there, voluptuous women recline and abandon themselves to ennui and daydreaming (fig. 40). A cultural marker of the American South, which Steinberg must have encountered in his extensive travels, rocking chairs recall the laziness of hot, humid summer afternoons that bring the time of endless tedium and endless dreaming. On the deep porch of an ornate wooden house, seven rocking chairs for children and adults are swaying empty, quiet witnesses of the domestic boredom and reveries descending at noontime.

A passionate observer of human postures and their larger cultural and social implications, Rudofsky traces the history of swings, hammocks, and rocking horses from classical Athens to Italy, modern India, and contemporary America.[27] He observes the therapeutic, soothing, and almost magical properties attributed to the act of swinging, concluding that it transforms, "by a kind of alchemy, motion into emotion."[28] This alchemical process, revealing how body and mind work together in resisting Cartesian dichotomies, comes across in Steinberg's drawings. Seated or swinging in a chair, the body fosters the gentle wanderings of the mind, which in turn transmogrifies the banality of boredom into the wonders of daydreaming.

FINITUDE AND INFINITY. Siegfried Kracauer's musings on *Langeweile* address boredom from the perspective of the modern split between work and leisure, a direct outcome of capitalism and the commodification of everyday life. Lacking the time to pursue *true* leisure as spiritual and intellectual growth, people invent the myth of a meaningful work ethic that at least allows them the dignity of some moral satisfaction.[29] To avoid the danger of mass boredom, whatever spare time is left outside work needs to be filled with distractions, which, at the beginning of the twentieth century, Kracauer identifies as advertisements, films, and radio. In this world of disruptions competing for one's attention, boredom turns into a form of resistance to facile diversions and the only way for individuals to regain control of their existence.[30] The alternative to mass entertainment, Kracauer proposes, is a full immersion into the wonderful banality of the everyday, into the close examination of the objects within one's reach. If one embraces the melancholy and sadness (*tristezza*) of a sunny afternoon spent indoors, one might surprisingly gain access—as de Maistre did—to rich ideas, projects, and a state of wonder: "Eventually, one becomes content to do nothing more than be with oneself, without knowing what one actually should be doing—sympathetically touched by the mere glass grasshopper on the tabletop that cannot jump because it is made of glass and by the silliness of a little cactus plant that thinks nothing of its own whimsicality. Frivolous, like these decorative creations, one harbors only an inner restlessness without a goal, a longing that is pushed aside, and a weariness with that which exists without really being."[31]

Only by deliberately exercising the patience "specific to legitimate boredom" can one experience a form of "bliss that is almost unearthly."[32] If entertainment is a collective pursuit, this state of daydreaming born from ennui can only be achieved in the solitude of one's domestic interior and the company of mundane objects.

If the front endpaper from *The Labyrinth,* an allegory of the American political and social system, sets the tone for the collection, the first drawing from *The New World* similarly establishes the premise of the entire book. A self-portrait of the artist with a thought bubble reading "Cogito, ergo Cartesius est," it is a critique of the supremacy of reason in the modern world, to which Steinberg proposes his alternative of "metaphysical drawings representing situations and problems."[33] Descartes is our own invention; he would not exist had we not assigned him his authority and entrusted him with our minds. (As Michael Haar writes in his analysis of Heidegger's concept of wonder, "the surprise and wonder of the Greeks has reversed itself to become Cartesian evidence and assurance."[34]) Another drawing from the collection shows a man (Descartes?) dreaming of himself. "I try not to make people reason," Steinberg muses, "but I try to make them jittery by giving them situations that are out of context and contain several interpretations."[35]

Dreaming and daydreaming resist the primacy of rational thinking as the only legitimate form of knowledge. Indeed, every creature, alive or inanimate, is entitled to dream. Born from the tedium of an ordinary existence or from a moment of identity crisis, these micro-reveries offer a glimpse into what it means to be in the world as a finite creature with hopes as well as limitations that both engender and inhibit one's dreams. Years after Steinberg publishes his drawings, the poet Joseph Brodsky, in a commencement address at Dartmouth College, will recommend to recent graduates that they fully admit and accept boredom in their lives, for it is a window onto time's infinity: "Boredom speaks the language of time, and it is to teach you the most valuable lesson in your life . . . the lesson of your utter insignificance."[36] Playing with "the voyage between perception and understanding," Steinberg's metaphysical drawings confront the viewer with their own finitude.[37]

With its eyes closed, a poor mutt has visions of prosperity, picturing himself in the garb of a gentleman, suit and fancy hat, fatter, nonchalant, and more confident. A fish dreams of another fish while catching or releasing one. On the next page, and at the opposite end of the evolution chain, a man dreams of a woman dreaming of him. The desire to possess is at the same time the desire to be possessed. Crossing and cutting each other, speech balloons and thought bubbles—what we say and what we think or dream—envelop the two women facing each other in a conversation, speaking elegantly written but intentionally illegible words (fig. 41).

Unremarkable and ordinary, they imagine themselves fancier and more sophisticated. Their—and our—existence unfolds between tall tales and dreams, facts and fictions, words and thoughts that give the measure of our human finitude. On the opposite page, a Parisian woman and a Sardinian one cannot escape the limitations of their places of origin, which are forever present in what they say and how they say it, one "speaking" a Paris street map, the other a map of her native island. Or perhaps they express the unspoken desire for a perpetual homecoming. A warning about the brevity of life and the way we waste it in useless pursuits: a man seated in a chair is

Figure 41. Saul Steinberg, *Untitled*, ca. 1960–63 (*left*), ink on paper, whereabouts unknown; Saul Steinberg, *Dialogue of Sardinia and Paris*, 1963 (*right*), ink, pencil, watercolor, crayon, and collage on paper, $25\frac{7}{8} \times 21$ in., private collection (drawing for *New Yorker* cover, 12 October 1963). Published in *The New World* (1965), 54–55. (© The Saul Steinberg Foundation / Artists Rights Society [ARS], New York)

looking at a television set, but instead of a screen he sees the words "Eheu! Fugaces Labuntur Anni" (Alas! The fleeting years slip by)—a belated admission, a thought, or a revelation.

In a form of visual object-oriented ontology *avant la lettre,* Steinberg's drawings give legitimacy and power to inanimate things. The viewing subject enters the magical state of tedium-turned-reverie, where objects come to life as characters in their own right. Like their human counterparts from comics and graphic novels, inanimate objects have their own dreams and desires, thinking and imagining through thought bubbles. These intimate aspirations and longings are kept hidden from humans behind the objects' conventional appearance.

No one is spared the existential crisis and the discontent with their own boundaries. Recalling Rudofsky's examination of swings, motions, and emotions, a banal rocking chair imagines itself a graceful rocking horse. A practical washing machine remembers being (or dreams of) an elaborate antique mechanism, ennobled by the patina of time, while a modern toaster replies, in wonder, "Wow!" (fig. 42).

Every creature aspires to become something else, better or different. A crooked circle would rather be a square, whereas a perfect circle dreams of a three-dimensional cone (fig. 43). A sturdy *E* imagines itself a slim, elegant, accented

Figure 42. Saul Steinberg, *Untitled,* 1961. Ink and magazine collage on paper, 14½ × 23 in. Beinecke Rare Book and Manuscript Library, Yale University. Originally published in the *New Yorker,* August 12, 1961. Republished in *The New World* (1965), 50. (© The Saul Steinberg Foundation / Artists Rights Society [ARS], New York)

French vowel (fig. 43). Loose thoughts become clearly outlined objects. Steinberg acknowledges his early fascination with the essence of the creative process: "My father was a box manufacturer. He had to pattern a piece of cardboard, which then was folded according to his instructions, and his machine made it into a box. Certainly, this was an influence for transforming a thought into an object."[38]

The hand that draws itself drawing, one of the many recurring themes in Steinberg's work, invites us to ponder not only the meaning of drawing qua drawing, as the artist suggests, but also the inherent tension between our limitations as finite beings and our longing to escape them. We create our own boundaries, our own windows into infinity, as Brodsky would put it, but from the most mundane reality, we also build castles in the air, daydreaming.

CLOSE AND FAR. The political establishment makes boredom operative at large

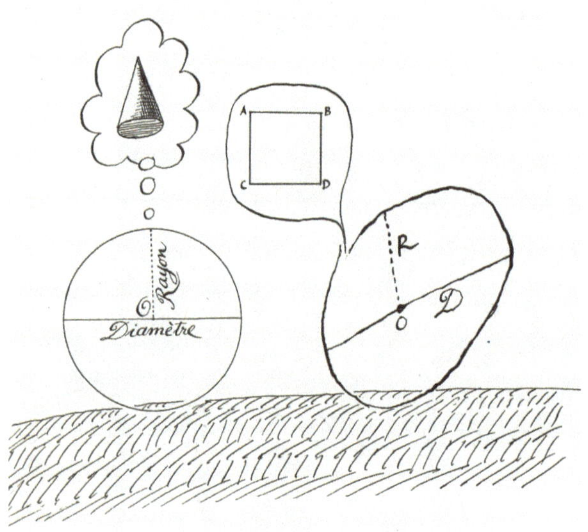

Figure 43. Saul Steinberg, *Untitled*, ca. 1961 (*left*), ink on paper, whereabouts unknown; Saul Steinberg, *Dream of E*, 1963 (*right*), ink and watercolor on paper, whereabouts unknown (drawing for *New Yorker* cover, 25 May 1963). Both republished in *The New World* (1965), 48, 147. (© The Saul Steinberg Foundation / Artists Rights Society [ARS], New York)

scales through standardization and repetition: urban and suburban developments, uniform housing projects indistinguishable from dull office buildings, mass media and advertising that enforce conformity and, subsequently, control. Trickling down into people's private lives, these norms affect how they conduct their everyday existence. Resistance, on the other hand, happens at a different level, the intimate scale of the body, the close-up examination of the world around, one's personal dreams—not unlike the way children experience and learn about the world through firsthand perception and bodily knowledge. Steinberg's drawings often have the deceiving appearance of children's representations of reality, an influence the artist himself recognizes (along with "Egyptian paintings, latrine drawings, primitive and insane art, Seurat . . . , embroidery, Paul Klee").[39] In addition to disguising the gravity of serious matters under an apparent innocence, the childlike drawing technique shows that the way children make sense of the world by mixing fact and fiction, reality and imagination, actuality and dream offers a productive path toward examining and resisting adult boredom. As Bachelard remarks in *The Poetics of Space*, "It is on the plane of the daydream and not on that of facts that childhood remains alive and poetically useful within us."[40] Closely examining and reinventing the world through childlike daydreaming is one of the techniques Steinberg proposes to resist the tedium of ordinary existence.

Bachelard elaborates on the relationship of the childhood house, memory, daydreaming, and boredom.[41] He recommends—counterintuitively—that it is salutary for a child "to learn to know the dialectics of exaggerated play and causeless, pure boredom."[42] (Bachelard's recommendations align with recent studies in child psychology showing evidence of the higher creativity levels achieved through children's unplanned and unprogrammed time.) The implicit argument is that the child's ennui is different from the adult's tedium, for it naturally and effortlessly veers into daydreaming. He recounts Alexander Dumas's childhood memory of crying out of sheer boredom. Without the grownup knowledge and vocabulary to explain the mood, the child does not know he is bored and simply states, "Dumas is crying because Dumas has tears."[43] Not the outcome of being alone but rather a deliberate choice to search for solitude, this mood is, unbeknownst to the child, a form of freedom. Of this story, Bachelard remarks, "But how well it exemplifies absolute boredom, the boredom that is not the equivalent of the absence of playmates. There are children who will leave a game to go and be bored in a corner of the garret. How often have I wished for the attic of my boredom when the complications of life made me lose the very germ of all freedom!"[44]

While Bachelard's position on boredom is influenced by the nineteenth-century French Romantic vision of ennui as a creative, aristocratic mood, his observations about how children take ownership of the world and their own emotions remain valid. Children learn (and adults remember) through sensorial experiences deriving from close-up interactions with things and objects. Without relying on Cartesian reason, Steinberg's drawings seize this form of embodied knowledge, offering a glimpse into tactics of inverting boredom and daydreaming. His particular drawing style invites multiple interpretations. Like the medieval jester whose status allows him to tell inconvenient truths, the childlike perspective disguises unpleasant facts under a deceivingly innocent outlook on the world. At the same time, it shows forms of knowledge that "shake prejudices" and make people "jittery."[45] Resistance to the tedium of conformity and norms is exercised at the personal and intimate scale of bodily experiences.

Closely related to childhood experiences, the theme of memory persists throughout Steinberg's work. A recurrent motif is the memory of his childhood home at number 4, Strada Palas, which he revisits consistently over the years.[46] The inversion of close and far, presence and absence, in the bodily construction of memories is one

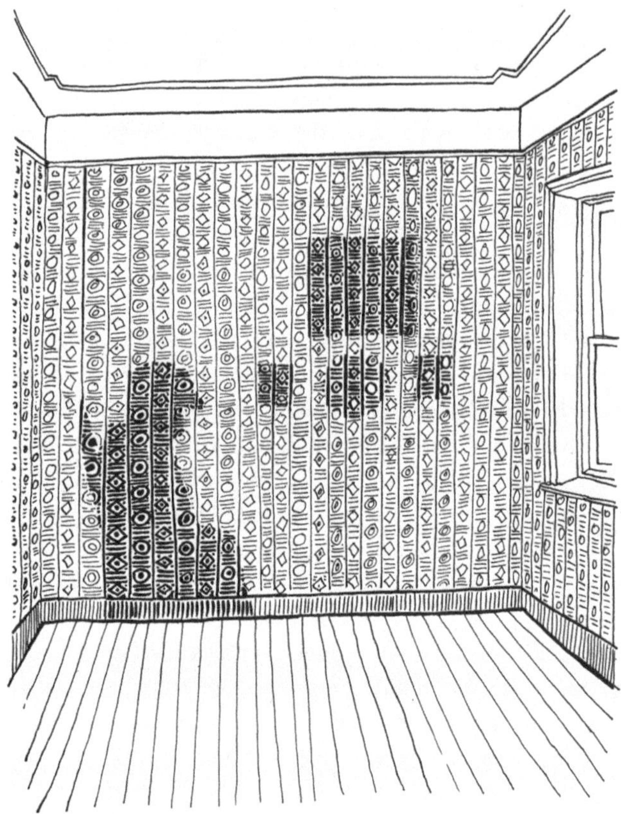

Figure 44. Saul Steinberg, *Untitled,* ca. 1947–49. Ink on paper. Whereabouts unknown. Originally published in *The Art of Living* (1949), 6. Republished in *Journal of the American Institute of Planners,* August 1961. (© The Saul Steinberg Foundation / Artists Rights Society [ARS], New York)

of Steinberg's main tactics for describing the nature of embodied spatial knowledge. A drawing published in the August 1961 issue of the *Journal of the American Institute of Planners* ties together the various threads connecting past and present, close and far, boredom and daydreaming.

The selection of drawings grouped under the title "Steinberg on the City" includes several pieces that examine not urban conditions, as the title suggests, but public and private interior spaces, typically stuffed with people, furniture, and objects. An anomaly in this context, a full-page drawing presents a one-point per-

Figure 45. Saul Steinberg, *Untitled*, 1960. Ink on paper. Whereabouts unknown. Published in *The Labyrinth* (1960), [238]. (© The Saul Steinberg Foundation / Artists Rights Society [ARS], New York)

spective of an empty room covered in patterned wallpaper with the outline of a window visible (fig. 44).

In stark contrast to Steinberg's other depictions of overcrowded interiors, this bare room dispenses with the abundance of details and information. The silhouette of a man seated in an armchair emerges from the faded wallpaper the way objects that have not changed positions in years leave marks on walls and floors. The absence inverts into a presence, like a ghost inhabiting space—not there, yet still present. In a strange twist, the silhouette is alive: a detail of the patterned wallpaper becomes its vigilant eye, forever open, looking out the window. Bored or daydreaming? The man in the armchair has spent too long being seated and waiting, so long that he left his bodily imprint on the wall while he was lost in reverie or the deepest ennui. But then, the open eye makes one wonder: are we looking at the presence of an absence or, perhaps, at a shadow cast on the wall, the shadow of someone we cannot see, someone outside the picture plane whose ephemeral presence is made visible through a shadow? Are we looking at the past or are we looking at the present? Time is built into the space and into the drawing itself, embedded in the repetitive gestures of depicting the minute details of the wallpaper and in the indelible marks left on the walls. The bare room is not empty; it contains the memories of its inhabitants, along with those of the inanimate objects that have populated it, but also the memories of the unseen yet palpable moods and atmospheres experienced in the space. Constructed through inversions and repetitions, the architectural representation of this room is simultaneously a riddle without answers and a contemplative act.

Riddles are everywhere. Just as boredom and daydreaming fold into each other through unexpected inversions, things turned upside down or inside out never stay the same. Walter Benjamin saw the inside of boredom as a "lustrous and colorful" silk within which we wrap ourselves when we dream, being at home "in the arabesque of its lining."[47] In his own way, through inversions, reflections, and shadows, Saul Steinberg stubbornly keeps looking in wonder for a sometimes twisted, often elusive, never straightforward truth (fig. 45).

Epilogue

INSIDE OUT

> *Boredom is a warm gray fabric lined on the inside with the most lustrous and colorful of silks. In this fabric we wrap ourselves when we dream.*
> —WALTER BENJAMIN, *The Arcades Project*

Boredom and time are intimately connected. At midcentury, the main protagonists of this book transform tedium into a critical and creative tool by embracing "the long while"—a perilous position in a world where efficiency means progress and time has a monetary value. Educated in the tradition of Modernism, Rudofsky, Venturi, Scott Brown, and Steinberg will soon become its unapologetic critics. Deployed differently by each of them, boredom presents a never-before-used conceptual frame to reimagine what architecture could become. A constant critic of the commodification of culture, Rudofsky turns toward a sensuous architecture, indifferent to ephemeral fashions—one that is attuned, instead, to the human body and its practices of inhabitation. Attempting to understand the effects of boredom on an urban scale, in his early projects Venturi introduces moments of stillness to overcome the tedium and alienation of modern public spaces. Scott Brown proposes the concept of deferred judgment as a way of creating space for critical reflection. Looking at the world with skepticism and serious humor, Steinberg transforms the boredom he finds in the environment into small acts of wonder.

The characters in this book all embraced and, at the same time, contested modern architecture, imagining new yet often divergent paths at a time when Modernism was at a stalemate. Their interest in the vernacular, for instance, takes different forms. Rudofsky looks at and idealizes traditional societies; Venturi and Scott Brown, criticizing him, embrace what they call the commercial vernacular; Steinberg delves with gusto into a particular vernacular shaped by urban habits and idiosyncrasies. The ripple effect of their midcentury explorations continues to inform and inspire decades later, past the postmodern moment with which they are involuntarily associated. Rudofsky's curatorial practices, which open up architecture to other practices and disciplines, are common today. Venturi's and Scott Brown's clever play with signs, symbols, colors, and flatness is taken to a different level by an architectural practice such as the Portuguese office Fala Atelier, which explicitly claims inspiration from Venturi's and Scott Brown's work. Steinberg's infinite ways of observing and analyzing the environment continue to be the subject of exhibitions all around the world, some of the most recent being *Saul Steinberg—Entre les lignes* (Centre Pompidou, Paris, 29 September 2021–28 February 2022) and *Saul Steinberg Milano New York* (Triennale di Milano, 15 October 2021–1 May 2022). Every generation seems to rediscover their work in unexpected ways. (Again, talking about them in present tense is also a form of paying homage to their legacy.)

Is there a place for boredom in today's architecture? The polemics between Ludwig Mies van der Rohe's "Less is more" and Robert Venturi's "Less is a bore" have not ended. In 2010, Danish architect Bjarke Ingels publishes *Yes Is More: An Archicomic on Architectural Evolution,* equal parts architectural manifesto, monograph of the Bjarke Ingles Group office, and promotional campaign. Situating himself within the genealogy of Mies van der Rohe, Robert Venturi, Philip Johnson, and Rem Koolhaas, Ingels uses the language of comic books, largely dismissing ideas that are not his as boring. Using the visual equivalents of brief tweets and text messages, he develops modes of representation that often reduce architectural concepts and experiences to one-dimensional formal diagrams.

Describing "The Mountain," one of the most celebrated projects of the firm, Ingels positions his idea as the antithesis of "a standard apartment slab next to a boring parking block."[1] In the "Infinity Loop," he changes the location of the rowhouses and apartments "from the boring Northeast to the sunny Southwest."[2] In "Urban Typography," the outcome of challenging the "depressingly boring" tower typology is the manipulation of exterior shapes into an oversized alphabet.[3] The outcome ("a giant town sign"[4]) is not fundamentally different from Venturi's proposal for a *bill-ding-board.* A hotel at the periphery stands out through its shape in plan (triangular, rather than rectangular) and façade treatment (suggesting the profiles of three Danish royal figures).[5] From certain angles, the building appears two-dimensional—indeed, a *decorated shed.* Seeing this project as the meeting point between Peter Zumthor and Andy Warhol, Ingels claims—ironically?—to have added a third category to Venturi's *duck* vs. *decorated shed,* which he calls *the princess:* "functional elements that independently seem benign constitute a collective iconic expression of another magnitude."[6] Unknowingly, or perhaps disinterested in more thoughtful pursuits, Ingels perpetuates the endless loop of the formal and rhetorical tedium he is trying so hard to overcome.

A different position is assumed by architects and designers such as Alberto Campo Baeza, John Pawson, Naoto Fukasawa, and Jasper Morrison, who—without specifically conceptualizing their work through the lens of boredom—cultivate and elevate the ordinary. The work of the Spanish architect Campo Baeza seems a stubborn exploration of white boxes. However, from their extreme asceticism and formal modesty emerges the exuberance of material and spatial experiences. Every project is a carefully constructed narrative joining inhabitants, landscape, and materials through the body of the house. The photographic essays that accompany each project systematically include the silhouette of a woman coming into or walking outside the frame. Techniques of visual storytelling articulate the embodied experience of the house.

Starting in 2006, Japanese designer Fukasawa and British designer Morrison have curated several shows under the title *Super Normal.*[7] Displayed on neutral white boxes, the objects exhibited come from different generations and periods but share the same quality: unsensational objects of the everyday, from paper clips and wastebaskets to grills and bicycles. Commenting on our contemporary assumption that "normal" has become the equivalent of "unstimulating" or "boring," the designers make an argument for ordinary objects that perform just as they should: naturally. Two intertwined ideas are at work in their approach: on the one hand, the absence of style and originality gives these objects the capacity to become invisible. On the other hand, by making them so "normal," they become extraordinary. The implicit statement is a critique of the interesting, of those seductive things that attract attention yet remain superficial, loud, and, ultimately, arbitrary. While the "authors" of the objects vary from completely anonymous makers to famous designers, the items all share the quality of being "a quietly seen unseen." Beauty and meaning, as Fukasawa and Morrison imagine them, are not inherent to forms or shapes but are found, instead, in the relationship between people, things, and time as lived presence.

British architect Pawson operates within the thick space where boredom folds into meditation. Usually described as Minimalist, his architecture recovers the unassuming qualities of mundane objects. His designs are built around the activities and habits of their inhabitants. From monastic life to food making, his work embraces the simple and elegant joys of the everyday. Not unlike Steinberg, who saw boredom as the engine of his creative pursuits, Pawson confesses: "I do sometimes think: 'What's next after architecture?' One's always trying to make the work better, but I don't know, maybe something different. I have a very low boredom threshold."[8] A professional photographer before becoming an architect, Pawson continues to work with photography as a means of conveying moods and atmospheres: "I like the everyday. I rarely photograph the spectacular view. Capturing small moments makes me feel less anxious about missing things."[9]

Boredom remains critical in contemporary architectural practice and discourse, as new technologies continually speed up the production and obsolescence of images. Quickly saturated with information presented in fleeting displays that are easy to produce, easy to delete, and easy to consume, as soon as our expectation of novelty and change fails to satisfy us, we fall back into the loop of boredom. In an environment inundated with visual stimuli, exercising our ability to experience boredom as a lengthy form of introspection might offer unforeseen avenues to engage with the immediate world.

This book was completed during a year when a global pandemic brought the world to a standstill. Between anxiety and boredom, prudence and recklessness, anger and defeat, despair and hope, laments for the past and dread of the future, we all learned to live one hour at a time. Time both dilated and contracted, leaving only the certainty of the bare present. Day after day, month after month, as the world was shrinking, the intensity of our feelings and emotions kept expanding. We were all trapped in the digital realm and accepted whatever fragments of reality were permitted. In a dissonant world where nothing made sense anymore, we suddenly confronted the infinity of time, becoming aware of our own finitude.

To close the loop, this book should end where it started, but, as Steinberg would have it, at a different altitude. Intrigued with the conundrum of boredom, Benjamin approaches it with what Rudofsky would call the "fingertip feeling," a form of embodied intuition and knowledge: "We are bored when we don't know what we are waiting for. That we do know, or think we know, is nearly always the expression of our superficiality or inattention."[10] So I ask, with Benjamin: Is it possible that "boredom is the threshold to great deeds"?[11]

NOTES

PROLOGUE

1. Studies in philosophy and aesthetics (Immanuel Kant, Arthur Schopenhauer, Søren Kierkegaard, Martin Heidegger, Sigfried Kracauer, Walter Benjamin, Giorgio Agamben, Lars Svendsen, Mark Kingwell), social sciences (Otto Fenichel, Orrin Klapp, Mihaly Csikszentmihalyi), critical theory and literary studies (Patricia Meyer Spacks, Elizabeth Goodstein, Reinhard Kuhn, Sianne Ngai), and visual arts (Jonathan Flatley, Tom McDonough, Julian Jason Haladyn) unpack boredom as an ontological concept of modernity. For the only book that has, to date, critically examined architecture and boredom, see Parreno, *Boredom, Architecture, and Spatial Experience.*

2. Heidegger, *Fundamental Concepts of Metaphysics,* 97–153.

3. Heidegger, *Fundamental Concepts of Metaphysics,* 135–53.

4. Haar, "Attunement and Thinking," 168–71; Held, "Fundamental Moods," 294–300.

5. Benjamin, *Arcades Project,* 107.

6. Burton, *Heaven and Hell,* 17.

7. *Oxford English Dictionary,* online edition, s.v. "boredom (n.)," last modified December 2022, https://www.oed.com; Göller, "Perpetual Style Change."

8. Göller, "Perpetual Style Change."

9. Le Corbusier, *Toward an Architecture,* 122.

10. Long, *Josef Frank,* 254.

11. Long, *Josef Frank,* 239 (letter from 2 March 1946).

12. Long, *Josef Frank,* 239 (letter from 2 March 1946), 240 (letter from 30 May 1946).

13. Bergquist and Michélsen, *Josef Frank: Spaces,* 102.

14. Bergquist and Michélsen, *Accidentism,* 20.

15. Bergquist and Michélsen, *Accidentism,* 24.

16. Mathews, *From Agit-Prop to Free Space,* 10, 68–71.

17. Mathews, *From Agit-Prop to Free Space,* 92.

18. Mathews, *From Agit-Prop to Free Space,* 88.

19. Chermayeff and Alexander, *Community and Privacy,* 73–79.

20. Chermayeff and Alexander, *Community and Privacy,* 77.

21. Chermayeff and Alexander, *Community and Privacy,* 79.

22. Heron, "Pathology of Boredom," 52.

23. Heron, "Pathology of Boredom," 52.

24. Rapoport and Kantor, "Complexity and Ambiguity," 211.

25. Rapoport and Kantor, "Complexity and Ambiguity," 214.

26. Mumford, "Case against Modern Architecture," 160.

27. Mumford, "Case against Modern Architecture," 160.

28. Mumford, "Case against Modern Architecture," 160.

29. Giedion, *Space, Time, and Architecture,* xxxii.

30. Giedion, *Space, Time, and Architecture,* xxxii–xxxiii.

31. Giedion, *Space, Time, and Architecture,* xxxiii.

32. Ginzburg, "Microhistory."

33. Ginzburg, "Morelli, Freud and Sherlock Holmes."

34. The concept of "thick description" was introduced by the philosopher Gilbert Ryle and developed further by the anthropologist Clifford Geertz in his book *The Interpretation of Cultures* (1973).

35. Haar, "Attunement and Thinking," 168.

PART I. WANDERING: BERNARD RUDOFSKY

1. Rudofsky, *Behind the Picture Window,* 5; Rudofsky, "Non ci vuole un nuovo modo," 7.

2. Rudofsky, *Behind the Picture Window,* 8.

1. GENEALOGIES OF BOREDOM

1. Rudofsky, *Behind the Picture Window,* 197.

2. Gumpert, *Anatomy of Happiness.* Rudofsky cites Gumpert in *Behind the Picture Window,* 193; his annotations can be found in *Now I Lay Me Down to Eat,* 38.

3. Gumpert, *Anatomy of Happiness,* 36.

4. Gumpert, *Anatomy of Happiness,* 38.

5. Gumpert, *Anatomy of Happiness,* 114–15.

6. Gumpert, *Anatomy of Happiness,* 115; Gumpert quoted in Rudofsky, *Behind the Picture Window,* 193.

7. Gumpert, *Anatomy of Happiness,* 261.

8. Tardieu, *Ennui.*

9. Rudofsky, Notebook B, box 1, Bernard Rudofsky Papers, ca. 1910–1987, Research Library, The Getty Research Institute, Los Angeles (hereafter cited as Rudofsky Papers).

10. Tardieu, *Ennui,* vii. See also Schopenhauer, *World as Will,* 312.

11. Tardieu, *Ennui,* 4.

12. Tardieu, *Ennui,* 260–61, 289.

13. Rudofsky, Notebook B, p. 935, Rudofsky Papers.

14. Kiven, "Philosophie"; Rudofsky, Notebook B, Rudofsky Papers.

15. Kiven, "Philosophie," 17.

16. Kiven, "Philosophie," 18.

17. Rudofsky, Notebook B, p. 940, Rudofsky Papers. Rudofsky's handwritten notebooks consistently use the abbreviation "A" for "American." See also Kiven, "Philosophie," 22.

18. Kiven, "Philosophie," 23.

19. Rudofsky, Notebook B, p. 942, Rudofsky Papers.

20. Rudofsky, *Behind the Picture Window,* 194.

21. Wim de Wit expands on this idea in his essay "Rudofsky's Discomfort."

22. Rudofsky, *Behind the Picture Window,* 199.

23. Rudofsky, *Behind the Picture Window,* 196.

24. Goodstein, *Experience without Qualities,* 99.

25. Gorer, *American People,* 143.

26. Kracauer, *Mass Ornament,* 332–33.

27. Heckscher, *Public Happiness,* 80–81.

28. Rudofsky, *Behind the Picture Window,* 196.

29. Marcuse, *One-Dimensional Man,* 5–9.

30. Adorno and Horkheimer, "The Culture Industry," in *Dialectic of Enlightenment,* 120–67.

31. Mumford, "The Challenge to Renewal," in *Conduct of Life,* 15.

32. Rudofsky, *Behind the Picture Window,* 199; Mumford, *Conduct of Life,* 15.

33. Mumford, *Conduct of Life,* 254.

34. Pieper, *Leisure.*

35. Pieper, *Leisure,* 59.

36. Russell, *In Praise of Idleness.*

37. De Grazia, *Of Time, Work and Leisure,* 19.

38. De Grazia, *Of Time, Work and Leisure,* 424.

39. De Grazia, *Of Time, Work and Leisure,* 303–12. Before de Grazia, Mumford has also

argued that the invention of the mechanical clock in medieval monasteries foreshadowed the Industrial Revolution. See Mumford, *Technics and Civilization,* 12–18.

40. De Grazia, *Of Time, Work and Leisure,* 327.
41. De Grazia, *Of Time, Work and Leisure,* 437.

2. CRITIQUES OF CONTEMPORARY TEDIUM

1. Rudofsky, *Behind the Picture Window,* 178.
2. Emmons, *Drawing Imagining Building,* 107.
3. Rudofsky, *Behind the Picture Window,* 10–11.
4. Rudofsky, *Behind the Picture Window,* 14–15.
5. Rudofsky, *Behind the Picture Window,* 15.
6. Rudofsky, *Behind the Picture Window,* 32.
7. Rudofsky, *Behind the Picture Window,* 13.
8. Rudofsky, *Now I Lay Me Down to Eat,* 13.
9. Rudofsky, *Behind the Picture Window,* 34–37.
10. Rudofsky, *Behind the Picture Window,* 117.
11. Scott, "Bernard Rudofsky."
12. Guarneri, *Bernard Rudofsky,* 100.
13. Rossi, *Bernard Rudofsky architetto,* 22.
14. De Wit, "Rudofsky's Discomfort," 120.
15. De Wit, "Rudofsky's Discomfort," 117.
16. De Wit, "Rudofsky's Discomfort," 98.
17. Rudofsky, *Now I Lay Me Down to Eat,* 14.
18. Rudofsky, *Behind the Picture Window,* 5.
19. Rudofsky, *Behind the Picture Window,* 6.
20. Rudofsky, *Behind the Picture Window,* 198.
21. Rudofsky, Notebook B, p. 941, Rudofsky Papers.
22. "Decorative Note," 100.
23. "The New House 194X," 69.
24. Mock, *Tomorrow's Small House,* 6.
25. Kennedy, *House,* 449.
26. Voight, "Modern Gardens," 118.
27. Feasley and Stuart, "Magazine Advertising," 21–23.
28. Isenstadt, *Modern American House,* 179–214.
29. Isenstadt, *Modern American House,* 203–9.
30. Nelson and Wright, *Tomorrow's House,* 169.
31. Boorstin, *Americans,* 345.

32. Kelly, *Expanding the American Dream,* 12.

33. Kelly, *Expanding the American Dream,* 12, 90–91.

34. Boorstin, *Image,* 259.

35. Kelly, *Expanding the American Dream,* 84.

36. This irony is seized upon by critics of suburbia such as Bernard Rudofsky, Daniel Boorstin, John Yeats, and William H. Whyte.

37. Whyte, *Organization Man,* 352.

38. Kelly, *Expanding the American Dream,* 84.

39. Whyte, *Organization Man,* 313; Riesman, *Lonely Crowd,* 80.

40. Whyte, *Organization Man,* 280.

41. Riesman, *Lonely Crowd,* 9.

42. Riesman, *Lonely Crowd,* v–vii.

43. Horkheimer and Adorno, *Dialectic of Enlightenment,* 149.

44. Rudofsky, *Behind the Picture Window,* 201.

45. Boorstin, *Image.*

46. Debord, *Society of the Spectacle,* 4.

47. Haladyn, *Boredom and Art,* 10–11.

48. Haladyn, *Boredom and Art,* 11.

49. Two more recent and detailed studies on the nature of midcentury privacy are Nelson, *Pursuing Privacy,* and Harju, "Picture Windows."

50. Boorstin, *Image,* 259.

51. Boorstin, *Americans,* 344–45.

52. Keats, *Crack in the Picture Window,* 21.

53. Keats, *Crack in the Picture Window,* 82.

54. Keats, *Crack in the Picture Window,* 143.

55. Friedan, *Feminine Mystique,* 20, 31, 243, 250–52, 283.

56. Friedan, *Feminine Mystique,* 246.

57. Kelly, *Expanding the American Dream,* 69–71.

58. Gorer, *American People,* 107. A student of Margaret Mead's, Geoffrey Gorer (1905–1985) was a British anthropologist who applied psychoanalytic techniques to anthropology. He moved to the United States in 1939.

59. Gorer, *American People,* 183. Rudofsky quotes directly from Gorer, in whose writings he finds the arguments that support his own in *Behind the Picture Window,* 195.

3. TACTICS OF RESISTING ENNUI

1. The topic appears in book chapters and various articles. In *Streets for People* (1969), Rudofsky dedicates an entire book to the theme of streets and street life. He also designs and

commercializes a line of footwear that exists to this day (Bernardo Sandals) and introduces original, if impractical, floors in the exhibitions he curates. All the houses he designs pay special attention to both interior and exterior ground planes.

2. Rudofsky, "Bread of Architecture," 28.

3. Rudofsky, "Before the Architects," 61. The same idea appears in *Behind the Picture Window,* 186.

4. Rudofsky, "L'architettura comincia con un pavimento" (my translation), 1.

5. Emmons, *Drawing Imagining Building,* 29.

6. Emmons, *Drawing Imagining Building,* 21–47.

7. Emmons, *Drawing Imagining Building,* 21–47.

8. Rudofsky, "Variazioni," 15 (my translation); Rudofsky, "Before the Architects," 61.

9. Rudofsky, "Variazioni," 14 (my translation). *Pianta* means a sole, a level in the house, and also a plant.

10. Rudofsky, "Variazioni," 15 (my translation).

11. Rudofsky, *Prodigious Builders,* 102–7.

12. Rudofsky, *Prodigious Builders,* 104.

13. Rudofsky, "Non ci vuole un nuovo modo."

14. Rudofsky, front matter, *Now I Lay Me Down to Eat.*

15. Rudofsky, "Non ci vuole un nuovo modo," 6.

16. Kierkegaard, *Either/Or,* 1:263, 291–92.

17. Rudofsky, "Giardino, stanza all'aperto," 71.

18. Rudofsky, "Non ci vuole un nuovo modo," 8.

19. Rossi, *Bernard Rudofsky architetto,* 76.

20. Rudofsky, *Prodigious Builders,* 106.

21. Rudofsky, *Prodigious Builders,* 107.

22. Rudofsky, "Non ci vuole un nuovo modo," 11.

23. Leatherbarrow, *Uncommon Ground,* 28.

24. Leatherbarrow, *Uncommon Ground,* 31.

25. Luigi Cosenza and Bernard Rudofsky, "Villa 'Oro,' Napoli—1934–1937," Luigi Cosenza Archives, accessed 29 April 2020, https://www.archivioluigicosenza.it/en/6/villa-oro-napoli-1934-1937.

26. Leatherbarrow, "Disorientation and Disclosure," 93.

27. Luigi Cosenza and Bernard Rudofsky, "Progetto per una villa, Positano—1937," Luigi Cosenza Archives, accessed 29 April 2020, https://www.archivioluigicosenza.it/en/18/progetto-per-una-villa-positano-1937.

28. Rudofsky, "Casa Guaruja," flat folder 7, Rudofsky Papers.

29. Rudofsky, "Three Patio Houses," 49.

30. Rudofsky, "Three Patio Houses," 49.

31. Rudofsky, "Three Patio Houses," 50–53.

32. Rudofsky, "Giardino, stanza all'aperto," 1–5, 70; "Notes on Patios"; "Three Patio Houses"; "The Conditioned Outdoor Room," in *Behind the Picture Window.*

33. Rudofsky, "Giardino, stanza all'aperto," 2–3 (my translation).

34. Williams, *Keywords,* 22.

35. Rudofsky, "Bread of Architecture."

36. Rudofsky, "Variazioni," 15 (my translation).

37. Zumthor, *Atmospheres,* 19.

38. Pallasmaa, "Space, Place, and Atmosphere," 19.

39. Pérez-Gómez, *Attunement,* 2.

40. *Oxford English Dictionary,* online edition, s.v. "atmosphere (n.)," last modified December 2022, https://www.oed.com.

41. Böhme, *Aesthetics of Atmospheres,* 2.

42. Among the most recent publications in the field are Bressani and Sprecher, "Atmospheres"; Pérez-Gómez, *Attunement;* Borch, *Architectural Atmospheres;* and Zumthor, *Atmospheres.*

43. Borch, "Introduction: Why Atmospheres?," in *Architectural Atmospheres;* Zumthor, *Atmospheres,* 11; Pérez-Gómez, *Attunement,* 1–13.

44. Böhme, "Atmosphere as the Subject Matter"; Böhme, *Aesthetics of Atmospheres;* Leatherbarrow, "Atmospheric Conditions," 96.

45. Rudofsky, *Now I Lay Me Down to Eat,* 12.

46. Forty, *Words and Buildings,* 174.

47. Forty, *Words and Buildings,* 174.

48. Forty, *Words and Buildings,* 174–87.

49. Rudofsky, "Giardino, stanza all'aperto," 4, 70.

50. Benjamin, *Arcades Project,* 155.

51. Rudofsky, *Prodigious Builders,* 246.

52. Rudofsky, *Now I Lay Me Down to Eat,* 13.

53. Rudofsky, *Prodigious Builders,* 12.

54. Rudofsky, *Prodigious Builders,* 103.

55. Rudofsky, *Now I Lay Me Down to Eat,* 12.

56. Rudofsky, *Prodigious Builders,* 103.

57. Rudofsky, "Three Patio Houses," 48–49.

58. Rudofsky, "Three Patio Houses," 49.

59. Rudofsky, "Three Patio Houses," 49.

60. Rudofsky, *Now I Lay Me Down to Eat,* 13.

61. Rudofsky, *Behind the Picture Window,* 198–99.

62. Plummer, *Experience of Architecture,* 7.

63. Plummer, *Experience of Architecture,* 21–24.

64. Felicity Scott observes that the installations for *Textiles, U.S.A.* built a dialogue between

the light fabrics floating in space and the floors in the indoor galleries, which were covered in men's suit fabric. See Scott, "Eye for Modern Architecture," 197.

65. Rudofsky, "Tokyo, on exhibition design," undated typed notes, p. 6, box 5, Lectures Japan, Rudofsky Papers.

66. Rudofsky, Casa Frontini blueprints, flat folder 5, Rudofsky Papers. See also Rudofsky, "Three Patio Houses," 50.

67. In their book *Tomorrow's House* (1945), George Nelson and Henry Wright dedicate a chapter to the family room, described as "the room without a name."

68. Rudofsky, "Bread of Architecture," 27.

69. Rudofsky, "Three Patio Houses," 60–61.

70. Rudofsky, undated typed notes of second lecture, p. 4, box 5, Lectures Japan. Original emphases.

PART II. WAITING: ROBERT VENTURI AND DENISE SCOTT BROWN

1. Robert Venturi, "Venturi MS. 'A,'" draft of *Complexity and Contradiction in Architecture,* p. 9, folder 225.RV.157, Venturi, Scott Brown Collection, Architectural Archives, University of Pennsylvania (hereafter cited as VSB Collection).

2. Venturi, "Venturi MS. 'A,'" VSB Collection.

3. Venturi, *Complexity and Contradiction in Architecture,* 1st ed., 6.

4. GENEALOGIES OF BOREDOM

1. Venturi, *Complexity and Contradiction in Architecture,* 2nd ed., 13.

2. Venturi, *Complexity and Contradiction in Architecture,* 2nd ed., 17.

3. McCoy, "Robert Venturi: To Whom It May Concern," 293–94.

4. Saffron, "Changing Skyline."

5. Venturi and Scott Brown, "Is and Ought," 38; Sebastian Jordana, "Interview: Robert Venturi and Denise Scott Brown, by Andrea Tamas," ArchDaily, 25 April 2011, accessed 29 August 2020, http://www.archdaily.com/130389/interview-robert-venturi-denise-scott-brown-by-andrea-tamas/. The interview with Tamas took place in August 2009.

6. Denise Scott Brown to Robert Venturi, box 70, folder 225.II.F.1037, VSB Collection; oral history interview with Robert Venturi by Peter Reed, 1 June–20 July 1991, pp. 1–2, Archives of American Art, Smithsonian Institution.

7. Undated document, folder 225.RV.113, VSB Collection.

8. Untitled catalogue, folder 225.II.F.1553, VSB Collection.

9. Scott Brown, "Learning from Africa," 26–29. In the interview by Andrea Tamas for ArchDaily, Scott Brown describes Vanna Venturi as "a socialist and a pacifist." To which Venturi adds, "And a Quaker."

10. Venturi, *Complexity and Contradiction in Architecture,* 2nd ed., 16.

11. Verplanck, "Silhouette and Quaker Identity," 48–49.

12. Attributed to George Fox, the founder of the Religious Society of Friends in the seventeenth century. See Garfinkel, "Letting in 'the World,'" 87n2.

13. Frederick B. Tolles suggests that "much of modern architecture . . . is only a reassertion of the principle which guided the builders of the early Quaker meeting houses." See Tolles, "'Of the Best Sort, but Plain,'" 74.

14. Venturi, "Upbringing among Quakers"; Venturi and Scott Brown, "Is and Ought."

15. Burt, "Philadelphia Plain and Fancy," 5.

16. Frost, *Quaker Family,* 217.

17. Garfinkel, "Letting in 'the World,'" 85.

18. Brinton, *Friends for 350 Years,* 165.

19. Brinton, *Friends for 350 Years,* 153–74, 103–4.

20. Garfinkel, "Letting in 'the World,'" 78.

21. Tolles, "'Of the Best Sort, but Plain'"; Fager, "Quaker Testimony"; Brinton, *Friends for 350 Years,* 163–74; Lavoie, "Reunified, Rebuilt."

22. Tolles, *Quakers and the Atlantic Culture,* 73; Frost, "From Plainness to Simplicity."

23. Boulding, *Friends Testimonies in the Home,* 25.

24. Frost, "From Plainness to Simplicity," 23.

25. Frost, "From Plainness to Simplicity," 37.

26. Philadelphia Yearly Meeting of the Religious Society of Friends, *Faith and Practice* (1961), 22–24, quoted in Fager, "Quaker Testimony," 4–5.

27. Philadelphia Yearly Meeting of the Religious Society of Friends, "Living in the World," accessed 29 August 2020, http://web.archive.org/web/20171019102233/http://www.pym.org/faith-and-practice/application-of-friends-testimonies/living-in-the-world/.

28. Frost, "From Plainness to Simplicity," 39.

29. Tolles, *Quakers and the Atlantic Culture,* 112.

30. Lavoie, "Reunified, Rebuilt," 22–29.

31. Lavoie, "Reunified, Rebuilt," 25.

32. Brinton, *Friends for 350 Years,* 166.

33. McCoubrey, "Three Paintings by Edward Hicks," 17.

34. Herman, "Eighteenth-Century Quaker Houses," 201.

35. Herman, "Eighteenth-Century Quaker Houses," 204.

36. Verplanck, "Silhouette and Quaker Identity," 52.

37. Verplanck, "Silhouette and Quaker Identity," 53–54.

38. The Episcopal Church, "What Makes Us Anglican? Hallmarks of the Episcopal Church," accessed 15 July 2020, https://www.episcopalchurch.org/library/article/what-makes-us-anglican.

39. Robert Venturi, "A Chapel for the Episcopal Academy, Merion, PA" (thesis), VSB Collection.

40. Two such examples are the Live Oak Meeting House in Houston, TX (2000), and the Chestnut Hill Friends Meeting House in Philadelphia, PA (2013).

41. Venturi, *Complexity and Contradiction in Architecture,* 2nd ed., 116.

42. Typed press release, 11 August 1966, 225.II.A, box 4, folder 6104.41, VSB Collection.

43. Alyssa Ribeiro, "Friends Neighborhood Guild," The Encyclopedia of Greater Philadelphia, accessed 5 November 2020, https://philadelphiaencyclopedia.org/archive/friends-neighborhood-guild/#13431.

44. "Senior Citizens Housing Loan Program: Policies and Guides for Project Design," Housing and Home Finance Agency, Community Facilities Administration, Washington, DC, 225.II.A, box 2, folder 6104.27, VSB Collection.

45. Typed press release, 11 August 1966, VSB Collection.

46. Venturi, *Complexity and Contradiction in Architecture,* 13.

47. Charlier et al., "Fatal Alchemy," 1402.

48. Lefebvre, *Toward an Architecture,* 22.

49. O'Neil, "Cynthia and the Moon," 1.

50. Charlier et al., "Fatal Alchemy."

51. *Oxford English Dictionary,* online edition, s.v. "antenna," https://www.oed.com.

52. "Ugly and ordinary" was Philip Johnson's description of Venturi and Scott Brown's entry for the 1967 Brighton Beach Housing Competition. See Fausch, "Context of Meaning," 214.

53. Venturi, *Complexity and Contradiction in Architecture,* 2nd ed., 116.

54. Vanel, "John Cage's Muzak-Plus," 109.

55. Notes on a construction drawing document, 225.II.A, box 2, folder 6104.08, VSB Collection.

56. Kracauer, *Mass Ornament,* 333.

57. Kracauer, *Mass Ornament,* 333.

5. CRITIQUES OF CONTEMPORARY TEDIUM

1. Venturi, *Complexity and Contradiction in Architecture,* 2nd ed., 16.

2. Venturi, *Complexity and Contradiction in Architecture,* 2nd ed., 16.

3. Alexander, *Notes on the Synthesis,* 4, and Heckscher, *Public Happiness,* 102. Venturi cites both sources in *Complexity and Contradiction in Architecture.*

4. Greg Lewis et al., "August Heckscher," Archives of the Century, accessed 20 January 2020, https://archivesofthecentury.org/myportfolio/august-heckscher-2/.

5. *These Are the Days* (1936); *A Pattern of Politics* (1947); *The Politics of Woodrow Wilson* (1956). In the 1950s and 1960s, Heckscher publishes extensively in journals such as *ALA Bulletin, Art Education, Music Educators Journal, Challenge,* and *The Bulletin of the Museum of Modern Art* on topics that range from libraries and the nation's cultural life to government and the arts.

6. Heckscher, *Public Happiness,* v. Subsequent references to this book will appear parenthetically in the text.

7. Venturi, *Complexity and Contradiction in Architecture,* 2nd ed., 124.

8. Venturi, *Complexity and Contradiction in Architecture,* 2nd ed., 126.

9. "Boredom Spells Trouble on the Line," *Life,* 1 September 1972, 30–38.

10. Venturi, *Complexity and Contradiction in Architecture,* 2nd ed., 130.

11. Venturi, *Complexity and Contradiction in Architecture,* 2nd ed., 129.

12. Krauss, "Grids," 50–52.

13. Krauss, "Grids," 57–63.

14. Venturi, *Complexity and Contradiction in Architecture,* 2nd ed., 130.

15. Venturi, *Complexity and Contradiction in Architecture,* 2nd ed., 132.

16. Venturi, *Complexity and Contradiction in Architecture,* 2nd ed., 90.

17. Venturi, *Complexity and Contradiction in Architecture,* 2nd ed., 130.

18. Venturi, *Complexity and Contradiction in Architecture,* 2nd ed., 132.

19. Venturi, "ARCH 512 Lecture XI: Composition. Proportion. Unity.," 6 April 1965, box 225.R.187, VSB Collection.

20. Venturi, *Complexity and Contradiction in Architecture,* 2nd ed., 130–31.

21. Venturi, *Complexity and Contradiction in Architecture,* 2nd ed., 130.

6. TACTICS OF RESISTING ENNUI

1. Venturi, Scott Brown, and Izenour, *Learning from Las Vegas,* 2nd ed., 87–93.

2. Scully, *Modern Architecture,* 263.

3. Finkelpearl, "Contemporary Confrontations."

4. Finkelpearl, "Contemporary Confrontations," 204.

5. Harries, *Ethical Function of Architecture,* 8.

6. Epstein and Klyukanov, "Interesting," 87.

7. Harries, *Ethical Function of Architecture,* 6–10.

8. Ngai, "Merely Interesting."

9. *Oxford English Dictionary,* online edition, s.v. "interest (n.)," last modified July 2022, and s.v. "interesting (adj.)," https://www.oed.com.

10. *Oxford English Dictionary,* online edition, s.v. "boredom (n.)."

11. Ngai, "Merely Interesting," 789.

12. Williams, *Keywords,* 22.

13. Meyer Spacks, *Boredom,* 23.

14. Kant, *Anthropology,* 130.

15. Kierkegaard, *Either/Or.*

16. Harries, *Between Nihilism and Faith,* 96–97.

17. Kierkegaard, *Either/Or,* 1:292.

18. Schlegel, *On the Study of Greek Poetry,* 21.

19. Schopenhauer, *World as Will,* 203, 314.

20. Heidegger, *What Is Called Thinking?,* 5.

21. Sontag, *Against Interpretation,* 101; Agamben, *Stanzas,* 5.

22. Plato, *Theaetetus* 155c–d (trans. Jowett).

23. Svendsen, *Philosophy of Boredom,* 143–50.

24. Deleuze and Guattari, *What Is Philosophy?,* 82.

25. Deleuze and Guattari, *What Is Philosophy?,* 82.

26. Judd, "Specific Objects"; Ruscha and Warhol quoted in Ngai, "Merely Interesting," 777 and 803; Kosuth, "Introductory Note."

27. Raposa, "Boredom," 77–82.

28. Ngai, "Merely Interesting," 778.

29. Ngai, "Merely Interesting," 813–14.

30. Venturi, Scott Brown, and Izenour, *Learning from Las Vegas,* 2nd ed., 101.

31. Letter from Denise Scott Brown to Robert Venturi, 12 July 1963, box 70, folder 225. II.F.1037, VSB Collection.

32. Scott Brown to Venturi, 12 July 1963, VSB Collection. Original emphasis.

33. Scott Brown, "On Pop Art," 186.

34. Scott Brown, "On Pop Art," 186.

35. Scott Brown, "Teaching Architectural History," 30.

36. Scott Brown to Venturi, 12 July 1963, p. 8, VSB Collection.

37. Scott Brown, "Planning the Powder Room."

38. Scott Brown, "Natal Plans."

39. Letter from Scott Brown to Erwin Gutkind, May 1960, p. 25, box 69, folder 225.II.F.1000, VSB Collection.

40. This 1960 letter informs the structure of Scott Brown's subsequent 1965 article, "The Meaningful City," where she revisits and refines the same arguments. See Scott Brown to Gutkind, May 1960, VSB Collection.

41. Scott Brown to Venturi, 12 July 1963, p. 8, VSB Collection.

42. Scott Brown, "Function of a Table."

43. Scott Brown to Gutkind, May 1960, VSB Collection.

44. Scott Brown, "Education in the 1970s."

45. Scott Brown, "On Pop Art," 184.

46. Scott Brown, "On Pop Art," 186.

47. Scott Brown to Venturi, 12 July 1963, VSB Collection.

48. Scott Brown, "Little Magazines," 223.

49. Scott Brown to Gutkind, May 1960, VSB Collection.

50. Scott Brown, "Form, Design and the City," 299.

51. Scott Brown, "Will Salvation Spoil," 71.

52. Russell and Vinsel, "Hail the Maintainers."

PART III. WONDERING: SAUL STEINBERG

1. See Chapsal, "Labyrinthe."

2. Gertrude Benson, "Painter Calls Art 'Silent Language,'" unidentified newspaper clipping, ca. 1956, Saul Steinberg Papers, Yale Collection of American Literature, Beinecke Rare Book and Manuscript Library, Yale University (hereafter Steinberg Papers); copy courtesy of The Saul Steinberg Foundation.

3. Girard and Laurie, *Exhibition for Modern Living.*

4. Reichek, "Steinberg on the City"; separatum not paginated.

5. Vanden Heuvel, "Straight from the Hand," 59.

7. GENEALOGIES OF BOREDOM

1. Hunter, *American Art,* 372.

2. Hunter, *American Art,* 372.

3. Sontag, "The Aesthetics of Silence," in *Styles of Radical Will,* 3–34.

4. Cage, *Silence,* 93.

5. Recent scholarship has examined the concept and relevance of boredom in midcentury art: see Flatley, *Like Andy Warhol;* McDonough, *Boredom;* Ngai, *Our Aesthetic Categories.*

6. Interview with Alberto Moravia republished in Moravia, *La Noia,* 303 (my translation).

7. Chtcheglov, "Formulary," 1–4.

8. Berryman, "Dream Song 14," in *Seventy-Seven Dream Songs,* 16.

9. Rose, "ABC Art," 57–61; Kramer, "Art of Boredom?"; Lippard, "After a Fashion," 625; Sontag, *Against Interpretation,* 303.

10. See the work of Frances Colpitt, Richard Lind, and Derek Matravers.

11. Flatley, *Like Andy Warhol,* 138–39.

12. Steinberg and Buzzi, *Reflections and Shadows,* 42.

13. Steinberg, "Chronology," 235.

14. Saul Steinberg, transcript of interview by Raymond Rosenthal and Moishe Ducovny for the American Jewish Committee Oral History Library, July–August 1960, Oral History Box 74, no. 4, New York Public Library, courtesy of The Saul Steinberg Foundation.

15. Letter from Saul Steinberg to Aldo Buzzi, New York, 16 March 1987, in Steinberg, *Lettere a Aldo Buzzi,* 158 (my translation).

16. Saul Steinberg, interview with Adam Gopnik, February 1986, Steinberg Papers.

17. For a detailed account of Steinberg's immigration ordeals, see Lalli, "Descent from Paradise."

18. Steinberg quoted in vanden Heuvel, "Straight from the Hand," 64.

19. Letter from Saul Steinberg to Aldo Buzzi, New York, 25 September 1972, in Steinberg, *Lettere a Aldo Buzzi,* 81.

20. Letter from Saul Steinberg to Aldo Buzzi, New York, 30 December 1957, in Steinberg, *Lettere a Aldo Buzzi,* 48.

21. Buzzi, "L'architetto Steinberg," 20–21 (my translation).

22. Blake, "Cartoon Critic," 108.

23. Frascari, "Horizons at the Drafting Table," 180–81.

24. Frascari, "Horizons at the Drafting Table," 183–84.

25. Rodman, *Conversations with Artists,* 181–85.

26. "Chronology," 1960, The Saul Steinberg Foundation, https://saulsteinbergfoundation.org/chronology/1960-yr/, accessed 5 August 2020. A portrait of Le Corbusier drawn by Steinberg on graph paper is published in the 3 May 1947 issue of the *New Yorker.*

27. Letter from Le Corbusier to Saul Steinberg, 1956, in Cohen, *Le Corbusier Le Grand,* 402–3. Francesca Pellicciari discusses Steinberg and Le Corbusier in "Saul Steinberg."

28. Bourdieu, *Outline of a Theory of Practice,* 89.

29. Bourdieu, *Outline of a Theory of Practice,* 95.

30. Saul Steinberg, "Notes about Dreams," formerly Uncat. Mss. 126, box 75, folder "Notes about Dreams," Steinberg Papers.

31. Steinberg, "Notes about Dreams," box 110, folders 2317–18, Steinberg Papers.

32. Steinberg, "Notes about Dreams," box 110, folders 2317–18, Steinberg Papers. Original strikethrough.

33. Saul Steinberg, transcript of remarks to Rolf Karrer-Kharberg for his film *Das Maskenhafte an Saul Steinberg: Bericht aus der Welt eines großen Zeichners* (The masked guises of Saul Steinberg: Report from the world of a great draftsman), Süddeutsche Rundfunk, 1968, box 128, folder 2446, Steinberg Papers, courtesy of The Saul Steinberg Foundation.

34. Steinberg, remarks to Karrer-Kharberg. Later in life, Steinberg will return to these ideas. See also Hughes, "World of Steinberg."

35. Formerly Uncat. Mss. 126, box/vol. 89, Steinberg Papers.

36. Formerly Uncat. Mss. 126, box/vol. 89, Steinberg Papers.

37. Teyssot, *Topology of Everyday Constellations,* 8.

38. Formerly Uncat. Mss. 126, box/vol. 89, Steinberg Papers; now box 121, folder 2356 (my translation).

39. Ciudad Trujillo journal, Steinberg Papers.

40. Ciudad Trujillo journal, Steinberg Papers.

41. Ciudad Trujillo journal, Steinberg Papers.

8. CRITIQUES OF CONTEMPORARY TEDIUM

1. Blake, "Cartoon Critic"; Lueder, "Saul Steinberg's 'Graph Paper Architecture,'" 209.

2. Preface to "Steinberg on the City," special issue, *Journal of the American Institute of Planners.*

3. Latour, "Why Has Critique," 231. Original emphasis.

4. Latour, "Why Has Critique," 237.

5. Latour, "Why Has Critique," 246.

6. Johnson, "Preface," *Built in USA: Post-war Architecture,* 9.

7. Steinberg, "Built in U.S.A.," 16.

8. Steinberg, "Built in U.S.A.," 19.

9. Letter from Saul Steinberg to Aldo Buzzi, 21 November 1960, in Steinberg, *Lettere a Aldo Buzzi.*

10. Chapsal, "Labyrinthe," 29.

11. Steinberg to Buzzi, 21 November 1960; Steinberg, remarks to Karrer-Kharberg.

12. Steinberg, remarks to Karrer-Kharberg.

13. Rodman, *Conversations with Artists,* 182.

14. Flaiano, *Solitudine del satiro,* 207 (my translation).

15. Steinberg, interview by Rosenthal and Ducovny, transcript, New York Public Library.

16. Kierkegaard, *Either/Or,* 1:258.

17. Kierkegaard, *Either/Or,* 1:258.

18. Rodman, *Conversations with Artists.*

19. Heckscher, *Public Happiness,* 254.

20. Venturi, *Complexity and Contradiction in Architecture,* 2nd ed., 54.

21. Baudrillard, *America,* 53.

22. Baudrillard, *America,* 27.

23. Baudrillard, *America,* 84.

24. In a 1968 interview, Steinberg defines the condition of the artist as that of a runaway "from their Main Street, from the family, from the culture, from the society that produced them." See Saul Steinberg, interview by Adrienne Clarkson, "Take 30 in New York," Canadian Broadcasting Company, January 1968, transcript, courtesy of The Saul Steinberg Foundation.

25. Letter from Saul Steinberg to Aldo Buzzi, 30 July 1958, in Steinberg, *Lettere a Aldo Buzzi.*

26. Saul Steinberg, unpublished interview by Mark Rosenthal, 1995, transcript courtesy of The Saul Steinberg Foundation.

27. For an in-depth examination of Steinberg's use of graph paper, see Lueder, "Saul Steinberg's 'Graph Paper Architecture.'"

28. Norman, "Saul Steinberg, MoMA," 11.

29. Steinberg's notes on the drawing "Types of Architecture," reproduced in *The Line / Types of Architecture / Shores of the Mediterranean / Cities of Italy,* n.p. "Types of Architecture" is a section from Steinberg's contribution to the Children's Labyrinth for the Tenth Milan Triennale (1954).

30. Steinberg, "Our False-Front Culture," 47.
31. Steinberg, "Our False-Front Culture," 48.
32. Mumford, "Case against Modern Architecture."
33. Mumford, "Case against Modern Architecture," 158, 161.
34. Steinberg, "Our False-Front Culture," 48.
35. Rykwert, *Judicious Eye.*
36. Rykwert, *Judicious Eye,* 8.
37. Nagourney, "Rubber Stamp Art," 80.
38. Nagourney, "Rubber Stamp Art," 80, 102.
39. Glueck, "Artist Speaks," 112.
40. See the website of The Saul Steinberg Foundation, https://saulsteinbergfoundation.org/search-artwork/?media=rubber-stamps, accessed 27 August 2020.
41. Letter from Saul Steinberg to Aldo Buzzi, 11 March 1980, in Steinberg, *Lettere a Aldo Buzzi.*

9. TACTICS OF RESISTING ENNUI

1. Vanden Heuvel, "Straight from the Hand," 59.
2. Letter from Saul Steinberg to Aldo Buzzi, New York, 9 April 1965, in Steinberg, *Lettere a Aldo Buzzi.*
3. Vanden Heuvel, "Straight from the Hand."
4. Maranda, "Riddles and Riddling," 127.
5. Aristotle quoted in Georges and Dundes, "Toward a Structural Definition," 111.
6. Georges and Dundes, "Toward a Structural Definition," 113.
7. Maranda, "Riddles and Riddling," 131.
8. Schopenhauer, *World as Will,* 260; Kierkegaard, *Either/Or,* 285 (1:257); Heidegger, *Fundamental Concepts of Metaphysics;* Benjamin, *Illuminations,* 91; Kracauer, *Mass Ornament,* 334.
9. *Oxford English Dictionary,* online edition, s.v. "daydream (n.)," last modified July 2022, https://www.oed.com.
10. Another definition of "daydream" is "to imagine oneself in another place, period, etc., as part of a daydream." See *Oxford English Dictionary,* online edition, s.v. "daydream (v.)."
11. See also Mihalache, "Three Ghosts and a Baldachin."
12. Vanden Heuvel, "Straight from the Hand," 59.
13. *Oxford English Dictionary,* online edition, s.v. "acedia (n.)," last modified July 2022, https://www.oed.com.
14. Early Christian theologians such as Evagrius of Pontus and Father John Cassian describe acedia as an evil or a demon.
15. Kuhn quoted in Spector, "Reinhard Kuhn."

16. De Maistre, *Journey around My Room,* 4.
17. Kracauer, *Mass Ornament,* 334.
18. Bachelard, *Poetics of Space,* 16.
19. Bachelard, *Poetics of Space,* 17.
20. De Maistre, *Journey around My Room,* 7–8.
21. De Maistre, *Journey around My Room,* 8–9.
22. Teyssot, "Boredom and Bedroom," 48.
23. Teyssot, "Boredom and Bedroom," 49.
24. Rykwert, "Sitting Position," 23–32.
25. Rudofsky, *Behind the Picture Window,* 69.
26. Rudofsky, *Behind the Picture Window,* 65.
27. Rudofsky, *Behind the Picture Window,* 71–75.
28. Rudofsky, *Behind the Picture Window,* 72.
29. Kracauer, *Mass Ornament,* 331–34.
30. Kracauer, *Mass Ornament,* 334.
31. Kracauer, *Mass Ornament,* 334.
32. Kracauer, *Mass Ornament,* 334.
33. Vanden Heuvel, "Straight from the Hand," 59.
34. Haar, "Attunement and Thinking," 169.
35. Vanden Heuvel, "Straight from the Hand," 66.
36. Brodsky, *On Grief and Reason,* 109.
37. Vanden Heuvel, "Straight from the Hand," 66.
38. Vanden Heuvel, "Straight from the Hand," 64.
39. Vanden Heuvel, "Straight from the Hand," 64.
40. Bachelard, *Poetics of Space,* 16.
41. Bachelard, *Poetics of Space,* 12–17.
42. Bachelard, *Poetics of Space,* 16.
43. Bachelard, *Poetics of Space,* 16.
44. Bachelard, *Poetics of Space,* 17.
45. Vanden Heuvel, "Straight from the Hand," 66.
46. See Mihalache, "Saul Steinberg's Stories of *Dor.*"
47. Benjamin, *Arcades Project,* 106.

EPILOGUE

1. Ingels, *Yes Is More,* 79.
2. Ingels, *Yes Is More,* 96.
3. Ingels, *Yes Is More,* 195.
4. Ingels, *Yes Is More,* 195.

5. Ingels, *Yes Is More,* 340.
6. Ingels, *Yes Is More,* 341–43.
7. Fukasawa and Morrison, *Super Normal.*
8. Sunshine, "Eye for Detail."
9. Sunshine, "Eye for Detail."
10. Benjamin, *Arcades Project,* 105.
11. Benjamin, *Arcades Project,* 105.

BIBLIOGRAPHY

ARCHIVAL SOURCES

Archives of American Art, Smithsonian Institution, Washington, DC.

The Bernard Rudofsky Papers, ca. 1910–1987. Research Library, The Getty Research Institute, Los Angeles, CA.

The Saul Steinberg Foundation, New York.

Saul Steinberg Papers. Yale Collection of American Literature, Beinecke Rare Book and Manuscript Library, Yale University, New Haven, CT.

Venturi, Scott Brown Collection. The Architectural Archives, University of Pennsylvania, Philadelphia, PA.

OTHER SOURCES

Adorno, Theodor W., and Max Horkheimer. *Dialectic of Enlightenment.* Translated by John Cumming. New York: Continuum, 1991.

Agamben, Giorgio. *The Man without Content.* Stanford, CA: Stanford University Press, 1999.

———. *Stanzas: Word and Phantasm in Western Culture.* Minneapolis: University of Minnesota Press, 1993.

Alexander, Christopher. *Notes on the Synthesis of Form.* Cambridge, MA: Harvard University Press, 1964.

Architekturzentrum Wien, ed., in association with The Getty Research Institute. *Lessons from Bernard Rudofsky: Life as a Voyage.* Basel: Birkhäuser, 2007. Exhibition catalog.

Bachelard, Gaston. *The Poetics of Space.* Translated by Maria Jolas. Boston: Beacon Press, 1994.
Baudrillard, Jean. *America.* Translated by Chris Turner. London: Verso, 1989.
Benjamin, Walter. *The Arcades Project.* Cambridge, MA: Harvard University Press, 2003.
———. *Illuminations.* Edited by Hannah Arendt. Translated by Harry Zohn. New York: Schocken Books, 1986.
———. *Reflections: Essays, Aphorisms, and Autobiographical Writings.* Edited and translated by Peter Demetz. New York: Harcourt Brace Jovanovich, 1978.
Bergquist, Mikael, and Olof Michélsen. *Accidentism: Josef Frank.* Basel: Birkhäuser, 2005.
———. *Josef Frank: Spaces.* Translated by Andy Nettleton. Zurich: Park Books, 2016.
Berryman, John. *Seventy-Seven Dream Songs.* New York: Farrar, 1964.
Blake, Peter. "Cartoon Critic." *Architecture,* no. 88 (September 1999): 106–9.
Böhme, Gernot. *The Aesthetics of Atmospheres.* London: Routledge, 2017.
———. "Atmosphere as the Subject Matter of Architecture." *Thesis Eleven,* no. 36 (2002): 113–26.
Boorstin, Daniel J. *The Americans: The Democratic Experience.* New York: Random House, 1973.
———. *The Image: Or, What Happened to the American Dream.* New York: Atheneum, 1962.
Borch, Christian, ed. *Architectural Atmospheres: On the Experience and Politics of Architecture.* Basel: Birkhäuser, 2014.
Boulding, Elise. *Friends Testimonies in the Home.* Philadelphia: Religious Education Committee, Friends General Conference, 1953.
Bourdieu, Pierre. *Outline of a Theory of Practice.* Translated by Richard Nice. Cambridge: Cambridge University Press, 1977.
Bressani, Martin, and Aaron Sprecher. "Atmospheres." *Journal of Architectural Education* 73, no. 1 (2019): 2–4.
Brinton, Howard H. *Friends for 350 Years.* 11th ed. Wallingford, PA: Pendle Hill Publications, 2002.
Brodsky, Joseph. *On Grief and Reason.* New York: Farrar, Straus and Giroux, 1995.
Built in USA: Post-war Architecture. Edited by Henry-Russell Hitchcock and Arthur Drexler. New York: Museum of Modern Art, 1952. Exhibition catalog.
Burt, Nathaniel. "Philadelphia Plain and Fancy." *Horizon* 5, no. 6 (1963): 4–15.
Burton, Neel. *Heaven and Hell: The Psychology of Emotions.* Exeter: Acheron Press, 2015.
Buzzi, Aldo. "L'architetto Steinberg." *Domus,* no. 214 (October 1946): 19–22.
Cage, John. *Silence: Lectures and Writings.* Middletown, CT: Wesleyan University Press, 1961.
Chapsal, Madeleine. "Le labyrinthe, c'est la spiral troublée: Entretien avec Steinberg." *La quinzaine littéraire,* 15 April 1966, 28–29.
Charlier, Philippe, Joël Poupon, Isabelle Huynh-Charlier, Jean-François Saliège, Dominique Favier, Christine Keyser, and Bertrand Ludes. "Fatal Alchemy." *BMJ: British Medical Journal* 339, no. 7735 (2009): 1402–3.

Chermayeff, Serge, and Christopher Alexander. *Community and Privacy: Toward a New Architecture of Humanism.* Garden City, NY: Doubleday, 1963.

Chtcheglov, Ivan. "Formulary for a New Urbanism." 1953. In *Situationist International Anthology,* translated and edited by Ken Knabb, 1–8. Berkeley, CA: Bureau of Public Secrets, 1981.

Cohen, Jean-Louis. *Le Corbusier Le Grand.* Paris: Phaidon, 2014.

Colpitt, Frances. "The Issue of Boredom: Is It Interesting?" *Journal of Aesthetics and Art Criticism* 43, no. 4 (1985): 359–65.

Debord, Guy. *The Society of the Spectacle.* Translated by Donald Nicholson-Smith. New York: Zone Books, 1995.

"Decorative Note." *Decorator and Furnisher* 25, no. 3 (1984): 100.

de Grazia, Sebastian. *Of Time, Work and Leisure.* New York: Twentieth Century Fund, 1962.

Deleuze, Gilles, and Felix Guattari. *What Is Philosophy?* Translated by Hugh Tomlinson and Graham Burchell. London: Verso, 2015.

de Maistre, Xavier. *A Journey around My Room and A Nocturnal Expedition around My Room.* Translated by Andrew Brown. Richmond, UK: Alma Classics, 2013.

de Wit, Wim. "Rudofsky's Discomfort: A Passion for Travel." In *Lessons from Bernard Rudofsky: Life as a Voyage,* edited by Architekturzentrum Wien in association with The Getty Research Institute, 98–125. Basel: Birkhäuser, 2007.

Dobriner, William M. *Class in Suburbia.* Englewood Cliffs, NJ: Prentice-Hall, 1963.

Emmons, Paul. *Drawing Imagining Building: Embodiment in Architectural Design Practices.* New York: Routledge, 2019.

Epstein, Mikhail, and Igor Klyukanov. "The Interesting." *Qui Parle* 18, no. 1 (2009): 75–88.

Fager, Charles E. "The Quaker Testimony of Simplicity." *Quaker Religious Thought* 14, no. 1 (1972): 2–30.

Fausch, Deborah. "The Context of Meaning Is Everyday Life: Venturi and Scott Brown's Theories of Architecture and Urbanism." PhD diss., Princeton University, 1999.

Feasley, Florence G., and Elnora W. Stuart. "Magazine Advertising Layout and Design: 1932–1982." *Journal of Advertising* 16, no. 2 (1987): 20–25.

Finkelpearl, Philip J. "Contemporary Confrontations." *Journal of the Society of Architectural Historians* 38, no. 2 (1979): 203–5.

Flaiano, Ennio. *La solitudine del satiro.* Milan: Adelphi, 1996.

Flatley, Jonathan. *Like Andy Warhol.* Chicago: University of Chicago Press, 2017.

Forty, Adrian. *Words and Buildings: A Vocabulary of Modern Architecture.* London: Thames & Hudson, 2000.

Frascari, Marco. "Horizons at the Drafting Table." *Chora,* 2007, 179–200.

Friedan, Betty. *The Feminine Mystique.* New York: W. W. Norton, 1963.

Frost, J. William. "From Plainness to Simplicity: Changing Quaker Ideals for Material Culture." In *Quaker Aesthetics: Reflections on a Quaker Ethic in American Design and Consumption,* edited by Emma Jones Lapsansky and Anne A. Verplanck, 16–42. Philadelphia: University of Pennsylvania Press, 2003.

———. *The Quaker Family in Colonial America: A Portrait of the Society of Friends.* New York: St. Martin's Press, 1973.

Fukasawa, Naoto, and Jasper Morrison. *Super Normal: Sensations of the Ordinary.* Baden: Lars Müller, 2007.

Garfinkel, Susan. "Letting in 'the World': (Re)Interpretive Tensions in the Quaker Meeting House." *Perspectives in Vernacular Architecture* 5 (1995): 78–92.

Geertz, Clifford. *The Interpretation of Cultures: Selected Essays.* New York: Basic Books, 1973.

Georges, Robert A., and Alan Dundes. "Toward a Structural Definition of the Riddle." *Journal of American Folklore* 76, no. 300 (1963): 111–18. https://doi.org/10.2307/538610.

Giedion, S. *Space, Time, and Architecture: The Growth of a New Tradition.* 5th ed. Cambridge, MA: Harvard University Press, 1967.

Ginzburg, Carlo. "Microhistory: Two or Three Things That I Know about It." *Critical Inquiry* 20, no. 1 (1993): 10–35. https://doi.org/10.1086/448699.

———. "Morelli, Freud and Sherlock Holmes: Clues and Scientific Method." *History Workshop* 9 (Spring 1980): 5–36.

Girard, Alexander, and W. D. Laurie. *An Exhibition for Modern Living.* Detroit: Detroit Institute of Arts, 1949.

Glueck, Grace. "The Artist Speaks: Saul Steinberg." *Art in America,* November–December 1970, 110–17.

Göller, Adolf. "What Is the Cause of Perpetual Style Change in Architecture?" In *Empathy, Form, and Space: Problems in German Aesthetics 1873–1893,* by Robert Vischer et al., translated by Harry Francis Mallgrave and Eleftherios Ikonomou, 193–226. Santa Monica, CA: Getty Center for the History of Art and the Humanities, 1994.

Goodstein, Elizabeth S. *Experience without Qualities: Boredom and Modernity.* Stanford, CA: Stanford University Press, 2005.

Gorer, Geoffrey. *The American People: A Study in National Character.* New York: Norton, 1964.

Gruen, John. "Saul Steinberg, Master of Wit and Fantasy." *ARTnews* 77, no. 5 (1978): 132–38.

Guarneri, Andrea Bocco. *Bernard Rudofsky: A Humane Designer.* Translated by David S. Tabbat. New York: SpringerWien, 2003.

Gumpert, Martin. *The Anatomy of Happiness.* New York: McGraw-Hill, 1951.

Haar, Michael. "Attunement and Thinking." In *Heidegger: A Critical Reader,* edited by Hubert L. Dreyfus and Harrison Hall, 159–71. Oxford, UK: Blackwell, 1992.

Haladyn, Julian Jason. *Boredom and Art: Passions of the Will to Boredom.* Winchester, UK: Zero Books, 2015.

Hanssen, Beatrice. *Walter Benjamin and the Arcades Project.* London: Continuum, 2006.

Harju, Bärbel. "Picture Windows: Architecture of Privacy and Surveillance." *e-cadernos CES* 27 (2017): 48–71. https://doi.org/10.4000/eces.2221.

Harries, Karsten. *Between Nihilism and Faith: A Commentary on "Either/Or."* Berlin: De Gruyter, 2010.

———. *The Ethical Function of Architecture.* Cambridge, MA: MIT Press, 1997.

Heckscher, August. *The Public Happiness.* New York: Atheneum, 1962.

Heidegger, Martin. *The Fundamental Concepts of Metaphysics: World, Finitude, Solitude.* Bloomington: Indiana University Press, 1995.

———. *What Is Called Thinking?* New York: Harper & Row, 1968.

Held, Klaus. "Fundamental Moods and Heidegger's Critique of Contemporary Culture." In *Reading Heidegger: Commemorations,* edited by John Sallis, 287–303. Bloomington: Indiana University Press, 1993.

Herman, Bernard L. "Eighteenth-Century Quaker Houses in the Delaware Valley and the Aesthetics of Practice." In *Quaker Aesthetics: Reflections on a Quaker Ethic in American Design and Consumption,* edited by Emma Jones Lapsansky and Anne A. Verplanck, 188–211. Philadelphia: University of Pennsylvania Press, 2003.

Heron, Woodburn. "The Pathology of Boredom." *Scientific American* 196, no. 1 (1957): 52–57. https://doi.org/10.1038/scientificamerican0157-52.

Hughes, Robert. "The World of Steinberg." *Time,* 17 April 1978, 92.

Hunter, Sam. *American Art of the 20th Century.* New York: H. N. Abrams, 1972.

Ingels, Bjarke. *Yes Is More: An Archicomic on Architectural Evolution.* Cologne: Evergreen, 2010.

Isenstadt, Sandy. *The Modern American House: Spaciousness and Middle-Class Identity.* New York: Cambridge University Press, 2006.

Judd, Donald. "Specific Objects." *Arts Yearbook* 8 (1965): 181–89.

Kant, Immanuel. *Anthropology from a Pragmatic Point of View.* Translated and edited by Robert B. Louden. Cambridge: Cambridge University Press, 2006.

Keats, John. *The Crack in the Picture Window.* Cambridge, MA: Riverside Press, 1956.

Kelly, Barbara M. *Expanding the American Dream: Building and Rebuilding Levittown.* Albany: State University of New York Press, 1993.

Kennedy, Robert Woods. *The House and the Art of Its Design.* New York: Reinhold, 1953.

Kierkegaard, Søren. *Either/Or.* Edited and translated by Howard V. Hong and Edna H. Hong. Princeton, NJ: Princeton University Press, 1987.

Kiven, Marcel. "La philosophie et l'histoire de l'ennui." *Bulletin de l'Institut Égyptien* (1918): 17–36.

Klapp, Orrin. *Overload and Boredom: Essays on the Quality of Life in the Information Society.* Westport, CT: Greenwood Press, 1986.

Kosuth, Joseph. "Introductory Note by the American Editor." *Art-Language* 1, no. 2 (1970): 1–4.

Kracauer, Siegfried. *The Mass Ornament: Weimar Essays.* Edited and translated by Thomas Y. Levin. Cambridge, MA: Harvard University Press, 1995.

Kramer, Hilton. "An Art of Boredom?" *New York Times,* 5 June 1966, D23.

Krauss, Rosalind. "Grids." *October* 9 (Summer 1979): 50–64.

Lalli, Mario Tedeschini. "Descent from Paradise: Saul Steinberg's Italian Years (1933–1941)." In "Modernity in the Cities of the Jews," edited by Christina Faccini. Special issue, *Quest: Issues in Contemporary Jewish History,* no. 2 (October 2011). http://www.doi.org/10.48248/issn.2037-741X/731.

Latour, Bruno. "Why Has Critique Run Out of Steam? From Matters of Fact to Matters of Concern." *Critical Inquiry* 30, no. 2 (2004): 225–48.

Lavoie, Catherine C. "Quaker Beliefs and Practices and the Eighteenth-Century Development of the Friends Meeting House in the Delaware Valley." In *Quaker Aesthetics: Reflections on a Quaker Ethic in American Design and Consumption,* edited by Emma Jones Lapsansky and Anne A. Verplanck, 156–87. Philadelphia: University of Pennsylvania Press, 2003.

———. "Reunified, Rebuilt, Enlarged, or Rehabilitated: Deciphering Friends' Complex Attitudes toward Their Meeting Houses." *Buildings & Landscapes: Journal of the Vernacular Architecture Forum* 19, no. 2 (2012): 20–52.

Leatherbarrow, David. "Atmospheric Conditions." In *Phenomenologies of the City: Studies in the History and Philosophy of Architecture,* edited by Henriette Steiner and Maximilian Sternberg, 85–100. London: Ashgate, 2015.

———. "Disorientation and Disclosure." *Interstices: Journal of Architecture and Related Arts* 12 (2011): 93–104.

———. *Uncommon Ground: Architecture, Technology, and Topography.* Cambridge, MA: MIT Press, 2002.

Le Corbusier. *Toward an Architecture.* Translated by John Goodman. Los Angeles: Getty Research Institute, 2007.

Lefebvre, Henri. *Toward an Architecture of Enjoyment.* Edited by Łukasz Stanek. Translated by Robert Bononno. Minneapolis: University of Minnesota Press, 2014.

Lind, Richard. "Why Isn't Minimal Art Boring?" *Journal of Aesthetics and Art Criticism* 45, no. 2 (1986): 195–97. https://doi.org/10.2307/430561.

Lippard, Lucy R. "After a Fashion: The Group Show." *Hudson Review* 19, no. 4 (1966): 620–26. doi:10.2307/3849195.

———. *Six Years: The Dematerialization of the Art Object from 1966 to 1972.* Berkeley: University of California Press, 1997.

Long, Christopher. *Josef Frank: Life and Work.* Chicago: University of Chicago Press, 2002.

Lueder, Christoph. "Saul Steinberg's 'Graph Paper Architecture': Humorous Drawings and Diagrams as Instruments of Critique." In *Laughing at Architecture: Architectural Histories of Humour, Satire and Wit,* edited by Michaela Rosso, 209–28. New York: Bloomsbury Publishing, 2018.

Maranda, Elli Köngäs. "Riddles and Riddling: An Introduction." *Journal of American Folklore* 89, no. 352 (1976): 127–37.

Marcuse, Herbert. *One-Dimensional Man.* Boston: Beacon Press, 1964.

Mathews, Stanley. *From Agit-Prop to Free Space: The Architecture of Cedric Price.* London: Black Dog, 2007.

Matravers, Derek. "Is Boring Art Just Boring?" *Journal of Aesthetics and Art Criticism* 53, no. 4 (1995): 425–26.

McCoubrey, John W. "Three Paintings by Edward Hicks." *Yale Art Gallery Bulletin* 25, no. 2 (1959): 16–21.

McCoy, Esther. "Robert Venturi: To Whom It May Concern." In *Piecing Together Los Angeles: An Esther McCoy Reader,* edited by Susan Morgan. Los Angeles: East of Borneo, 2012.

McDonough, Tom, ed. *Boredom: Documents of Contemporary Art.* Cambridge, MA: MIT Press, 2017.

Meyer Spacks, Patricia. *Boredom: The Literary History of a State of Mind.* Chicago: University of Chicago Press, 1995.

Mihalache, Andreea. "The Act and Art of Architectural Critique: A Drawing, a House, and a Sign." *The Plan Journal* 2, no. 1 (2017): 25–38.

———. "Musings on Boredom, Midcentury Architecture, and Public Spaces." *The Plan Journal* 5, no. 1 (2020): 119–38.

———. "Saul Steinberg's Stories of *Dor.*" In *Confabulations: Storytelling in Architecture,* edited by Paul Emmons, Marcia F. Feuerstein, and Carolina Dayer, 80–86. New York: Routledge, 2017.

———. "Three Ghosts and a Baldachin: Boredom and (Day)Dreaming in Two Drawings by Saul Steinberg." In *Ceilings and Dreams: The Architecture of Levity,* edited by Paul Emmons, Federica Goffi, and Jodi La Coe, 197–211. New York: Routledge, 2020.

Moravia, Alberto. *Boredom.* Translated by Angus Davidson. New York: New York Review, 1999.

———. *La Noia.* Florence: Giunti Editore, 2019.

Mumford, Lewis. "The Case against Modern Architecture." *Architectural Record* 131 (April 1962): 155–62.

———. *The Conduct of Life.* New York: Harcourt, Brace, 1951.

———. *Technics and Civilization.* New York: Harcourt, Brace, 1934.

Nagourney, Peter. "Rubber Stamp Art." *Journal of Popular Culture* 15, no. 3 (1981): 80–103.

Nelson, Deborah. *Pursuing Privacy in Cold War America.* New York: Columbia University Press, 2002.

Nelson, George, and Henry Niccolls Wright. *Tomorrow's House: How to Plan Your Post-War Home Now.* New York: Simon and Schuster, 1945.

"New House 194X, The." *Architectural Forum,* September 1942, 65–152.

Ngai, Sianne. "Merely Interesting." *Critical Inquiry* 34, no. 4 (2008): 777–817.

———. *Our Aesthetic Categories: Zany, Cute, Interesting.* Cambridge, MA: Harvard University Press, 2012.

———. *Ugly Feelings*. Cambridge, MA: Harvard University Press, 2004.

Norman, Will. "Saul Steinberg, MoMA, and the Unstable Cultural Field." *Italian Modern Art* 3 (January 2020): 1–21.

Olendorf, Donna. *Something about the Author*. Vol. 69. Detroit: Gale, 1992.

O'Neil, Edward N. "Cynthia and the Moon." *Classical Philology* 53, no. 1 (1958): 1–8.

Pallasmaa, Juhani. "Space, Place, and Atmosphere: Peripheral Perception in Existential Experience." In *Architectural Atmospheres: On the Experience and Politics of Architecture*, edited by Christian Borch, 19–41. Basel: Birkhäuser, 2014.

Parreno, Christian. *Boredom, Architecture, and Spatial Experience*. London: Bloomsbury, 2021.

Pellicciari, Francesca. "Critic without Words: Saul Steinberg e l'architettura." Thesis, Istituto Universitario di Architettura di Venezia, 2005.

———. "Saul Steinberg, l'archittetura e il 'piccolo padre' Le Corbusier." *Abitare* 467 (2006): 110–17.

Pérez-Gómez, Alberto. *Attunement: Architectural Meaning after the Crisis of Modern Science*. Cambridge, MA: MIT Press, 2016.

Pieper, Josef. *Leisure, the Basis of Culture*. New York: Pantheon Books, 1964.

Plato. *Theaetetus*. Translated by Benjamin Jowett. Rockville, MD: Serenity Publishers, 2009.

Plummer, Henry. *The Experience of Architecture*. London: Thames & Hudson, 2016.

Rapoport, Amos, and Robert E. Kantor. "Complexity and Ambiguity in Environmental Design." *Journal of the American Institute of Planners* 33, no. 4 (1967): 210–21.

Raposa, Michael L. "Boredom and the Religious Imagination." *Journal of the American Academy of Religion* 53, no. 1 (1985): 75–91.

Reichek, Jesse. "Steinberg on the City." *Journal of the American Institute of Planners* 28, no. 3 (1961): 246–91.

Riesman, David. *The Lonely Crowd: A Study of the Changing American Character*. New Haven, CT: Yale University Press, 1950.

Rodman, Selden. *Conversations with Artists*. New York: Devin-Adair, 1957.

Rose, Barbara. "ABC Art." *Art in America* 53, no. 5 (1965).

Rossi, Ugo. *Bernard Rudofsky architetto*. Napoli: CLEAN edizioni, 2016.

Rudofsky, Bernard. "L'architettura comincia con un pavimento." *Domus*, no. 122 (February 1938): 1.

———. "Before the Architects." *Design Quarterly*, no. 118–19 (1982): 60–63.

———. *Behind the Picture Window*. New York: Oxford University Press, 1955.

———. "The Bread of Architecture." *Arts and Architecture* 69, no. 10 (1952): 27–29, 45.

———. "Giardino, stanza all'aperto: A proposito della Casa Giardino a Long Island, NY." *Domus*, no. 272 (July–August 1952): 1–71.

———. "Non ci vuole un nuovo modo di costruire, ci vuole un nuovo modo di vivere." *Domus*, no. 123 (March 1938): 6–15.

———. "Notes on Patios." *New Pencil Points*, no. 24 (June 1943): 44–47.

———. *Now I Lay Me Down to Eat: Notes and Footnotes on the Lost Art of Living.* New York: Anchor Books, 1980.

———. *The Prodigious Builders: Notes Toward a Natural History of Architecture with Special Regard to Those Species That Are Traditionally Neglected or Downright Ignored.* New York: Harcourt Brace Jovanovich, 1977.

———. *Streets for People: A Primer for Americans.* Garden City, NY: Doubleday, 1969.

———. "Three Patio Houses." *New Pencil Points,* no. 24 (June 1943): 48–65.

———. "Variazioni." *Domus,* no. 124 (April 1938): 14–15.

Russell, Andrew, and Lee Vinsel. "Hail the Maintainers." *Aeon,* 7 April 2014. Accessed 20 March 2020. https://aeon.co/essays/innovation-is-overvalued-maintenance-often-matters-more.

Russell, Bertrand. *In Praise of Idleness and Other Essays.* London: George Allen & Unwin, 1935.

Rykwert, Joseph. *The Judicious Eye: Architecture Against the Other Arts.* Chicago: University of Chicago Press, 2008.

———. *The Necessity of Artifice.* New York: Rizzoli, 1982.

Saffron, Inga. "Changing Skyline: An Elegant Redesign for Ben Franklin—and Venturi." *Philadelphia Inquirer,* 26 August 2013. Accessed 6 August 2014. http://articles.philly.com/2013-08-26/news/41446205_1_denise-scott-brown-robert-venturi-benjamin-franklin-museum.

Schlegel, Friedrich. *On the Study of Greek Poetry.* Translated and edited by Stuart Barnett. Albany: State University of New York Press, 2001.

Schopenhauer, Arthur. *The World as Will and Representation.* Translated by E. F. J. Payne. 2 vols. New York: Dover, 1966.

Scott, Felicity. "Bernard Rudofsky: Allegories of Nomadism and Dwelling." In *Anxious Modernisms,* edited by William Goldhagen, Sarah Legault, and Réjean Legault, 215–37. Cambridge, MA: MIT Press, 2000.

———. "An Eye for Modern Architecture." In *Lessons from Bernard Rudofsky: Life as a Voyage,* edited by Architekturzentrum Wien in association with The Getty Research Institute, 172–209. Basel: Birkhäuser, 2007. Exhibition catalog.

Scott Brown, Denise. "Education in the 1970s: Teaching for an Altered Reality." *Architectural Record* (October 1970): 128–33.

———. "Form, Design and the City." *Journal of the American Institute of Planners* 28, no. 4 (1962): 297–99.

———. "The Function of a Table." *Architectural Design* 37 (April 1967): 154.

———. "Learning from Africa." *Zimbabwean Review,* July 1995, 26–29.

———. "Little Magazines in Architecture and Urbanism." *Journal of the American Institute of Planners* 34, no. 4 (1968): 223–32.

———. "The Meaningful City." *AIA Journal,* no. 43 (January 1965): 27–32.

———. "Natal Plans." *Journal of the American Institute of Planners* 30, no. 2 (1964): 161–66.

———. "On Pop Art, Permissiveness, and Planning." *Journal of the American Institute of Planners* 35, no. 3 (1969): 184–86.

———. "Planning the Powder Room." *AIA Journal* 47, no. 4 (1967): 81–83.
———. "Teaching Architectural History." *Arts and Architecture* 84, no. 5 (1967): 29–30.
———. "Will Salvation Spoil the Dodge House?" *Architectural Forum,* October 1966, 68–71.
Scully, Vincent. *Modern Architecture and Other Essays.* Edited by Neil Levine. Princeton, NJ: Princeton University Press, 2005.
Sontag, Susan. *Against Interpretation, and Other Essays.* New York: Farrar, Straus and Giroux, 1966.
———. *Styles of Radical Will.* New York: Farrar, Straus and Giroux, 1969.
Spector, Robert D. "Reinhard Kuhn: *The Demon of Noontide: Ennui in Western Literature.*" Review of *The Demon of Noontide: Ennui in Western Literature* by Reinhard Kuhn. *World Literature Today* 51, no. 3 (1977): 507.
Steinberg, Saul. "Built in U.S.A.: Post-War Architecture, 1945–52." *ARTnews* 51, no. 10 (1953): 16–19.
———. "Chronology." In *Saul Steinberg.* New York: Whitney Museum of American Art, 1978. Exhibition catalog.
———. *The Discovery of America.* New York: Alfred Knopf, 1992.
———. *4 Leporellos—The Line / Types of Architecture / Shores of the Mediterranean / City of Italy.* Zurich: Nieves, 2014.
———. *The Labyrinth.* New York: Harper and Brothers, 1960.
———. *The New World.* London: Hamish Hamilton, 1965.
———. "Our False-Front Culture." *Look,* 9 January 1968, 46–49.
———. *The Passport.* New York: Random House, 1979.
———. "Rubber Stamps." *New Yorker,* 3 December 1966, 56–61.
———. "Steinberg on the City." *Journal of the American Institute of Planners* 27, no. 3 (1961).
Steinberg, Saul, and Aldo Buzzi. *Lettere a Aldo Buzzi 1945–1999, a cura del destinatario.* Milan: Adelphi, 2002.
———. *Reflections and Shadows.* New York: Random House, 2002.
Sunshine, Becky. "An Eye for Detail: Architect John Pawson's Photographs." *Guardian,* 19 November 2017. Accessed 19 March 2020. https://www.theguardian.com/lifeandstyle/2017/nov/19/an-eye-for-detail-architect-john-pawsons-photographs.
Svendsen, Lars. *A Philosophy of Boredom.* London: Reaktion Books, 2004.
Tardieu, Émile. *L'ennui: Étude psychologique.* Paris: F. Alcan, 1913.
Teyssot, Georges. "Boredom and Bedroom: The Suppression of the Habitual." *Assemblage,* no. 30 (August 1996): 44–61.
———. *A Topology of Everyday Constellations.* Cambridge, Mass.: MIT Press, 2013.
Tolles, Frederick B. "'Of the Best Sort, but Plain': The Quaker Aesthetic." *American Quarterly* 11, no. 4 (1959): 484–502.
———. *Quakers and the Atlantic Culture.* New York: Macmillan, 1960.

Tomorrow's Small House. Edited by Elizabeth Mock. New York: Museum of Modern Art, 1945. Exhibition catalog.

vanden Heuvel, Jean. "Straight from the Hand and Mouth of Steinberg." *Life,* 10 December 1965, 59–70.

Vanel, Herve. "John Cage's Muzak-Plus: The Fu(Rni)Ture of Music." *Representations* 102, no. 1 (2008): 94–128.

Venturi, Robert. *Complexity and Contradiction in Architecture.* New York: Museum of Modern Art; Garden City, NY: Doubleday, 1966.

———. *Complexity and Contradiction in Architecture.* 2nd ed. New York: Museum of Modern Art, 1977.

———. "Upbringing among Quakers." In *Growing Up Italian,* edited by Linda Brandi Cateura, 195–201. New York: William Morrow, 1997.

Venturi, Robert, and Denise Scott Brown. "Is and Ought: Interview with Denise Scott Brown and Robert Venturi." *Perspecta,* no. 41 (December 2008): 37–41.

Venturi, Robert, Denise Scott Brown, and Steven Izenour. *Learning from Las Vegas.* 2nd ed. Cambridge, MA: MIT Press, 1998.

Verplanck, Anne. "The Silhouette and Quaker Identity in Early National Philadelphia." *Winterthur Portfolio* 43, no. 1 (2009): 41–78.

Vinegar, Aron. *I Am a Monument: On "Learning from Las Vegas."* Cambridge, MA: MIT Press, 2008.

Voight, L. B. "Modern Gardens: Indoor-Outdoor Living Based on a Well-Conceived Design." *Landscape Architecture Magazine* 42, no. 3 (1952): 116–19.

Whyte, William Hollingsworth. *The Organization Man.* New York: Simon and Schuster, 1956.

Williams, Raymond. *Keywords: A Vocabulary of Culture and Society.* New York: Oxford University Press, 1985.

Wölfflin, Heinrich. *Principles of Art History: The Problem of the Development of Style in Later Art.* Translated by M. D. Hottinger. New York: Dover, 1950.

———. *Renaissance and Baroque.* Ithaca, NY: Cornell University Press, 1967.

Zumthor, Peter. *Atmospheres: Architectural Environments, Surrounding Objects.* Basel: Birkhäuser, 2006.

INDEX

Page numbers in italics refer to illustrations.